The Bell *Magazine and the Representation of Irish Identity*

The Bell Magazine and the Representation of Irish Identity

OPENING WINDOWS

Kelly Matthews

FOUR COURTS PRESS

Set in 11.5 pt on 13.5 pt Centaur for
FOUR COURTS PRESS LTD
7 Malpas Street, Dublin 8, Ireland
www.fourcourtspress.ie
and in North America by
FOUR COURTS PRESS
c/o ISBS, 920 N.E. 58th Avenue, Suite 300, Portland, OR 97213.

A catalogue record for this title
is available from the British Library.

ISBN 978–1–84682–323–7

Printed in England
by Antony Rowe Ltd, Chippenham, Wilts.

Contents

Acknowledgments

The research that forms the basis of this book was funded by a Vice Chancellor's Research Scholarship from the University of Ulster. I thank Professors Robert Welch and Jan Jedrzejewski for encouraging me to apply as a doctoral research student, and for their guidance throughout my time at UU. My doctoral supervisors, Bruce Stewart, Frank Sewell, and Willa Murphy, were invaluable sources of advice and expertise, and my examiners, Clair Wills and Elmer Kennedy-Andrews, both offered critical but constructive feedback which helped my thesis grow into a fully-fledged book. I am also grateful to the libraries of the University of Ulster, Trinity College Dublin, Queen's University Belfast, Boston College, Boston University, Harvard University; and to the Linen Hall Library, Belfast, and the Donegal County Library, Letterkenny for access to their collections of materials related to *The Bell*, its editors and contributors. In particular, I thank librarians Janet Peden and Frank Reynolds for making sure my access to *The Bell* was not interrupted during major construction work at the University of Ulster's Coleraine campus.

Anthony Cronin and Val Mulkerns, former Associate Editors of *The Bell*, generously agreed to talk to me about their work on the magazine in the 1950s, and I very much enjoyed our conversations. Martin Fanning, at Four Courts Press, has consistently been responsive and attentive, and I appreciate the work of the two anonymous readers who reviewed my initial manuscript; their questions and suggestions greatly improved the final book. My colleagues in the English department at Framingham State University have been universally encouraging and supportive. My department chair, Elaine Beilin, was instrumental to my revision process, suggesting a number of important changes that resulted in a stronger introductory chapter.

It was only towards the end of my doctoral research that I became conscious of the overlap between the time period of this study and the term in office that my great-grandfather, Francis P. Matthews, served as US Ambassador to Ireland. I am very grateful to his son, my grandfather, Francis P. Matthews, Jr, and to my grandmother, Helen Spencer Matthews, for making it possible for me to begin my study of Irish literature so many years ago, and for supporting my initial research on *The Bell* during my postgraduate year at Trinity College Dublin. I thank my parents, Pat Matthews and Patty Matthews, for supporting me in all my pursuits. I am especially grateful to my husband, Ronnie Millar, for believing in me from the start, and to my sons, Rory and Andrew Millar, who cheerfully accepted every child care arrangement that allowed me to spend time researching and writing – and who kept me on my toes by asking how many pages I had completed each day when I returned home. I hope this book will live up to their expectations.

Foreword

The Bell is often referred to as a literary review, the equivalent of *Horizon*. But though it solicited contributions from its readers and carried short stories and poems from what are referred to as established writers it did not primarily exist to publish new writing. Neither was it concerned with the issues of the day. Wartime censorship, if nothing else, ensured that it did not discuss the issues and ideologies which underlay the conflict then raging. But denying itself, or being denied these things, it became the most important Irish periodical journal published in the twentieth century. It also became, which is rare among periodicals, an agent in what was discussed, not by editorializing about it but by the mere fact of opening its pages to the description of things as they were.

Documentary was a favoured form everywhere in the 1930s and 1940s. In the 30s new classes, new forms of social organization and mass culture had appeared and whole schools of writing had been founded and flourished on a documentary base. And in the 40s there were the new experiences of wartime which affected millions. It was part of *The Bell's* implicit assumptions that the Ireland its readers lived in had not been described and that too much Irish life had been seen through the haze of nostalgia for an invented past or idealism about a projected future. In its first editorial Sean O'Faoláin wrote, 'This is your magazine. Only the people can create an image of themselves.' And if they didn't respond in such publishable numbers as was hoped others could be commissioned. The early documentaries tended to have simple declarative titles such as 'I live in a slum' or 'I lost a leg'. There were also 'Days in the Life' of working people of various descriptions. Later attempts to document how the Irish spent their time would include surveys of leisure activities to which Flann O'Brien contributed descriptions of the dance-halls and the pubs, the latter showing more knowledge and intimacy than the former.

Only after some time, Kelly Matthews says in her needed book, did *The Bell* begin to develop its role 'as an instrument of direct criticism both cultural and political'. When it did, she insists, the question of Irish identity became the most important to be discussed and she speaks of '*The Bell's* attempts to influence the formation of a post-colonial Irish identity'. Now that we are so entirely subsumed into the neo-liberal capitalist world where the possession of the English language is agreed on all sides to be a commercial advantage (which is the all-important consideration) we do not have to worry about this any longer.

The Bell lasted fourteen years though there were gaps and re-incarnations. The most important change that occurred in that time was probably the changeover from Sean O'Faoláin to Peadar O'Donnell as Editor. O'Faoláin, a man of great talent and considerable diplomatic charm both in print and in person, was, among his other literary avocations, a natural editor; whatever his other abilities Peadar O'Donnell, ex-revolutionary and polemicist-turned-novelist, was not. When I joined him in the early 50s as Associate Editor his interest in *The Bell* was diminishing, as were its finances, which were a mystery to which only he had the key. There was also much less interest in it among the writing community, whose most professional and talented members had been departing from Ireland since the war's end. The depressed and miserable Ireland of the post-war, which furnished both its readers and contributors, was not a favourable breeding-ground for a magazine. Magazines must deal to some extent in some sort of optimism. Kelly Matthews, in the only uncertain section of an otherwise assured book, seems a little mystified by *The Bell's* demise but there is no mystery about it. *The Bell* died of dullness, not its own, but that of the country to which it belonged. As John Montague put it in his autobiographical book, *Company*, 'Ireland seemed to be the slough of despond ... Cronin's editorials of the period sound like a foghorn in thick mist, as if the island were drowning.'

Anthony Cronin, April 2012

CHAPTER ONE

Introduction

OPENING WINDOWS

In his first editorial for *The Bell*, founding editor Sean O'Faoláin told his read-ers that the magazine was theirs to construct, and that the picture of Life that emerged would be their own creation. In the spirit of documentary real-ism, O'Faoláin threw open the magazine's doors and welcomed the contribu-tions of anyone in Ireland with a story to tell. He would later state, in a note that preceded a series of articles on six of the new nation's religious denomi-nations: 'It is part of the regular policy of *The Bell* to open as many windows as possible on the lives of as many people as possible, so that we may form a full and varied picture of modern Ireland'.[1] In the years that followed, *The Bell* explored the complexity of Irish identity and engaged with questions of national culture from multiple angles. *The Bell's* editors often regarded them-selves as working outside or against the aesthetics of literary modernism, yet much of their work connected to Irish identity articulates modernist concerns: addressing fragmentation, examining the world from multiple perspectives at once, and bringing conflicting elements of contemporary experience together to form a multi-faceted representation of modern life. Reading *The Bell* is much like viewing a Cubist painting of mid-twentieth century Irish society: each issue is a collection of divergent voices, bound together by the common thread of their Irish identity. Month after month, the magazine's editors consciously pre-sented a complex and inclusive version of modern Ireland, one that could embrace both rural and urban realities, Gaelic and European influences, North-ern and Southern traditions, wealthy and poor social classes, and many other seemingly contradictory aspects of Irish culture. O'Faoláin made his activist intentions clear when he wrote to fellow writer and *Bell* editor Frank O'Connor in the early days of the magazine:

> If I can get the BELL to take in every sort of person from Kerry to
> Donegal, and bind them about you and me and Peadar [O'Donnell]
> and Roisin [Walsh] do you not see that we are forming a nucleus? Take

---

1 Note preceding Revd Matthew Bailey, 'What It Means to be a Presbyterian: Credo – 1', *The Bell* 8:4 (July 1944), p. 298.

the long view – bit by bit we are accepted as the nucleus. Bit by bit we can spread ideas, create *real* standards, ones naturally growing out of Life and not out of literature and Yeats and all to that. [...] I am doing a spot of real construction.[2]

The Bell also opened a window on the world outside Ireland for those stifled by Emergency-era economic stagnation and by wartime restrictions on communication with combatant Europe and America. In one edition of his popular column for *The Bell*, 'The Open Window', Michael Farrell, writing as 'Gulliver', described a Dublin shopgirl who had come to be known as 'Kingstown Kate' because of her frequent trips to Dun Laoghaire to watch the mail boat coming in or going out. 'I suppose', Farrell wrote, 'that girl simply feels tortured by the same claustrophobia that has fallen on us all since the War began. There's nothing romantic about it. It is just personality craving light and space, and air'.[3]

Over its fourteen years of publication, *The Bell* successfully promoted a new version of Irish identity by opening windows on the lives of Irish men and women from a wide variety of rural and urban environments, social classes, religious backgrounds, occupations and professions. Side by side with documentary articles written by ordinary citizens from all walks of life, the magazine's editors offered their readers an extensive range of essays, poems and short stories by established and emerging writers from Ireland and abroad. The differences between these varied genres of writing, however, often produced tensions that *The Bell*'s editors found difficult to resolve. Moreover, the editors' focus on literary realism as the basis for an authentic representation of Irish identity made them hesitant to accept the aesthetic challenge of literary modernism and other avant-garde movements that were on the rise in Europe and America. When O'Faoláin, in the statement quoted above, vowed to 'form a full and varied picture of modern Ireland', he meant that *The Bell* would use literary realism as the basis for an authentic representation of contemporary Irish identity. As experimental and modernist techniques emerged in writing submitted to the magazine, O'Faoláin and his fellow editors repeatedly refused to endorse them. While *The Bell* argued energetically for a new definition of Irishness for an increasingly modernized Irish society, its editors nonetheless shrank from the aesthetic challenges of modernism in new forms of art and literature.

In this study of *The Bell*, I draw upon a range of critical approaches in order to open up material within the magazine for examination and discussion. Building upon previous studies of Irish cultural history in the twentieth century, I

---

2 O'Faoláin, undated letter to Frank O'Connor, Gotlieb Archival Research Center.   3 Farrell, 'The Open Window: A Monthly Perambulation Conducted by Gulliver', *The Bell* 6:1 (April 1943), p. 81.

emphasize *The Bell*'s underlying project of identity formation, which can best be understood in broadly post-colonial terms. In doing so, I bring a new perspective to the magazine, and read it as a collaborative endeavour, the collective work of editors, writers, and readers combined. As a periodical, *The Bell* presents a challenge to the critical reader's fixed ideas about genre. It is neither the work of one editor alone, nor an arbitrary assemblage of contributors' writings. Moreover, the periodical continually engages in dialogue with its readers and allows readers themselves to contribute to its content in ways which are unavailable within other literary genres. While I have built upon the foundations established by previous studies of Irish literary magazines and Irish culture in the mid-twentieth century, my aim is to approach *The Bell* in a new way, one which does not ignore the influence of trailblazing editors Sean O'Faoláin, Frank O'Connor, Peadar O'Donnell and their staff, nor the strong voices of individual contributors, but which develops a holistic criticism of *The Bell* as a publication in its entirety, comprising editorials, articles, stories, poems, illustrations, advertisements and letters from readers both within Ireland and overseas.

There exist few theoretical models for considering the periodical as a literary genre, or for studying a magazine as a self-contained literary text. Yet new ground is being broken by initiatives such as Oxford's Modernist Magazine Project, which takes a 'historicizing and materialist approach' to the study of twentieth-century periodicals.[4] Margaret Beetham suggests such a mode of reading when she writes that the critical reader must attempt to reconstruct the experience of the periodical reader of the era studied, examining, when possible, the end-papers, advertisements, and other material available to subscription holders of a magazine.[5] Beetham's initial work towards a theory of the periodical is useful to a study of *The Bell* in its discussion of several aspects of the periodical that set it apart from other literary forms.[6] The heterogeneity of the periodical, Beetham notes, prevents the text from being situated, as in traditional literary criticism, in the *oeuvre* of a particular author. Even the most domineering editor has a limited amount of power in relation to the other parties involved in production of the periodical.[7] Then, too, the role of a periodical reader is different to that of a reader of other literature. As Beetham points out, the contents of a periodical are not designed to be read in order, and most readers do not read every piece in a given issue; thus, the periodical 'is a form which

4 Peter Brooker and Andrew Thacker, 'General Introduction' in *The Oxford critical and cultural history of modernist magazines, volume I, Britain and Ireland, 1880–1955*, ed. by Brooker and Thacker (Oxford, 2009), p. 9. 5 Margaret Beetham, 'Towards a Theory of the Periodical as a Publishing Genre', in *Investigating Victorian journalism*, ed. by Laurel Brake, Alec Jones and Lionel Madden (London, 1990), p. 23. 6 Beetham's critical work focuses on women's magazines of the nineteenth century. See Beetham, *A magazine of her own? Domesticity and desire in the woman's magazine, 1800–1914* (London, 1996). 7 Beetham, 'Towards a Theory of the Periodical', p. 25.

openly offers readers the chance to construct their own texts'.[8] The periodical is open, furthermore, in the sense that it invites the reader 'to intervene directly' in the writing of the text itself, 'by writing letters, comments and other contributions'.[9] *The Bell* was particularly notable in this area, in that its editors frequently appealed to readers, in various ways, to submit their own writing for publication in the magazine. In an early draft of his first editorial, O'Faoláin went so far as to tell readers: '[W]hether you know it or not, you are writing every line you read'.[10] The fact that the periodical is an open, rather than closed, form, Beetham writes, makes it both 'a potentially creative form for its readers' and 'a potentially disruptive kind of text'.[11] Finally, she notes that the nature of a periodical as a serial publication implies that each issue can also be read as a self-contained text, so that the periodical 'is both open-ended and end-stopped'.[12] This aspect of *The Bell* becomes important when we consider editorial choices such as the production of special issues, and the juxtaposition of articles within individual issues of the magazine.

Richard Kearney, editor of the Irish literary journal *The Crane Bag* from 1977 to 1985, has differentiated between the novel, the newspaper, and what he calls the magazine-journal by examining their varying periodicities and authorial voices. Whereas the voice of the novel is subjective, and the voices in a newspaper are objective, the magazine-journal tries to be both, to 'respond to the objective world of facts while retaining something of the imaginative richness of subjective interpretation'.[13] Likewise, the magazine-journal, appearing regularly (unlike a novel) but not daily (unlike a newspaper), allows for more measured reflection on the events it records.[14] O'Faoláin alluded to this aspect of the magazine-journal when he rejected a piece by O'Connor on the novelist Gerald O'Donovan: 'It has the "immediate reaction" quality, not the "considered reaction" quality – and the first is first-class for the Daily Paper, but the Monthly wants much more'.[15] In Kearney's final formulation, 'The purpose of a magazine is [...] *dialogue*, and by extension, *community*'.[16] Here we are reminded of Beetham's proposition that periodical readers are invited to intervene directly in the construction of the periodical text. In attempting to represent the full range of its readers' daily lives, *The Bell* both responded to a contemporary Irish society in flux and created its own version of community amidst the changing cultural landscape of Ireland in the 1940s and 50s.

In the context of scholarship on Irish literary culture in the mid-twentieth century, *The Bell* suffers from a paradoxical dilemma. On the one hand, the mag-

8 Ibid., p. 26. 9 Ibid., p. 27. 10 O'Faoláin, draft of 'This Is Your Magazine', Gotlieb Archival Research Center. 11 Beetham, 'Towards a Theory of the Periodical', p. 27. 12 Ibid., p. 29. 13 Richard Kearney, *Transitions: narratives in modern Irish culture* (Dublin, 1988), p. 267. 14 Kearney, *Transitions*, p. 267. 15 O'Faoláin, undated letter to O'Connor, Gotlieb Archival Research Center. 16 Kearney, *Transitions*, p. 268 [emphasis Kearney's].

azine is so well-known that the prevailing perception among literary commentators is that it has been more than adequately analyzed. Brian Fallon, for example, writes in *An age of innocence*, his survey of Irish culture from 1930 to 1960, that
'*The Bell* has been so often discussed, and appears in so many studies, biogra-
phies and other contexts, that to write about it here at length is probably redundant and even boring'.[17] Indeed *The Bell* is so often mentioned as the most influential Irish literary magazine of its time that this phrase itself has become a
commonplace. A review of the existing literature, however, reveals that although
The Bell is frequently cited and praised, there exists little criticism of its role as
an instrument of cultural representation and transformation for the Ireland of
the 1940s and 50s. In his introduction to the only published full-length book
on *The Bell*, an anthology of selected stories, poems, and articles, Sean McMahon states that

> An institution as significant and as influential as *The Bell* really demands
> a book-length history [...]. That history should it ever come to be writ-
> ten would have a lot to say as well about the Ireland of the Forties and
> early Fifties; for if ever a magazine held the mirror up to nature and
> showed Ireland her own face, *The Bell* did.[18]

More recently, in his encyclopaedic survey of Irish literary magazines from 1710
to 1985, Tom Clyde states that 'although it has attracted more comment than
any other publication in this study, the definitive work on *The Bell* has still to be
written'.[19] It is my intention to fill this critical gap, and my hope that this new
study of *The Bell* will reinvigorate discussion of the magazine and its impact on
Irish society.

THE BELL AND MID-TWENTIETH-CENTURY IRELAND

Founded in October 1940, *The Bell* came to life during the constrictive years of
the Emergency, and continued as a monthly publication – apart from its hiatus
in 1948–50, and one brief stint as a quarterly – until the end of 1954. A review
of the magazine's contents offers insights into mid-twentieth century events
such as political and moral censorship, debates over the Irish language, and considerations of the newly drawn border between Éire and Northern Ireland. It
also opens a window onto the mid-twentieth-century Irish literary landscape.

---

17 Fallon, *An age of innocence: Irish culture, 1930–1960*, p. 232.   18 *The best from* The Bell: *great Irish writing*, ed. by Sean
McMahon (Dublin, 1978), p. 8.   19 Tom Clyde, *Irish literary magazines: an outline history and descriptive bibliography* (Dublin,
2003), p. 46.

O'Faoláin, already a successful novelist, founded *The Bell* with the help of fellow writers Frank O'Connor and Peadar O'Donnell, among others. Young writers such as John Hewitt, Brendan Behan, Maura Laverty and John Montague published their early work in the magazine, and more established authors such as Patrick Kavanagh, W.R. Rodgers, and Liam O'Flaherty found there a paying forum for their work as well. In one memorable issue of the magazine, short stories by Kate O'Brien and Brian Friel appear within a few pages of one another. But it is not primarily as a repository of valuable writing that *The Bell* will be viewed in this book. Rather, this study will focus on the magazine's simultaneous efforts towards the representation and transformation of popular conceptions of Irish identity in the mid-twentieth century, a time of social and technological change, when essentialist versions of Irishness largely dominated political and cultural discourse.

The Bell figures prominently in every study of mid-twentieth-century Irish culture, whether it is presented as an example of resistance to cultural stagnation or as a sign of sustained literary progress – in other words, whether it is seen as the exception or the rule. Therefore *The Bell* plays an important role in the current debate over the interpretation of Irish cultural life in the 1940s and 50s. This debate began in 1971 when the historian F.S.L. Lyons used the image of Plato's cave to describe the isolated state of Irish culture during the Second World War, in what has become an enduring metaphor for mid-twentieth century Ireland:

> It was as if an entire people had been condemned to live in Plato's cave, with their backs to the fire of life and deriving their only knowledge of what went on outside from the flickering shadows thrown on the wall before their eyes by the men and women who passed to and fro behind them.[20]

In the decades since, several historians have worked to complicate Lyons' image of the cave-dwelling Irish, though most have concurred that the mid-century was marked by a high degree of cultural isolation and stagnation. In the late 1980s, R.F. Foster and J.J. Lee reinforced Lyons' claims: Foster wrote of the 'cultural chauvinism and insularity of the Free State',[21] and Lee extended Lyons' assessment to the pre-war era, pointing out that 'Ireland had already intellectually isolated herself in large measure since independence'.[22] In Lee's view, it was Ireland's post-colonial condition, not her neutrality, that engendered insularity.

Others, however, have disagreed. Writing in 1998, the journalist Brian Fallon refuted Lyons' claims of cultural stagnation by listing the many achievements

---

20 F.S.L. Lyons, *Ireland since the Famine* (London, 1971), pp 557–8. 21 R.F. Foster, *Modern Ireland, 1600–1972* (London, 1988), p. 535. 22 J.J. Lee, *Ireland, 1912–1985: politics and society* (Cambridge, 1989), p. 260.

of Irish writers and artists of the time.[23] Along these lines, Diarmaid Ferriter has argued that statements about the conservatism of the mid-twentieth century do 'little justice to the complex layers of Irish society during this era'.[24] Most recently, Bryan Fanning has countered claims of intellectual insularity by analyzing the underpinning philosophies of *Studies* and *Christus Rex*, two Catholic quarterlies of the day.[25] Indeed, poets and writers of the mid-century occasionally disagreed among themselves as to the extent of cultural conservatism. John Montague, for example, in his poem 'The Siege of Mullingar, 1963', famously rewrote the refrain from Yeats' 'September 1913' to argue that 'Puritan Ireland' had been nothing more than 'A myth of O'Connor and O'Faoláin'.[26]

The work of literary critics Terence Brown and Clair Wills has laid the groundwork for an interdisciplinary approach to Irish cultural history in the twentieth century. Brown's assessment of the mid-century is largely in line with Lyons' view that cultural development was in abeyance from the end of the Civil War until the economic revival of the 1960s.[27] More recently, Wills has examined Irish cultural life during the Second World War, and uncovers signs of life amid the strictures of supply shortages and wartime censorship.[28] Both Brown and Wills take a broad view of Irish culture, combining literary criticism with historical research to produce studies that are at once descriptive and analytical. Brown's efforts are wide-ranging, an attempt, as he writes in his preface, at 'a preliminary mapping of the territory' so that others may follow.[29] Wills pays him due homage, noting that his chapter on the Emergency is still 'the best analysis of Irish literary culture in the war years' before stating that her own work aims 'to expand and interrogate Brown's concise and illuminating analysis'.[30] In this study, I intend to extend their approach to cultural history with a specific focus on one key publication of the Emergency era. This examination of *The Bell*'s project to represent and transform Irish identity will show how the magazine itself shaped and responded to changes in Irish society during a crucial time in the development of Irish national culture.

When *The Bell* began publication in 1940, Ireland had been politically independent from Britain for only eighteen years. The Irish Free State, established in 1922, had survived the bloody and bitter Civil War and had gradually grown into a stable society, albeit a society whose political conservatism and economic deprivations soon led to disillusionment for those who had hoped that an inde-

23 Brian Fallon, *An age of innocence: Irish culture, 1930–1960* (Dublin, 1998).   24 Diarmaid Ferriter, *The transformation of Ireland, 1900–2000* (London, 2004), p. 359.   25 Bryan Fanning, *The quest for modern Ireland: the battle of ideas, 1912–1986* (Dublin, 2008).   26 John Montague, 'The Siege of Mullingar, 1963', in *Selected poems* (Toronto, 1986), p. 62.   27 Terence Brown, *Ireland: a social and cultural history, 1922–2002* (London, 2004).   28 Clair Wills, *That neutral island: a cultural history of Ireland during the Second World War* (London, 2007).   29 Brown, *Ireland*, p. xxii.   30 Wills, *That neutral island*, p. 429.

pendent Ireland would be a vibrant and flourishing nation. The post-Civil War government, led by W.T. Cosgrave and the Cumann na nGaedheal party (which later joined with smaller parties to form Fine Gael), imposed law and order and was careful to exercise restraint in government spending. Yet even during these grim times, the effort to delineate an Irish culture distinct from Britain – an effort which had previously culminated in the Irish Literary Revival of the early twentieth century – was on the rise. The Irish Ireland movement of the 1920s continued to gather strength throughout the 1930s, as the Gaelic League and its supporters strove to restore the Irish language as the new nation's primary mode of public and private speech, drawing on Douglas Hyde's imperative to 'de-Anglicise' Irish culture in order to reclaim an essential 'Irishism' that had been diluted by centuries of English colonial rule.[31] The Free State government's insistence on Irish as the primary language to be used in the National Schools, for example, was based on its opposition to the dominance of the English language and culture throughout the bureaucratic structures of the fledgling state.

In the 1930s, the Irish Ireland movement was championed by Daniel Corkery, a leading academic who had mentored both O'Faoláin and Frank O'Connor as young men, but who had come to represent, in their eyes, a dangerously conservative and reactionary view of Irish identity. O'Faoláin, in particular, had a complicated relationship with Corkery, as the two had competed in 1931 for a prestigious academic post at University College Cork, which Corkery won, to O'Faoláin's bitter disappointment.[32] Corkery's first major critical work, *The hidden Ireland*, proposed to reveal the spirit of 'Irish Ireland' through the study of eighteenth-century Gaelic poetry.[33] Later, in his influential work *Synge and Anglo-Irish literature*, Corkery claimed that the 'three great forces' which defined 'the Irish national being' were religious consciousness, Irish nationalism, and rural life. He rejected as 'alien-minded' any Irish literature which did not keep these three elements to the fore, and he expected that in truly Irish writing they would be 'breaking in on every page'.[34]

The general trend towards social and political conservatism would continue with the rise to power of Eamon de Valera, whose newly founded party Fianna Fáil won the largest number of seats in Dáil Eireann in 1932. Fianna Fáil, with de Valera as its leader, remained the governing party for sixteen years, until 1948, and de Valera was a driving political force throughout much of the mid-twentieth century. Historians are divided, however, as to the extent of his government's impact on mid-century Irish culture. Brown writes that de Valera 'enthusiastically shared

31 Brown, *Ireland*, pp 44–67; Douglas Hyde, 'The Necessity for De-Anglicizing Ireland', speech delivered to National Literary Society, Dublin, 25 November 1892, in *Irish political documents, 1869–1916*, ed. by Arthur Mitchell and Padraig Ó Snodaigh (Dublin, 1989). 32 See Maurice Harmon, *Sean O'Faolain: a life* (London, 1994), pp 90–5. 33 Daniel Corkery, *The hidden Ireland* (Dublin, 1924), p. 23. 34 Corkery, *Synge and Anglo-Irish literature* (Cork, 1931), pp 19–25.

Irish Ireland's vision of national possibility, preferring an Ireland of frugal, God-fearing country folk to any absorption of the country into industrial Europe'.[35] Ferriter, on the other hand, argues that 'Social historians should be sceptical of the phrase "de Valera's Ireland", often used to describe the 1930s and 1940s'.[36] Like Fallon, Ferriter finds evidence of opposition to Fianna Fáil's conservative agenda, not only in the work of prominent writers and artists, but also in the efforts of Catholic social theorists of the day. Despite his assertion that 'cultural vitality' continued to exist in Ireland, however, Ferriter concedes that 'The reality was that de Valera believed in state control of all areas of Irish life'.[37]

Advances in state control of Irish life can most clearly be seen in two initiatives of the 1930s: the economic war with Britain, under which de Valera's government restricted trade and attempted to establish agricultural self-sufficiency, to the detriment of many small farmers;[38] and the work of the Board of Literary Censors, which was established by the Irish Censorship of Publications Act of 1929 and arguably became, in the words of Senator Sir John Keane, a full-blown 'literary Gestapo' under de Valera's government.[39] By the time *The Bell* tackled the Censorship in a series of vehemently oppositional editorials, letters and essays in 1942, over 1,600 books, many of them by well-respected Irish authors, had been banned from sale or distribution in Ireland on the grounds of moral indecency. Indeed, *The Bell's* role in the debate over the Censorship has been widely celebrated and discussed, and stands as one of its most significant contributions to the development of an independent-minded literary and intellectual culture in the 1940s. Michael Adams' *Censorship: the Irish experience* devotes an entire chapter to the magazine's activist efforts, led by Sean O'Faoláin, to limit the power of the Board of Literary Censors.[40] Since I will be arguing for a new examination of *The Bell's* project of cultural representation, I will address the magazine's anti-Censorship campaign in the context of its opposition to conservative ideas of Irish identity as they were promoted and institutionalized by the actions of the Censors, especially their banning of *The Tailor and Ansty*, which had first been serialized in the pages of *The Bell*.

The editors of *The Bell* had a conflicted and sometimes contradictory relationship to ideas about modernity, modernization, and modernist movements in

35 Brown, *Ireland*, p. 133.   36 Ferriter, *Transformation*, p. 358.   37 Ferriter, *Transformation*, pp 360, 365.   38 See Brown, *Ireland*, pp 131–4.   39 Sir John Keane, Seanad debates, November–December 1942, quoted in Michael Adams, *Censorship: the Irish experience* (Alabama, 1968), p. 86. Throughout this study, the term 'Censorship', when capitalized, signifies the Board of Literary Censors as constituted by the Irish Censorship of Publications Act of 1929.   40 Adams, *Censorship*, pp 81–95. See also Brad Kent, 'Shaw, *The Bell*, and Irish Censorship in 1945', *The Annual of Bernard Shaw Studies* 30 (2010). While Adams' is still the main work in this area, Daniel P. Johnson's unpublished doctoral thesis 'Censorship and publishing in Ireland in the 1930s and 40s' (University of Ulster, 2001) is a useful resource, especially for its discussion of O'Faoláin's 65 *Bell* editorials, with particular focus on the Seanad's Censorship debate of 1942. *The Bell's* role in the debate over the Censorship will be discussed in more detail in Chapter Four.

art and literature. Across the developed world, especially in the years after the Second World War, technological and industrial advances had resulted in rapid social change. As a result of increasing industrialization, workers converged on cities; extended families diminished in importance, in favour of the nuclear family; and societies worldwide became increasingly similar. In Ireland, modernization has often been understood as the opponent of tradition, and tradition has been equated with 'the discourse of the nation'. [41] Yet nationalism and modernity need not be viewed as irreconcilable. In the pages of *The Bell*, which was undeniably a national and nationalist endeavour, writers and editors grappled with the implications of modernization for their emerging society. Rather than regressing, as Corkery, de Valera and others suggested, into nostalgia for a pre-colonial agrarian past, O'Faoláin and his fellow editors consistently confronted the challenges of modernity with which their new nation was faced. These included the increasing migration of rural workers to Irish and English cities and towns, technological advances in communication and transportation, and the juxtaposition of social groups which had previously existed in relative isolation from one another. In the face of rapid changes in post-revolutionary Ireland, *The Bell* provided a forum for writers from all strata of Irish society to document and discuss their own experiences of modernity. Its editors embraced both tradition and modernization without viewing these two realities as mutually exclusive (as indeed they were not for many *Bell* writers and readers).

Yet, paradoxically, *The Bell*'s editors, with rare exceptions, adhered to traditional forms of literary expression, and shunned modernist or experimental movements in poetry, fiction, and art. Indeed, *The Bell*'s editors frequently argued amongst themselves, and with contributors such as Belfast poets John Hewitt and Roy McFadden, over the expression of nationalism in poetry and over the formal experimentation practiced by modernist writers in England, Europe and America. One of the contradictions that emerges in *The Bell*'s trajectory is that the magazine's editors consistently embraced the representation of modernity even while they argued against departures from literary realism in both poetry and fiction. Arguably, modernism's challenge to representational modes of literature threatened the editors' belief in the power of representation, and of documentary realism, to transform conceptions of national identity.

PRECURSORS TO THE BELL

Rather than accept the essentialist versions of Irish identity that were prevalent in popular discourse in the 1930s, 40s and 50s, *The Bell*'s editors continually asked

---

41 Conor McCarthy, *Modernisation, crisis and culture in Ireland, 1969–1992* (Dublin, 2000), pp 14–18.

what Irishness meant in the context of a post-colonial society that was rapidly becoming more urban, modern and industrialized. In doing so, they took up questions that had previously been debated in the pages of the *Irish Statesman*, edited by Æ, and the short-lived journal *Ireland To-Day*, both of which published political and critical commentary alongside creative literary work. In every issue of the *Irish Statesman*, which ran weekly from 1923 to 1930, Æ (who also wrote under his given name, George Russell) penned lengthy editorials on political developments in the newly independent Irish Free State. In addition, he published poetry, short stories and letters from both established and emerging Irish writers, including early poems by Frank O'Connor and Patrick Kavanagh, as well as work by O'Faoláin, including his early short story 'In Lilliput'.[42] In the late 1920s, while O'Faoláin was studying at Harvard on a Commonwealth Fellowship, he corresponded several times with Æ, who reaffirmed him in his 'wish to devote [himself] to literature' and wrote, reassuringly: 'I think that you have a great talent'.[43] O'Faoláin's vociferous opposition to the Censorship in the 1940s may be seen as one way in which *The Bell* followed on from the work of the *Irish Statesman*, which voiced strong objection to the Censorship of Publications Act in 1929.[44] When the *Irish Statesman* announced in 1930 that it would cease publication, its founder, the agricultural reformer Sir Horace Plunkett, concluded his remembrances of the magazine with the hope that another liberal-minded literary periodical would arise to take its place: 'My prayer is that the example the *Irish Statesman* has set may be taken to heart, and that before long the gap it has left will be adequately filled'.[45] It seems clear that when O'Faoláin, O'Connor, O'Donnell and their colleagues founded *The Bell*, they aimed to fill the void left by the *Irish Statesman*'s demise.

Like the *Irish Statesman*, *Ireland To-Day*, which ran from 1936 to 1938, was rooted in a clearly articulated political agenda, in this case, republicanism, as espoused by its editor, Jim O'Donovan. Its political and cultural commentary was similar to that which *The Bell* would later publish, and its list of contributors included future *Bell* editors O'Faoláin, O'Connor, and O'Donnell, as well as future *Bell* writers Liam O'Laoghaire and Owen Sheehy Skeffington. *Ireland To-Day* billed itself as 'the first lay monthly magazine that has dealt with Social, Economic, National and Cultural matters, together with a strong literary intrusion of story, poems and a much-appreciated book section'.[46] Like the *Irish Statesman*, *Ireland To-Day* was more overtly political than literary; its creative contributions are described as an 'intrusion', rather than a central focus of the magazine. In the issue of

---

42 Frank Shovlin, *The Irish literary periodical, 1923–58* (Oxford, 2003), pp 18–36.   43 Æ, letter to Sean O'Faoláin, 20 May 1927.   44 *The Bell*'s opposition to the Censorship is discussed in more detail in Chapter Four.   45 Sir Horace Plunkett, 'Notes and Comments: *The Irish Statesman* Ends', *Irish Statesman* 14:6 (12 April 1930), p. 106.   46 'Editorial', *Ireland To-Day* 2:1 (January 1937), pp 3–4.

Ireland To-Day for October 1936, however, there can be seen one early manifesta-
tion of the debate over Irish identity which would become a focal point for *The
Bell*. Under the title 'Is an Irish Culture Possible?' Dr James Devane, author of *Isle
of destiny: the clash of cultures*, published in 1936, explores the debate between
Corkery and O'Faoláin which had recently emerged in the pages of the *Dublin
Magazine* : 'Ireland stands at the cross roads. Guides beckon her to differing ways.
One invites her to the land of cosmopolitan culture. The other to hidden Ireland'.[47] In other words, Devane saw O'Faoláin as standing for the assimilation of
Ireland into modern Europe, while Corkery advocated a return to pre-colonial
Irish identity. Devane concludes that 'If Ireland is to achieve anything she must
look back rather than forward'.[48] O'Faoláin himself responded, in the same issue
of *Ireland To-Day*, with a statement of his beliefs about the need for a forward-
looking, inclusive version of Irish identity, based on the representation of 'the
actuality of the Ireland in which we live'.[49] Of those who, like Corkery and
Devane, would try to idealize the Irish past, O'Faoláin wrote:

> They hate the truth because they have not enough personal courage to
> be what we all are – the descendants, English-speaking, in European
> dress, affected by European thought, part of the European economy, of
> the rags and tatters who rose with O'Connell to win under Mick Collins
> – in a word, this modern Anglo-Ireland.[50]

Here O'Faoláin suggests that an authentic version of modern Irishness, one
which acknowledges both the Irish peasantry as well as English and European
influences, is the only way 'to create something real on the basis of reality'.[51] It
was an argument that he had made elsewhere, as in the pages of the modernist
magazine *Motley* in 1933, when he acknowledged that 'The Gaelic revivalist, the
Irish-Irelander, the would-be Separatist, every brand of active Nationalist dis-
likes the word [Anglo-Ireland] so thoroughly that he ends by disliking his own
people, almost, indeed, by disliking himself'.[52] Such a statement prefigures the
founding mission of *The Bell*, which would aim to address this break in the Irish
psyche and to resolve what O'Faoláin and others saw as a national identity crisis.

The differences between *The Bell* and predecessors such as *Ireland To-Day* and
the little magazine *Motley* are chiefly those of focus, scope and longevity. Both
of these earlier periodicals were rooted in clearly delineated perspectives –
Ireland To-Day in O'Donovan's republicanism, *Motley* in the promotion of its
founding organization, the newly established Gate Theatre. Mary Manning, the

47 James Devane, 'Is an Irish Culture Possible?', *Ireland To-Day* 1:5 (October 1936), p. 21. 48 Ibid., p. 24. 49
O'Faoláin, 'Commentary on the Foregoing', *Ireland To-Day* 1:5 (October 1936), p. 32. 50 Ibid. 51 Ibid. 52 O'Faoláin,
'Letter from a Novelist to an Idealist', *Motley* 2:7 (November 1933), p. 4.

editor of *Motley*, published 19 issues of 16 pages each between March 1932 and
May 1934. Manning wrote film reviews and ran literary competitions, but her
main purpose for the magazine was the promotion of the Gate and its theatrical productions. One contributor, trade unionist Louie Bennett, who would later
debate with O'Faoláin in the pages of *The Bell*, suggested an expansion of *Motley's*
mission, such as would later be undertaken by *The Bell*: 'I should like to see
MOTLEY carried on as a bigger venture, not limited to dealing with one art,
but serving it as an open forum for the youth of Ireland to speak their mind on
life and all the arts'.[53] As Nicholas Allen has shown, O'Faoláin's letters to
O'Donovan, *Ireland To-Day's* editor, suggest that he, too, felt the need for a more
ambitious and more independent-minded Irish literary magazine. Allen speculates that O'Faoláin's growing frustration with the exclusivity of the republican
agenda promoted by *Ireland To-Day* spurred him toward the foundation of *The
Bell* as an openly inclusive literary magazine after *Ireland To-Day* ran out of funds.
Furthermore, Allen suggests that witnessing the demise of O'Donovan's journal taught O'Faoláin much about successful strategies for keeping *The Bell* afloat
after its initial launch in 1940.[54] In contrast to *Ireland To-Day*, *The Bell* was managed by an established board, not by one editor alone, and O'Faoláin worked
assiduously to treat his contributors as professionals, prodding them to write
their best and keep to deadlines, offering a relatively generous pay scale of one
guinea per 1,000 words to recognize their efforts.[55]

While *The Bell* took some of its native political impulses from the *Irish Statesman* and *Ireland To-Day*, it was also modelled on two foreign predecessors, the
nineteenth-century Russian periodical *Kolokol*, and the British literary journal
Horizon, which began publication in 1939, just one year before *The Bell's* appearance. *Kolokol*, whose title translates as *The Bell*, was edited by Russian émigré
Alexander Herzen from 1857 to 1868, and has recently been chronicled by Helen
Williams, who describes Herzen as a leading figure in the nineteenth-century
cultural debates between 'the so-called Slavophiles with their messianic view of
the destiny of Russia, and the "Westernizers," who looked to western Europe
for inspiration'.[56] O'Faoláin referred to this very debate in one of his *Bell* editorials, drawing an analogy between the nineteenth-century Slavophiles and those
he saw as modern-day 'Celtophils' – bureaucrats who propagated literary censorship and other strictures in the name of Irish nationalism.[57] Like *The Irish
Statesman* and *Ireland To-Day*, *Kolokol* was less a literary magazine than a political
one, a monthly collection of 'editorial articles, a mixture of news, political and

53 Louie Bennett, Letter, *Motley* 1:4 (September 1932), p. 16.   54 Nicholas Allen, *Modernism, Ireland and Civil War* (Cambridge, 2009), pp 193–4.   55 O'Faoláin, undated letter to Frank O'Connor, Gotlieb Archival Research Center.   56
Helen Williams, 'Ringing the Bell: Editor-Reader Dialogue in Alexander Herzen's *Kolokol*', *Book History* 4 (2001), p.
116.   57 Sean O'Faoláin, 'The Stuffed-Shirts', *The Bell* 6:3 (June 1943), p. 190.

social comment, and other items such as leaked official documents'.⁵⁸ Perhaps its most significant connection to *The Bell* was its intention to represent the voice of the Russian people: 'Its pages were opened to all Russians of goodwill who were invited both to listen to the bell and to "ring it themselves"'.⁵⁹ O'Faoláin would later make use of a similar metaphor, inviting Irish men and women from all walks of life to take part in *The Bell*'s project of building a new national culture, and to 'make this bell peal out a living message'.⁶⁰

In England, concerns about the effect of the Second World War on the cultural climate produced the literary journal *Horizon*, whose layout, contents and structure clearly served as a blueprint for *The Bell*. As early as 1943, Denys Val Baker compared the two magazines in his first annual *Little Reviews Anthology*: '[T]here are hopeful signs that the *Bell*, which is closely modelled, it would seem, on *Horizon*, will find a much-needed place in Irish literature of to-day'.⁶¹ In 1946, Conor Cruise O'Brien measured *The Bell* less favourably against its English counterpart when he wrote that *Horizon* was the product of English high culture, while *The Bell* was written for 'the lettered section of the Irish petty bourgeoisie'.⁶² *Horizon* has been the topic of a monograph by Michael Shelden, who places his study of the journal in the context of the life of its founding editor, Cyril Connolly, 'in a way which blends literary history with criticism and biography'.⁶³ In so doing, Shelden aims to fill a gap in Connolly's previously published biography, and to bring to light the contributions of other writers and editors to *Horizon*, especially Peter Watson, who, along with Stephen Spender, helped to found the magazine. According to one contemporary advertisement for the magazine, *Horizon* was intended to 'provide readers with enjoyment and writers with opportunity, and to maintain a high literary standard during the war'.⁶⁴ It had no political agenda to press, and no particularly national perspective to express. Its contents were a mix of essays, poems, short stories and art reviews, with a monthly editorial 'Comment' written by Connolly as a frontispiece. It seems likely that Connolly's editorials, which differed from those of other little magazines in their extensive and often witty commentary on cultural life, inspired O'Faoláin's use of the form in *The Bell*. Indeed, *The Bell*'s own editorials were so lively that they tend to overshadow most critics' appreciation of the magazine's contents; as Sean McMahon has noted, 'One excellent anthology of *Bell* material would be the collected editorials of [O'Faoláin and O'Donnell]'.⁶⁵

The Bell's writers and editors were keenly aware of their native and foreign literary predecessors. References to *Horizon* appear frequently in the pages of

58 Williams, 'Ringing the Bell', p. 120.   59 Ibid., p. 120.   60 Sean O'Faoláin, 'This Is Your Magazine', *The Bell* 1:1 (October 1940), p. 6.   61 Denys Val Baker, *Little reviews, 1914–43* (London, 1944), p. 44.   62 Donat O'Donnell [Conor Cruise O'Brien], 'Horizon', p. 1030.   63 Michael Shelden, *Friends of promise: Cyril Connolly and the world of Horizon* (London, 1990), p. 10.   64 Ibid., p. 2.   65 McMahon, *The best from* The Bell, p. 9.

The Bell, both in advertisements for the journal itself and in allusions to particular articles printed therein; O'Faoláin once described *Horizon* as *The Bell*'s 'London counterpart'.[66] In February 1942, *Horizon* published an 'Irish number' which included articles by O'Faoláin, Frank O'Connor, and others, and which was summarized and praised in a paragraph-long editorial note in *The Bell*.[67] In September 1942, a second editorial note appeared, promising to 'repay the compliment [...] with an English Number of *The Bell*'.[68] For the editors of *The Bell*, it was important to vie for equality with their English counterpart by publishing a corresponding issue to balance the scales. In promising an 'English Number', *The Bell* would take on the subjective viewpoint previously reserved for the colonial power, and submit England to the role of object, for a change.

But the 'English Number' never appeared. In October, an editorial note on the topic reported that 'Owing to difficulties of communication we shall have to postpone for a month or two the proposed "English Number" of *The Bell* which we are planning by way of a courtesy reply to the "Irish Number" of *Horizon*'.[69] Seven prospective English authors were listed, nonetheless, along with their tentative topics, and it seemed that the eventual appearance of the 'English Number' was assured. It was only in February 1943 that *The Bell* was forced to abandon its preparations for a reciprocal response to *Horizon*:

> There are so many apparently unsurmountable [*sic*] war-time difficulties in the way of producing the 'English Number' of *The Bell* that we have decided to alter our plan. Chiefly, illness and unforeseen commitments are holding up several of our contributors, and we do not care to keep readers waiting indefinitely on our promise. We have developed what we hope is an even better scheme – a series of *International Numbers*. In these all the promised English contributions will, we trust, duly appear, together with contributions representing other lands.[70]

While the excuses of illness and unforeseen commitments are undoubtedly valid, it seems likely that wartime censorship may have also played a part, as the Irish government's policy of neutrality steadfastly denied permission to print anything sympathetic to either Allies or Axis.[71] Furthermore, O'Faoláin privately wrote of the financial difficulties of paying English writers at English rates, a situation exacerbated by the lack of agreed Irish Serial Rights, which had not yet been legally established after the achievement of political independence.[72]

66 O'Faoláin, 'On Editing a Magazine', p. 96. 67 Editorial note, *The Bell*, 3:6 (February 1942), p. 429. 68 Editorial note, *The Bell*, 4:6 (September 1942), p. 456. 69 Editorial note, *The Bell*, 5:1 (October 1942), p. 67. 70 Editorial note, *The Bell*, 5:5 (February 1943), p. 342. 71 See Wills, *That neutral island*, pp 274–7. Wartime censorship is further discussed at pp 142–4. 72 O'Faoláin, letter to Frank O'Connor, 19 September 1942, Gotlieb Archival Research Center.

Thus, the editors' focus had shifted, due at least in part to Ireland's neutrality and its post-colonial condition, from centring on England as a direct literary counterpart, to portraying the former colonial power as only one of many voices in the contemporary literary world. *The Bell's* proposed 'English Number' episode stands as one demonstration of the tensions inherent in its attempt to create a new version of Irish identity in the post-colonial era.

IDENTITY, REPRESENTATION, TRANSFORMATION:
A DISCUSSION OF TERMS

In writing about conceptions of Irishness in the mid-twentieth century, I have chosen to emphasize the word 'identity' rather than 'society' or 'culture' because I have become convinced, in studying *The Bell*, that what was at stake for the writers and editors of the magazine was the very definition of what it meant to be Irish at a time when independence from Britain was less than two decades old, and when the assertion of neutrality in the Second World War had drawn a line between Ireland and her European and American contacts. I am aware of the pitfalls of an attempt to write about identity as a fixed concept within cultural and literary discourse: identity is a notoriously slippery idea, and even Erik Erikson, the American psychoanalyst who popularized the term 'identity' through his work on the psychological stages of the life cycle, hesitated to offer a finite definition, but hastened to point out that 'The more one writes about this subject, the more the word becomes a term for something as unfathomable as it is all-pervasive'.[73]

The widespread use of the term 'identity' can be traced to Erikson's writings of the 1960s, in which he theorized that individual identity formation is the main psychological task of childhood, and that subsequent problems experienced in adulthood can be traced to undue prolongation of, or regression to, one of the many potential crisis points of identity formation. In Erikson's use of the term, identity is itself a multi-faceted proposition, a self-concept which he describes as 'a process "located" *in the core of the individual* and yet also *in the core of his communal culture*'.[74] Erikson's focus on the dual nature of identity as being based both in individual and collective experiences lends itself to a consideration of identity formation as related to the literary process, in which the individual writer must simultaneously work at self-expression as well as communication to a larger cultural community if he or she wishes to find a reading audience. Erikson's description of identity as a process, 'always changing and developing', also highlights the dynamic nature of identity formation:

73 Erik Erikson, *Identity: youth and crisis* (London, 1968), p. 9.   74 Erikson, *Identity*, p. 22 (emphasis Erikson's).

> [I]n psychological terms, identity formation employs a process of simultaneous reflection and observation, a process taking place on all levels of mental functioning, by which the individual judges himself in the light of what he perceives to be the way in which others judge him in comparison to themselves and to a typology significant to them; while he judges their way of judging him in the light of how he perceives himself in comparison to them and to types that have become relevant to him.[75]

Erikson suggests that this process is for the most part unconscious, 'except where inner conditions and outer circumstances combine to aggravate a painful, or elated, "identity-consciousness"'.[76] Such a description of identity-consciousness – alternately painful and elated – seems particularly fitting for the writers of mid-twentieth-century Ireland.

Although his description focuses, as does much of modern psychoanalysis, on the individual, Erikson acknowledged that the concept of identity carried wider social implications. In particular, he described the development of a positive group identity within populations that have been subjected to political oppression. In such cases, Erikson noted, it is often writers who become 'artistic spokesmen and prophets' for a group's identity, for it is they who decide that 'a certain painful identity-consciousness may have to be tolerated' in order to come to a new understanding of the group's position in relation to the dominant majority. Erikson's discussion focuses on the work of African-American writers such as W.E.B. DuBois, Ralph Ellison, and James Baldwin, whose writing attempted to recapture the 'surrendered identity' which had been taken from them over centuries of enslavement and institutional racism. He further offers the example of Indian subjects of the British Empire, who were forced into a 'revolution of awareness' of their group identity by Gandhi's activism.[77] Thus Erikson's work intersects with the work of post-colonial theorists such as Frantz Fanon, who argued that the first goal of the 'native intellectual' must be 'to see clearly the people he has chosen as the subject of his work of art', and who commented on the native's need to defend his or her national culture in order to establish its right to exist alongside the uncontested culture of the colonizer.[78] More recently, the concept of group identity has been explored in relationship to cultural studies, and its implications for the understanding of cultural expression have been discussed by a number of theorists. Many, in common with Erikson, stress the dynamic nature of identity itself. Stuart Hall, for example, argues

75 Ibid., pp 22–3. 76 Ibid., p. 23. 77 Ibid., pp 296–8. Erikson cites American historian C. Vann Woodward on the concept of 'surrendered identity'. 78 Frantz Fanon, *The wretched of the earth*, trans. by Constance Farrington (London, 1967; repr. 1990), pp 168, 182.

against an 'essentialist' view of identity when he writes that identity 'does *not* signal that stable core of the self, unfolding from beginning to end through all the vicissitudes of history without change; the bit of the self which remains always-already "the same", identical to itself across time'.[79] Rather, Hall argues, the formation of group identity is continually responsive to societal change, and is free to develop and evolve as conditions warrant.

Hall's cautionary stance against an essentialist definition of identity calls to mind the version of Irish identity promoted by Daniel Corkery, whose insistence on a rigid definition of Irish identity based on nationalism, religion and the land was anathema to O'Faoláin and the other editors of *The Bell*. Rather than limit Irish identity to a few core elements, O'Faoláin made it clear, in a 1931 review of Corkery's *Synge and Anglo-Irish literature* published in *Criterion*, that he was opposed to any attempt at a narrow definition of what it meant to be Irish:

> One inevitably asks: Is Dublin not Ireland? Its drawing-rooms, its broth-els, as well as its churches and its chapels? Is a garden-party in the Viceregal lodge not a piece of Ireland? As well as the grand-stand at Punchestown, or an Irish Jew frying kidneys for his wife's breakfast, or an old poet on top of his castle playing at Alastor, or a ship from Rio de Janeiro drawing up by the Cork jetties? Suffice it to say that the writer believes that Mr. Corkery has over-simplified and over-idealized Irish life.[80]

Such a statement prefigures *The Bell*'s insistence on an inclusive approach to representations of Irish identity. O'Faoláin again attacked Corkery in the pages of the *Dublin Magazine* in 1936, equating his cultural exclusivism with the racial programs of Nazism.[81] As *The Bell*'s founding editor, O'Faoláin would eventually realize his ambition to publish a wide range of perspectives drawn from diverse experiences of Irish daily life. His list of rhetorical questions in the review quoted above mirrors a typical Table of Contents from one of *The Bell*'s monthly issues, in which documentary articles such as 'A Hundred Years of Irish Fisheries' stood side by side with 'Dublin Street Rhymes' and 'Fairyhouse', a description of the Irish Grand National steeplechase.

In his famous St Patrick's Day radio address of 1943, Eamon de Valera, like Corkery, cast Irish identity as existing in a romanticized rural past, waiting to be reclaimed by Irish men and women of the present day. 'The ideal Ireland', he said, was 'a land whose countryside would be bright with cosy homesteads,

79 Stuart Hall, 'Introduction: Who Needs Identity?', in *Questions of cultural identity*, ed. by Stuart Hall and Paul du Gay (London, 1996), p. 3.   80 O'Faoláin, review of *Synge and Anglo-Irish literature* by Daniel Corkery, *Criterion* 11 (October 1931), p. 142.   81 Shovlin, *The Irish literary periodical*, pp 54–5.

whose fields and villages would be joyous with the sounds of industry.'[82] In the
lines that followed, de Valera invoked St Patrick, the Young Irelanders, the Gaelic
League and the Irish Volunteers, all committed, in de Valera's words, to the ideal
Ireland he described. Thus he traced an ideological lineage that included
Catholicism, nationalism, and the Irish language, and connected that lineage to
his Irish listeners in 1943, rooting them firmly in their heroic past. But for
O'Faoláin and his fellow editors, de Valera's vision of the ideal rural republic
was not liberating, but limiting. Rather than accept the popular version of
national identity as static and, as de Valera often described it, truly Irish – a
phrase which implied a conception of racial purity disturbingly similar to those
being put forward in Nazi Germany – *The Bell* advocated a broadened spectrum
of Irish identity, one that would accommodate not only rural realities but also
urban life, and that would give voice to the experiences of writers from all
denominations and all strata of Irish society.

The collaborative structure of a magazine such as *The Bell* lends itself particularly well to the articulation of group identity. In *The Bell*, established authors
found their work published alongside that of emerging writers, as well as non-
specialist members of the public who often used first-person declarative sentences as titles, for example, 'I Live in a Slum' or 'I Lost a Leg'.[83] As O'Faoláin
wrote in his first editorial, 'This is Your Magazine': 'Only the people can create
an image of themselves'.[84] In the context of a collaborative process, identity formation is necessarily present- and future-oriented: drawing on history, language
and culture as resources, but always facing forward, towards what the people
aspire to become. In contrast to Corkery and de Valera, the editors of *The Bell*
asked their contributors to keep their eyes on the present, to represent the
authenticity of their current lives and experiences, and not to be lured into nostalgia for an Ireland that may never have existed.

In studies of Irish literature, the use of the term 'identity' remains controversial. Peter McDonald takes issue with the tendency of post-colonial critics
to equate Irish identity with a sense of victimization:

> For the Irish, it seems, a 'sense of selfhood' is inevitably a recognition
> of the 'bondage' they have suffered, and suffer; to deny the oppression
> is either to have failed to achieve an 'affirmative consciousness' of who
> one is, or to have been hoodwinked into believing that one has not been
> hoodwinked.[85]

82 Eamon de Valera, 'Address by Mr de Valera, 17 March 1943', RTÉ Archives 83 'I Live in a Slum', *The Bell* 1:2 (November 1940); F.N., 'I Lost a Leg', *The Bell* 12:2 (May 1946). 84 O'Faoláin, 'This Is Your Magazine', *The Bell* 1:1 (October 1940), pp 5–9 (p. 7). 85 Peter McDonald, *Mistaken identities: poetry and Northern Ireland* (Oxford, 1997), p. 9.

McDonald's discussion further highlights the difficulty of writing about identity in light of the recent history of Northern Ireland, where identity and politics are inextricably intertwined. Yet his repudiation of the negative identity assigned by the Irish colonial past, and his willingness to engage with ideas of identity in his critique of Northern Irish poetry, would seem to suggest that he accepts that identity continues to be an issue in interpretations of Irish literature. In doing so, he takes up Seamus Deane's suggestion that the construction of a post-colonial Irish identity must not be based on backward-looking definitions of Irishness: 'it is still true that the desire to rewrite or reread our history in the light of a Utopian future or of an Edenesque past from which all these repellent features [of industrialized modernity] have been eliminated, is dangerous'.[86] In Deane's view, a positive post-colonial Irish identity can be formed, and true independence from Britain established, only '[i]f the Irish could forget about the whole problem of what is *essentially* Irish'.[87] We can be sure that O'Faoláin and his fellow editors would have agreed with Deane's assertion that 'Identity is here and now, not elsewhere and in another time'.[88]

It was Erikson who coined the phrase 'identity crisis', which he explained as 'designating a necessary turning point, a crucial moment, when development must move one way or another, marshalling resources of growth, recovery and further differentiation'.[89] I would argue that Irish society in 1940, fresh after the declaration of neutrality in the Second World War, and only eighteen years after independence, faced just such a crisis. Irish identity itself was a contested terrain, with conservative figures such as Corkery and de Valera, not to mention the assembled editorial boards of the various religious periodicals, aligned in favour of a narrowly defined, essentialist version of Irishness built around the image of a socially conservative, Gaelic, Catholic, self-sufficient rural community; against more liberal writers and commentators such as the editors of *The Bell*, who used their magazine to promote a more complex, inclusive version of Irish identity.

The idea of identity as a process of becoming, rather than as a state of being, is particularly relevant to the version of Irish identity advanced by the editors and writers of *The Bell*. One striking feature of the magazine's editorial content is the number of times that the theme of the nation as infant, child, or adolescent is repeated, providing a sense of development that parallels Erikson's depiction of identity formation throughout the life cycle of any given individual. In his early editorials, O'Faoláin maintained that Ireland, as a newly independent country, was still in its infancy, and that its identity had to be constructed out of whole cloth, not patched together from the tatters of pre-revolutionary ideals and images. In a play on the word 'Emergency' as chosen by the Irish government to

---

86 Seamus Deane, 'Remembering the Irish Future', *The Crane Bag* 8:1 (1984), p. 86.   87 Ibid., p. 90 (emphasis Deane's).   88 Ibid., p. 91.   89 Erikson, *Identity*, p. 16.

denote the Second World War, O'Faoláin wrote, in 1941, that 'we are, to-day, in this emergent Ireland living experimentally' because 'the forms of life are still in their childhood'.[90] Ten years later, Mary Beckett, a short story writer from Belfast, compared the 'adolescence' of the Republic with the 'retarded development' of Northern Ireland, inviting a comparison to Erikson's description of the undue prolongation of a crisis point in identity formation: 'As for us here we don't have growing pains for the simple reason that we don't grow'.[91] Towards the end of *The Bell*'s publishing run, in 1953, Associate Editor Anthony Cronin wrote that in comparison to 'adult countries' such as France, the Irish 'pre-occupation with our nationhood has become a sort of obsessional neurosis'.[92] The painful awareness of being in an early stage of identity development — to use Erikson's term, the identity-consciousness — voiced by *Bell* editors and contributors speaks of the need for a positive formation of Irish identity, one that would contrast with essentialist and predetermined ideas of Irishness.

When *The Bell* put forward its representation of a complex and inclusive Irish identity, its agenda was nothing less than transformational. The term 'transformation', almost as slippery as 'identity', has been used in both the active and passive senses in discussions of twentieth-century Irish culture. In examining the relationship between representation and transformation, this study will rely primarily on the active sense of the word, as it is used in Luke Gibbons' collection of essays, *Transformations in Irish culture*. In his introduction, Gibbons asserts that paintings, novels and other works of art are best viewed not as mere windows on social reality, nor simply as exercises in escapism. Rather, he argues, 'I insist on the transformative capacity of culture in society, its power to give rise to what was not there before'.[93] Though Gibbons' essays are primarily concerned with visual media such as film and television, his analysis of the transformative power of art is equally applicable to literary depictions of Irish life such as those found in *The Bell*. His description of the power of representation is particularly relevant:

> Culture *transforms* what it works on: it does not produce it *ex nihilo*. Representations draw their 'raw materials' from extra-cultural spheres of activity (such as politics, economics, kinship systems), but then subject them to symbolic transformations of their own making.[94]

90 O'Faoláin, 'Attitudes', *The Bell* 2:6 (September 1941), pp 11–12.   91 Mary Beckett, 'The Young Writer', *The Bell* 17:7 (October 1951), p. 19. Beckett went on to predict a future child-adult relationship between Northern Ireland and the Republic: 'If ever the leading strings are removed we'll suffer agony in every soft muscle, and you, by then an adult society, will probably have little patience with us'.   92 Anthony Cronin, 'Nationalism and Freedom', *The Bell* 18:11 (Summer, 1953), pp 12, 15.   93 Luke Gibbons, *Transformations in Irish culture* (Cork, 1996), p. 8. The word 'culture' here appears to be interchangeable with 'art' or 'artistic representation'.   94 Ibid., p. 11.

For Gibbons, it was the generic format of television programmes such as *The Riordans* and *The Late Late Show*, for example, which allowed them to deal sympathetically with controversial subjects such as marital breakdown and illegitimacy, thus challenging prevailing social attitudes that encouraged secrecy around these topics.[95] Similarly, I would argue, it was *The Bell*'s overtly inclusive editorial policy, with its call for contributions from all members of Irish society, which challenged essentialist definitions of Irish identity and allowed the magazine to promote a more complex, multi-faceted version of Irishness than those that were prevalent in mid-twentieth-century popular and political discourse.

'Transformation' has also been used in the titles of studies of Irish literature and culture in the twentieth century, such as Robert Welch's *Changing states: transformations in modern Irish writing* and Ferriter's *The transformation of Ireland, 1900–2000*.[96] Here, 'transformation' is used in a more passive sense, denoting the changes wrought by encroaching modernization. This sense of the word is also important to this study, particularly in the discussion of post-war modernization in Chapter Five. As the magazine evolved over the course of its fourteen-year run, its role as an agent of transformation diminished somewhat, and its editorials and essays were often reactive, commenting on changes in technology and media as well as on Ireland's increasingly active role in international affairs.

NATIONAL CULTURE AND POST-COLONIAL DISCOURSE

While authors such as Liam Kennedy have disputed whether Ireland can accurately be described as a post-colonial nation, other contemporary critics such as Anne McClintock have suggested that the continued partition of Northern Ireland negates the 'post-' prefix entirely.[97] Regardless of where one's political sympathies lie in this debate, post-colonial discourse does shed light on the situation in which *The Bell*'s writers and editors found themselves in the post-revolutionary period of the 1940s and 50s. When *The Bell* took up the mission of representing and transforming Irish identity, it did so within a society that was decidedly post-colonial in a cultural sense.

Kennedy's argument against rigid use of the post-colonial perspective can, in fact, be very useful to a discussion of *The Bell*'s project of cultural representation and transformation. Kennedy solidly confirms that 'The indiscriminate use of an ill-defined, umbrella term like colonialism, when reconstructing the past, can distort as well as illuminate'.[98] But there is much to be found in post-

---

95 Ibid., pp 11–12, 57–67, 78–9.   96 Robert Welch, *Changing states: transformations in modern Irish writing* (London, 1993). 97 Anne McClintock, 'The Angel of Progress: Pitfalls of the Term "Post-colonialism"', *Social Text* 31/32 (1992), pp 84–98.   98 Liam Kennedy, 'Modern Ireland: Post-Colonial Society or Post-Colonial Pretensions?', *Irish Review*

colonial discourse which does indeed illuminate the cultural project of *The Bell* in the context of an Irish society which had been self-governing for less than twenty years, and which had newly asserted its political independence in the form of neutrality during the Second World War. Likewise, there is much evidence that the editors of *The Bell* would have agreed with Kennedy's belief that the over-emphasis on Anglo-Irish relations detracts from a clear understanding of Irish society in the post-colonial era. As this book will show, *The Bell* frequently aimed to widen the perspective of its Irish readers, whether through its 'International Numbers', of which the March 1943 issue would be the first, or through O'Faoláin's series of 'One World' editorials, with their ranging focus on countries as disparate as Canada, Yugoslavia and Denmark. It remains the case, however, that *The Bell* emerged in a post-colonial cultural context, and the application of post-colonial theory thus enables a new reading of the magazine.

Before independence, Irish literature had witnessed the folkloric Irish Literary Revival, led in large part by W.B. Yeats and Lady Gregory, during which they and other writers (most notably John M. Synge) attempted to inspire Irish cultural nationalism by translating ancient Irish folklore into English-language poetry and prose. In many ways, the work they produced fuelled the rise of an indigenous Irish identity, and encouraged Irish men and women to campaign for full independence from Britain. In contrast to Revival-era writers such as Yeats and Gregory, however, *The Bell's* editors attempted to document Irish life without idealizing its traditional or primitive elements. In comparing their efforts, we may refer to Sinéad Garrigan Mattar's discussion of the Irish Literary Revival, which usefully defines primitivism as an 'idealist fiction' whose formulation tells us more about the society that creates it than about the populations it is supposed to represent.[99] Mattar differentiates between romantic primitivism, such as that practised by Yeats and Gregory, which seeks to portray the Irish peasantry as 'ostensibly more innocent, more pure, and more "natural"' than civilized society; and modernist primitivism, such as that of J.M. Synge, which idealizes rural life precisely 'because it is seemingly *other* to civilization'.[1] The intentions of *The Bell's* editors did not, however, place them squarely in one or the other of these two camps. Rather, *The Bell's* achievement was to bring the discussion of Irish identity into a post-colonial context: not to depict Irish life as it was lived in an idealized past, nor to document ways of life and language which would exist only, as Synge had written, 'for a few years more' in Ireland,[2] but to convey the state of Irish life at a time of transition, and to invite readers both inside and outside Ireland to embrace the complex-

13 (Winter, 1993), pp 116–117. 99 Sinéad Garrigan Mattar, *Primitivism, science, and the Irish Revival* (Oxford, 2004), p. 246. 1 Ibid., pp 3–4. 2 J.M. Synge, *The playboy of the western world: a comedy in three acts* (Boston, 1911), p. vii.

ity of Irish identity in the Emergency era. For the writers of *The Bell*, the newly independent state stood, in 1940, 'at the beginning of its creative history, and at the end of its revolutionary history'.[3]

The concept of the nation as infant, rather than ancient, permeated the pages of *The Bell*, and gave rise to writing that was often documentary in intent, as *The Bell's* writers and editors strove to portray Irish life in the present, not in some glorious past. The same intent was voiced two decades later, by Frantz Fanon, in his anti-colonial treatise *The wretched of the earth*:

> It is not enough to try to get back to the people in that past out of which they have already emerged; rather we must join them in that fluctuating movement which they are just giving a shape to, and which, as soon as it has started, will be the signal for everything to be called in question.[4]

As O'Faoláin frequently reminded his readers, 'We are a young nation, and this is a young magazine, and we must both start at the bottom and build up'.[5] Whereas the pre-revolutionary nation needed to derive strength from the epic history of native culture, *The Bell* urged its post-independence Irish readers to turn their attention to the present project of creating a new national culture, one that would be free from colonial influences as well as from colonial preoccupations. Again, Fanon's ideas are instructive:

> A national culture is not a folklore, nor an abstract populism that believes it can discover the people's true nature. [...] A national culture is the whole body of efforts made by a people in the sphere of thought to describe, justify and praise the action through which that people has created itself and keeps itself in existence.[6]

In its focus on newness and present action, *The Bell* was an exemplar of Fanon's precepts for post-colonial literature. Declan Kiberd has noted the 'remarkable similarity' between Irish history after independence and Fanon's phases of post-colonialism.[7] Time and again, *The Bell* exhorted its writers and readers to keep their eyes forward, to turn their attention to the task of creating a new, independent national culture, and in this way the magazine falls squarely within the boundaries of post-colonial discourse.

The Bell emerged in the context of a national moment of uncertainty, at a time when Irish writers, critics and political leaders were divided as to the direc-

3 Sean O'Faoláin, 'Standards and Taste', *The Bell* 2:3 (June 1941), p. 6. 4 Fanon, *The wretched of the earth*, pp 182–3. 5 Sean O'Faoláin, 'Answer to a Criticism', *The Bell* 1:3 (December 1940), p. 6. 6 Fanon, *The wretched of the earth*, p. 188. 7 Declan Kiberd, *Inventing Ireland* (London, 1995), pp 551–2.

tion of Irish society and the shape of Irish identity. The political philosopher Hannah Arendt wrote of such turning points as moments 'when not only the later historians but the actors and witnesses, the living themselves, become aware of an interval in time which is altogether determined by things that are no longer and by things that are not yet'.[8] Homi K. Bhabha and others have written about the stance of the post-colonial writer, who occupies a tenuous position in regard to the binary opposition between colonizer and colonized, becoming a complex actor in the spaces between these two rigidly defined categories. Accordingly, Bhabha has described the post-colonial fixation on newness in terms of an interstitial awareness of time.[9] O'Faoláin's command that Irish writers discard the old symbols and invent new ones was indicative of *The Bell*'s focus on newness, which was especially intent in its early days. Furthermore, Bhabha's work on 'hybrid' examples of literary and artistic discourse would seem to accommodate *The Bell* as a complex, multi-faceted representation of post-colonial Irish identity.

Yet *The Bell* was more than simply representational. A central point of this book is that *The Bell* not only represented Irish identity, but also acted to transform it. In this connection one may refer to Gibbons' argument that culture acts as a transformative force on society, not merely as an aesthetic reflection: 'Cultural representations do not simply come after the event, "reflecting" experience or embellishing it with aesthetic form, but significantly alter and shape the ways we make sense of our lives'.[10] National transformation was undeniably a part of *The Bell*'s agenda, along with its declared focus on representation. By presenting various aspects of Irish life that did not always find their images in the mainstream (for example, slum dwellers and prisoners), and by persistently including voices from all strata of Irish society (for example, Ascendancy Protestants and Ulster Orangemen as well as Gaelic speakers), *The Bell* consciously tried to create a more complex and inclusive version of Irish identity than those that were prevalent at the time.

It is *The Bell*'s willingness to embrace complexity that marks it as a post-colonial text. In 1931, Corkery famously decried Irish identity as 'a quaking sod':

> Everywhere in the mentality of the Irish people are flux and uncertainty. Our national consciousness may be described, in a native phrase, as a quaking sod. It gives no footing. It is not English, nor Irish, nor Anglo-Irish.[11]

8 Hannah Arendt, *Between past and future: eight exercises in political thought*, Enlarged Edition (Middlesex, 1968), p. 9. 9 Homi K. Bhabha, *The location of culture* (London, 1994). 10 Gibbons, *Transformations in Irish culture*, p. 8. 11 Corkery, *Synge and Anglo-Irish literature*, p. 14.

The editors of *The Bell* were not threatened by what Corkery described as the 'flux and uncertainty' of mid-twentieth-century Irish life. Time and again the magazine solicited articles by writers from various sections of Irish society, printing, for example, a symposium on the 'five strains' of influence on Irish heritage (Gaelic, Classical, Norman, Anglo-Irish and English), and, later, a series on the religions of the contemporary nation: Presbyterian, Church of Ireland, Catholic, Unitarian, Quaker and Jewish. Rather than lament the lack of a unified national consciousness, as Corkery had done, *The Bell* proposed for Ireland a multi-faceted identity, a multiplicity of voices that had been interwoven throughout history and carried into the present day. As such, the magazine represents a break with the narrow forms of nationalist Irish discourse which predominated in the 1930s, and a willingness to acknowledge the diversity of influences on contemporary Irish society.

In advancing this particular assessment of *The Bell*, I disagree with Gerry Smyth, who in his metacritical work *Decolonisation and criticism* takes *The Bell* to task for parroting the received colonial modes of literary discourse. Smyth's book is most successful in its delineation of the 'liberal' versus 'radical' modes of decolonization, and the necessity of negotiating the pitfalls of the two in order to emerge in some 'Third Space' which offers the most promising way forward. For Smyth, the 'liberal' mode of decolonization is little more than a mirror image of colonialism itself, in which the institutions and government structures of the colonizers are adopted wholesale by the native government once the colonial power has withdrawn. In Smyth's view, liberal decolonization is problematic because it precludes the possibility of true equality between the colonizing and colonized cultures, given that their relationship will always be founded on opposition.[12] Smyth argues that liberal decolonization is inferior to radical decolonization, which aims to overthrow colonial assumptions of native inferiority and to celebrate difference and otherness. Yet the 'radical' mode of decolonization, though more effective in eradicating the received structures of colonial oppression, is only slightly preferable, in Smyth's assessment:

> In its more militant moments this second mode came to register as a need to shed, violently if need be, the material and intellectual trappings of subordination, and to embrace/construct instead a pristine pre-history which would serve as both Edenic cause and Utopian goal of nationalist activity.[13]

One example would be the renewed interest in epic Gaelic folklore, which was championed by the Irish Literary Revival in the early twentieth century.[14]

12 Smyth, *Decolonisation and criticism: the construction of Irish literature* (London, 1998), p. 16.   13 Ibid., p. 17.   14 A second

Smyth's argument against *The Bell* depends on his assessment of the magazine's published criticism as being hopelessly stuck in a liberal decolonizing mode of discourse.

There are several flaws, however, in Smyth's line of reasoning. First, his limited focus on *The Bell*'s book reviews rules out consideration of the several other forms of literary criticism that appeared in the magazine's pages over its fourteen years of publication. These include, for example, 'New Writers' and 'The Belfry', in which O'Faoláin and Poetry Editor Frank O'Connor printed advice for emerging short story writers and poets, alongside their stories and poems; 'Personal Anthologies', in which prominent writers were asked to name their favourite poems and poets, with full explanation; and 'Time and Poetry', in which contemporary poems were paired with older, 'time-tested' poems for comparison. *The Bell* also published a series of debates between O'Faoláin and Geoffrey Taylor, its second Poetry Editor, on the topic of 'Sense and Nonsense in Poetry', that is, realism and abstraction. Although it is true that *The Bell* followed the standard practice of reviewing a number of books each month in terms of their content and merit, which, as Smyth points out, is 'a format that may be traced back to the literary and cultural journals of the late eighteenth century',[15] such experimental features as 'The Belfry' and 'New Writers', for which there exist no parallels in other literary magazines of the period, certainly represent a break with tradition. Contrary to Smyth's abridged description, *The Bell* pioneered quite a few divergent critical tactics which mark a separation from the received, colonial modes of literary criticism.[16]

A second flaw is that Smyth chooses to pit *The Bell* against *Kavanagh's Weekly*, a short-lived journal written and published by Patrick Kavanagh, although it is not clear that an assessment of the two journals is served by placing them in opposition to each other in this way. Although Smyth not unfairly characterizes *The Bell*'s tone as 'smug' and 'urbane' in contrast to Kavanagh's 'iconoclastic' approach to criticism,[17] he neglects to consider the fact that Kavanagh himself was an active contributor to *The Bell*, publishing nineteen poems there, as well as essays, book reviews, and a serialized version of *Tarry Flynn*. His journal and *The Bell* were fundamentally different in character, with *Kavanagh's Weekly* almost entirely authored by Kavanagh himself, and appearing for only thirteen weeks in 1952. A final flaw in Smyth's analysis is that it follows the common pattern of equating the editors' personal political history with that of *The Bell*, falling back on O'Faoláin and O'Donnell's involvement in the revolution of 1916 as an explanation for their editorial actions some twenty-five years later: 'O'Faoláin,

example would be the campaign to restore the Irish language, which is discussed at pp 123–31. 15 Smyth, *Decolonisation*, p. 115. 16 'New Writers' and 'The Belfry' are discussed at pp 47–51, and approaches to poetry are discussed at pp 74–83. 17 Smyth, *Decolonisation*, pp 115, 116.

after all, had participated in the military struggle, and in 1940 was still close enough to the actual events of the revolution and its aftermath for those events to bear significantly on his intellectual profile'.[18] The tone of Smyth's analysis conveys the critical distance felt by today's critics from O'Faoláin's work, and stands in contrast to earlier, more affectionate appraisals published in the 1960s and 70s, but it is nonetheless rooted in an understanding of the magazine as the product of its editor's authorship, an understanding which is problematic in itself. As we will see, the tendency to equate the editors' lives with the life of the magazine undercuts a full appreciation and analysis of *The Bell's* evolution throughout its fourteen-year span.

SCHOLARSHIP ON THE BELL AND IRISH LITERARY MAGAZINES

To date, studies of *The Bell* have tended to take one of two approaches: treating the magazine as the work of founding editor Sean O'Faoláin alone, or attempting to catalogue the multitude of voices and perspectives provided by *The Bell's* many contributors over its fourteen-year lifespan. Many commentators have focused on O'Faoláin's powerful personality, and have treated *The Bell* as a product of O'Faoláin's authorship, much like a novel or essay collection. There are obvious pitfalls to this approach, not the least of which is the significant difference between the collaborative act of gathering and editing short material for a monthly magazine, and the solitary act of writing a sustained, substantial, creative piece of prose. Another pitfall is the fact that O'Faoláin served as editor for only the first six years of the magazine. During this time he was undoubtedly a dominant presence in the writing and editing of *The Bell*, but other staff members contributed heavily to its content and perspective. *The Bell's* Editorial Board, for example, included the novelists Maurice Walsh and Peadar O'Donnell, and its successive Poetry Editors, Frank O'Connor, Geoffrey Taylor, and Louis MacNeice, were all well-established writers who helped shape the magazine's literary agenda.[19]

After O'Faoláin resigned his editorship in 1946, *The Bell* was edited for eight years by Peadar O'Donnell, who receives comparatively little attention from most critics of the magazine. Privately, O'Faoláin remarked to O'Connor that he and O'Donnell had wrestled over editorial control from the very beginning of *The Bell's* publication: 'Of course Peadar would love to write the whole bloody thing.'[20] Once O'Donnell assumed the editor's chair, however, he was, in the

18 Ibid., p. 114.   19 The other listed members of the Editorial Board were Roisin Walsh and Eamonn Martin. See *The Bell* 1:5 (February 1941), masthead, p. 1. O'Connor's work as Poetry Editor is further discussed at pp 47–51, Taylor's at pp 74–83. MacNeice's stint as Poetry Editor is briefly discussed at pp 94–5.   20 O'Faoláin, undated

words of Val Mulkerns, 'the least enthusiastic editor you can possibly imagine', and he left much of the day-to-day work of running *The Bell* to his Associate Editors: first H.A.L. (Harry) Craig, then Anthony Cronin, then Mulkerns, and, for the final months of publication, Cronin again.[21] The magazine was always a collaborative effort, not the work of one man alone, as O'Faoláin wryly acknowledged when he wrote, in a 1944 editorial: 'A magazine, I found, is a ship in whose running the passengers and the crew may have a great deal of say. It is a highly democratic vessel'.[22]

The second, somewhat less common, approach to *The Bell* is to critique it as a repository of work by the great writers of its time, a 'valuable anthology', in the words of Richard Furze, who wrote a PhD thesis on *The Bell* at University College Dublin in 1974.[23] This approach appropriately honours the publishing record of *The Bell*, in which Irish writers found a forum for publication amid the straitened atmosphere of the Emergency, and in whose pages several important Irish authors of the time were printed, including John Hewitt, Brendan Behan, Maura Laverty, and Patrick Kavanagh. It leaves room, however, for a more analytical appraisal of *The Bell*'s achievement as an instrument of cultural representation and transformation.

While the first approach treats *The Bell* as monolithic, the work of a single mind (O'Faoláin's), the second approach results in an impression of cacophony, a patchwork of great authors interspersed with 'filler' pieces by lesser-known scribes. When the existing scholarship on *The Bell* is examined, it becomes clear that a new approach to the magazine is needed. While it is certainly useful to bear in mind the personal and publishing history of *The Bell*'s founding editor, it is important to avoid an excessive focus on O'Faoláin's influence. *The Bell* was read throughout Ireland, by a wide spectrum of readers from all sectors of Irish society, as well as by readers in England and America, and it seems unlikely that all of these were drawn solely by O'Faoláin's personality. Meanwhile, it is equally important to avoid the dissipation of critical energy that results from the understandable urge to quantify *The Bell*'s achievement in terms of the sheer volume of significant pieces published in its 131 monthly issues.

Criticism of *The Bell* began to be printed before the magazine was more than a few years old, and first appeared in the pages of *The Bell* itself. In characteristically self-reflexive form, O'Faoláin commissioned a series of articles on Irish

letter to Frank O'Connor, Gotlieb Archival Research Center. 21 Mulkerns interview, 13 November 2008. Editorial staff changes will be further discussed in Chapter 3. 22 O'Faoláin, 'On Editing a Magazine', p. 93. O'Faoláin also proposed sharing his editorial responsibilities, on occasion: at one stage, he asked Patrick Kavanagh and Frank O'Connor to serve as guest editors for special issues of the magazine, though this plan apparently never materialized (O'Faoláin, letter to Frank O'Connor, 3 November 1943, Gotlieb Archival Research Center). 23 Richard A. Furze, Jr., 'A Desirable Vision of Life: A Study of *The Bell*, 1940–1954' (unpublished doctoral thesis, University College Dublin, 1974), p. 156.

printed media, and included his own publication as the final topic in the series. The result was a stinging review of the extent of his influence on the content of *The Bell* – a review which likely led to much of the subsequent focus on O'Faoláin's editorial personality as the driving force behind the magazine. As Vivian Mercier wrote in his oft-cited 'Verdict on *The Bell*',

> For Sean O'Faoláin *is* THE BELL. He is not just a figurehead – he is the magazine, as you find out after, or before, you have written one article for it. He writes his own Editorial, all 3,000 words of it; he usually has another piece – a lecture, short story or what not – under his own name; he writes the little blurb in italics which appears at the head of most BELL contributions; and if I am not careful, he will write most of this article too.[24]

Mercier somewhat satirically takes O'Faolain and his fellow editors to task for giving too much unwanted 'free criticism and advice' to the new writers they publish.[25] He is nonetheless among the first to point out how multi-faceted *The Bell* aims to be: 'It fulfils for Ireland the functions which in England, e.g., are carried out by a multiplicity of periodicals – some monthly, some weekly'.[26] As such, he provides an early assessment of *The Bell*'s cultural importance to Ireland in the Emergency era, a time when censorship, paper shortages, and communication difficulties effectively sealed off the island from most British and American print media.

Subsequent appraisals of *The Bell* leaned heavily towards Mercier's focus on O'Faoláin as the dominant force behind the magazine. Honor Tracy, who served briefly as an editorial assistant (and who later became O'Faoláin's lover), writes that O'Faoláin 'stands out in Dublin like a rock in foaming seas'.[27] In the Summer and Autumn, 1960, issues of *Kilkenny Magazine*, James Delehanty eulogized *The Bell* by paying tribute to its founding editor: 'he it was who had given us every month something to sharpen our minds on, something genuinely of modern Ireland, whether we liked it or not (and very often we didn't)'.[28] In Spring, 1976, a special issue of *Irish University Review* celebrated O'Faoláin's life and work, including an article on his editorship of *The Bell* written by Dermot Foley, based on the author's personal recollections of encountering the magazine as a young librarian in County Clare.[29] In the same volume, Hubert Butler,

---

24 Vivian Mercier, 'The Fourth Estate: VI. – Verdict on "The Bell"', *The Bell* 10:2 (May 1945), pp 156–67, at p. 157. 25 Mercier, 'The Fourth Estate: VI', p. 158. *The Bell*'s advice to new writers and poets is discussed in more detail at pp 47–51. 26 Mercier, 'The Fourth Estate: VI', p. 159. 27 Honor Tracy, *Mind you, I've said nothing!: forays in the Irish republic* (London, 1953), p. 56. 28 James Delehanty, 'The Bell: 1940–1954 [1]', *Kilkenny Magazine* 1 (Summer 1960), p. 37. 29 Foley, 'Monotonously Rings the Little Bell', *Irish University Review* 6:1 (Spring, 1976), pp 54–62.

The Bell's book reviewer in 1951–2, personally thanks O'Faoláin for taking so many Anglo-Irish writers under his wing.[30] For his part, Mercier contributes an apology for his 'rather brash "Verdict on *The Bell*"' from thirty years before, and praises O'Faoláin's professionalism as an editor and as a writer.[31]

Perhaps the best-known studies of O'Faoláin's life and work are the critical introduction and the biography by Maurice Harmon, published in 1966 and 1994, respectively.[32] *The Bell* figures more prominently in the biography than in Harmon's earlier analysis of O'Faoláin's work as a writer, perhaps because *The Bell* years, as Harmon calls them, were more focused on managing the magazine than on producing original creative work. While the biography charts O'Faoláin's friendship and falling out with fellow editor Frank O'Connor, his attempt to steer *The Bell* through a libel lawsuit, and his affair with Honor Tracy, Harmon's earlier analysis gives only five pages to O'Faoláin's tenure at *The Bell*, stating that 'The whole difficulty for the writer was that this period really was one of pause before change'.[33]

At the opposite end of the spectrum are those studies of *The Bell* which attempt to catalogue its achievements in terms of the number of authors published, or the number of significant poems, short stories and essays in its pages, and which often fall short of a coherent analysis of the magazine. Sean McMahon acknowledges this inevitable weakness in the introduction to his anthology *The best from* The Bell. It must be noted, however, that by collecting many of the best examples of short stories, poems, and essays from *The Bell*, McMahon successfully avoids the pitfall of focusing excessively on editorial voices: only two of Sean O'Faoláin's editorials, his first and last, appear amid the 41 pieces McMahon chooses to anthologize, and he includes none of O'Faoláin's short stories, citing their availability in print elsewhere and his desire to give space to other writers.[34] Richard Furze's unpublished 1974 PhD thesis, on the other hand, is a pertinent example of an overly quantitative approach. As Clyde has noted, 'Any attempt to summarise the achievement of *The Bell* is immediately faced with an obvious problem: how to condense without reductionism, how to represent without endless lists?'.[35] Furze's study, along with Rudi Holzapfel's *Index to contributors to* The Bell, do provide ample information on *The Bell's* impressive list of published authors. Holzapfel's *Index*, in particular, usefully lists every contributing writer, along with article titles and initials to indicate genre ('p' for poem, 'ss' for short story, for example).[36] Yet Furze's description of *The Bell* also

30 Hubert Butler, 'The Bell: An Anglo-Irish View', *Irish University Review* 6:1 (Spring 1976). 31 Vivian Mercier, 'The Professionalism of Sean O'Faoláin', *Irish University Review* 6:1 (Spring 1976), p. 45. 32 Maurice Harmon, *Sean O'Faolain: a critical introduction* (Notre Dame, 1966); *Sean O'Faolain: a life*. 33 Harmon, *A critical introduction*, p. 53. 34 McMahon, *Best from* The Bell, pp 6–7, p. 12. 35 Clyde, p. 193. 36 Holzapfel, *An index of contributors to* The Bell. Holzapfel later commented that he would additionally have liked to index *Bell* articles by subject, but that available funds

reveals an unfulfilled ambition, to analyze the development of the magazine in terms of its evolution over fourteen years of publication. Tracing *The Bell's* evolution is one of the goals of this book, and will be further discussed in Chapters Two and Three.

Recent studies of literary periodicals have demonstrated that there is much more to be gained from an analysis of *The Bell* than a portrait of Sean O'Faoláin's editorship or a catalogue of important authors in the 1940s and 50s. For example, two important surveys published in 2003, one by Tom Clyde and the other by Frank Shovlin, set the stage for an expansion of interest in Irish literary magazines, and both have argued for a new critical approach to the field. More recently, Ballin's new study of Irish, Welsh, and Scottish periodicals has usefully brought genre theory to bear on considerations of periodical texts, and discusses *The Bell* in the context of other literary magazines of its era, while Bryan Fanning's philosophical analysis of five twentieth-century periodicals contrasts *The Bell's* preoccupations with those of ecclesiastical and secular journals.

Not surprisingly, Clyde cites a documentary impulse as the initial spur to producing his *Bibliography*, an impulse which will be familiar to any researcher who has spent time poring through the pages of long-forgotten literary magazines: 'During my earlier researches, it became clear that much valuable material was locked up in journals, and that greater use could be made of this exciting primary material if some sort of practical guide was available'.[37] But he also reveals his belief in the transformative cultural discourse of the literary magazine, and his desire to bring this discourse into the wider critical arena so that it can be properly discussed and analyzed:

> An essential quality of the journals is their *currency*; they are simultaneously the training ground for new writers, a forum in which established writers have licence to experiment, a sounding-board for whatever issues – political, ethical, artistic – agitated sensibilities at the time, and of course a vital source of data in their poems, sketches, advertisements, letters, reviews, obituaries and satires. On a deeper level, ILMs [Irish literary magazines] constitute an important medium by which intellectual élites have carried on the discourses from which have emerged key concepts of nationality.[38]

Clyde goes on to describe Irish literary magazines as an essential mechanism in the development of the type of 'imagined community' described by Benedict Anderson as central to the idea of the modern nation.[39] In the absence of a fully

and resources limited the scope of his efforts. See his *Author Index 3* (Blackrock, Co. Dublin: Carraig Books, 1985). 37 Tom Clyde, *Irish literary magazines: an outline history and descriptive bibliography* (Dublin, 2003), p. vii. 38 Ibid., p. xi. 39 Ibid.

developed theory of the literary periodical as a form in itself, Clyde draws an analogy to Anderson's discussion of the newspaper and its role in forming an 'imagined community' of readers – an anonymously linked, secular community of individuals bound together by a common identity.[40] This analogy is particularly pertinent to *The Bell*, in its conscious project of aiding in the development of Irish identity in the post-independence era. As this study will show, *The Bell*'s readership was distributed across the entire island of Ireland and overseas, so the impact of its construction of Irish identity was widely felt.

Like Beetham and Clyde, Shovlin argues persuasively, in his survey of twentieth-century Irish literary magazines, for 'the emergence of a field of study which examines the literary periodical as a distinct genre'.[41] Shovlin emphasizes the importance of Irish literary magazines as part of the 'material history' of the country, citing Brown,[42] and, like other critics, he situates *The Bell* at the intersection of O'Faoláin's literary career and his political development. Shovlin writes that 'O'Faoláin experimented throughout his career with a wide variety of forms: short story, novel, historical biography, drama, poetry, travel writing', and speculates that editorship of *The Bell* was O'Faoláin's attempt to experiment with a new genre, in order to see if it would fit his artistic needs.[43] In Shovlin's analysis, *The Bell*'s status as a miscellany becomes a solution to O'Faoláin's dissatisfaction with other genres, as well as with post-revolutionary Ireland. The miscellany's inherent heterogeneity provides a vehicle for O'Faoláin's need to express his competing impulses as a writer, and to describe the varied aspects of mid-century Irish culture.

A similar survey, Ballin's 2008 study of twentieth-century Irish, Welsh and Scottish literary magazines, provides a delineation of the miscellany form, which Ballin distinguishes from two other periodical genres, the review and the little magazine. As Ballin notes in an earlier article on *The Bell* and the *Irish Statesman*, 'Common characteristics of the [miscellany] genre [...] include, as we have already seen, the mixing of factual and creative writing, together with a sharp focus on internal Irish affairs, matched against a lively interest in the world outside Ireland'.[44] Ballin perceptively points out that in the miscellany periodical, 'texts can be strategically arranged by editors, providing explicit or (more usually) implicit comments on one another', which suggests that miscellany editors, far from being passive collectors of diverse material, actively shape their readers' perceptions in their decisions both about content and about structure.[45] In contrast to the authoritative voice of the review, the miscellany is defined by

40 Benedict Anderson, *Imagined communities: reflections on the origin and spread of nationalism*, Revised Edition (London, 1991), p. 35.   41 Shovlin, *The Irish literary periodical*, p. 9.   42 Ibid., p. 11.   43 Ibid., p. 102.   44 Malcolm Ballin, 'Transitions in Irish Miscellanies Between 1923 and 1940: *The Irish Statesman* and *The Bell*', *International Journal of English Studies* 2:2 (2002), p. 30.   45 Ibid.

its commitment to dialogue, 'both in its overt readership relations and also in the interplay between varieties of texts displayed closely together in the same publication'.[46] Such a description well fits the initial outlook of *The Bell*, whose editors told readers that 'This Is Your Magazine' and invited contributions from all quarters of Irish society.[47]

While all of these valuable surveys place *The Bell* in the context of discussion about the development of the Irish literary periodical, they necessarily leave the door open for closer analysis of this particular magazine in its entirety. Recent discussions of *The Bell* are less overtly sympathetic to O'Faoláin than those published in the 1960s and 70s, but they continue to assign many of *The Bell*'s characteristics to O'Faoláin's personality, often focusing on his early experiences as a soldier in the Irish revolution. O'Faoláin's literary background and temperament are certainly important to *The Bell*'s editorial stance and content. It is necessary to bear in mind, however, that editorship and authorship are quite different acts of creativity. It is important also to remember that O'Faoláin did not create *The Bell* alone. From the earliest days of the magazine's founding, he collaborated with fellow editors and writers to construct *The Bell* as a project of cultural representation and transformation. As Shovlin states suggestively, in concluding his chapter on *The Bell*: 'There is still much to be learned about the state of mid-century Irish society and politics from a close examination of the journal's pages'.[48]

A NOTE ON STRUCTURE

In light of the need for a thorough analysis of *The Bell*, and for a discussion of its attempts to influence the formation of post-colonial Irish identity, this study strives to maintain a balance between chronological and thematic organization. One danger in attempting to analyze the entire body of writing published in the magazine is the potential for repetition, since themes that are first discussed in *The Bell* in the early 1940s often resurface for further examination as the years go by, editors change, and the cycle of publication, as well as of cultural and political life, brings old topics back to the fore. Another danger is the temptation simply to describe the contents of the magazine, and to chart, chronologically, the rise in prominence of writers such as John Hewitt and Patrick Kavanagh, whose careers *The Bell* helped to promote by providing a paying venue for publication in the 1940s and 50s. In structuring my discussion in terms of both the chronology of *The Bell*'s publication run, and the development of its

46 Malcolm Ballin, *Irish periodical culture, 1937–1972: genre in Ireland, Wales and Scotland* (New York, 2008), p. 73.   47 *The Bell*'s initial policy is discussed in Chapter Two.   48 Shovlin, *The Irish literary periodical*, p. 116.

attempts to influence mid-twentieth-century Irish identity, I have tried to steer a course between Scylla and Charybdis: between ignoring chronology, on the one hand, and falling into a pattern of mere description on the other. One aim of this book is to provide a history of *The Bell*, and to this end Chapters Two and Three examine the tensions inherent in the initial structure of the magazine and its evolution over its fourteen-year publishing run, from 1940 to 1954. Chapters Four and Five offer a developmental view of *The Bell*'s construction of post-colonial Irish identity. Internally, these chapters are less strictly observant of chronology than the opening chapters, though they are sequenced according to the arc of the magazine's career. It is my intention to expand on the work of cultural historians such as Brown and Wills, who have done so much to bring the achievements of mid-century Irish writers to light. While Brown hoped to map the terrain, and Wills to extend his analysis, I would hope that my own work illuminates the period still further, and provides a detailed exploration of *The Bell* and its efforts to represent and transform Irish identity in the mid-twentieth century.

CHAPTER TWO

Truth versus art: tensions between representation and transformation

The first issue of *The Bell* proclaimed itself a new development in Irish literature, a bold experiment in the literary life of the young nation. Even the magazine's advertisements crackled with the excitement of a new venture: the New Ireland Assurance Company declared that *The Bell*'s début 'bespeaks confidence in our people and the stability of our State',[1] and the men's clothier Frank Hugh O'Donnell, under the heading 'OYEZ! OYEZ!! OYEZ!!!', stated that 'it is but fitting that in this the new Ireland those of us who seek to express beauty in the products we manufacture should be associated with those Irish writers who within these pages seek to interpret the Irish mind'.[2]

In *The Bell*'s opening editorial, titled 'This Is Your Magazine', founding editor Sean O'Faoláin declared that the symbolic figures popularized by the Irish Literary Revival – Róisín Dubh, Cathleen Ní Houlihan, the Shan Van Vocht – were dead. The old images no longer held meaning for contemporary Ireland: 'All our symbols have to be created afresh, and the only way to create a living symbol is to take a naked thing and clothe it with new life, new association, new meaning, with all the vigour of the life we live in the Here and Now'.[3] Above all else, *The Bell* was determined to maintain a focus on the present, not on the glorious past celebrated and mythologized by an earlier generation of Irish writers. O'Faoláin explained the editors' choice of the magazine's title: 'Any other equally spare and hard and simple word would have done; any word with a minimum of associations'.[4] In a letter to Frank O'Connor, who became *The Bell*'s first Poetry Editor, O'Faoláin wrote that he had wanted the title to be *You*, or *Now*, and that Peadar O'Donnell had suggested *Us*, while O'Faoláin's wife Eileen had proposed a compromise: *All of Us*.[5] As he approached *The Bell*'s first publication, O'Faolain believed that the final title would be *This Ireland*, but told O'Connor:

> I hate the self-conscious use of the word Ireland in a title, but it happens because we have no symbols of our own and use the English language which prevents our own language from conveying the Irishry of

1 New Ireland Assurance Company, Ltd, advertizing in *The Bell* 1:1 (October 1940), p. 1. 2 Frank Hugh O'Donnell, advertising in *The Bell* 1:1 (October 1940), 4. 3 O'Faoláin, 'This Is Your Magazine', pp 5–6. 4 Ibid., p. 5. 5 O'Faoláin, undated letter to Frank O'Connor, Gotlieb Archival Research Center.

a paper, e.g. Je Suis Partout is obviously not an Italian paper, but YOU, or US etc. is not obviously Irish – and for good reasons one needs that.[6]

Thus the focus on representing a distinct and contemporary Irish identity was clear from the outset of the magazine's publication. O'Faoláin was never fully satisfied with the working title, however, and added, in an aside to O'Connor: 'If a brain-wave strikes you before next Friday it can be used'.[7] Shovlin suggests that, eventually, *The Bell* was chosen as a title partly because it paid homage to the Russian journal *Kolokol* [*The Bell*], Alexander Herzen's similarly pro-democracy, anti-authoritarian magazine of the mid-nineteenth century.[8]

Any assessment of *The Bell*'s impact on mid-twentieth century Irish identity must be tempered by an acknowledgment that the magazine's circulation numbers were relatively small. Though *The Bell* sold out every copy of its first issue, its print run was initially limited by the wartime paper shortage to 5,500 copies, and estimates put later figures for circulation at 2,000 to 3,000.[9] O'Faoláin claimed that true circulation, accounting for library use and the passing of copies between friends, was closer to 30,000, but this figure was probably inflated by an uncharacteristic bout of editorial exuberance: to assume that each monthly issue changed hands ten times seems overly optimistic. Following the same line of reasoning, O'Faoláin estimated that the readership of the London magazine *Horizon* was roughly 70,000, which he interpreted as indicating that *The Bell*'s circulation was proportionately stronger, given the far smaller size of Ireland's population in relation to Britain's. Whatever the true numbers, O'Faoláin declared that *The Bell*'s readership was 'satisfyingly small' and stated that 'the smallness of circulation is in inverse ratio to the independence of the paper'.[10]

O'Faoláin's assertion of independence was made at a time when most Irish periodicals, be they daily newspapers or weekly magazines, served as mouthpieces for religious or political organizations. There were several religious magazines serving a large readership in Ireland in the 1930s, 40s and 50s: the *Irish Rosary*, for example, was the vehicle of the Irish Vigilance Association, a pro-Censorship organization, and was edited by members of the Dominican Order;[11] the *Catholic Bulletin* was founded and edited by Senator Patrick J. Keohane, a right-wing supporter of the Censorship;[12] and the *Standard*, a weekly Catholic magazine, boasted a circulation of about 50,000 in 1939.[13] Irish daily newspapers, meanwhile, were largely oriented in terms of political parties. The *Irish*

6 Ibid. 7 Ibid. 8 Shovlin, 'Between the Sheets: Material Production and Cultural Politics in the Irish Periodical Press, 1922–58', in *New voices in Irish criticism*, ed. P.J. Mathews (Dublin, 2000), p. 201. 9 For more on circulation numbers and paper supply, see Chapter 3. 10 Sean O'Faoláin, 'On Editing a Magazine', *The Bell* 9:2 (November 1944), pp 95–6. 11 Adams, *Censorship*, p. 15. 12 Ibid., p. 67. 13 J.H. Whyte, *Church and state in modern Ireland* (Dublin, 1971), pp 70–1.

Press, for example, was founded by de Valera in 1931 with the express purpose of drumming up support for his new party, Fianna Fáil, and its opposition to the Anglo-Irish Treaty. In his history of the *Irish Press,* Mark O'Brien demonstrates that throughout the 1930s and 40s,

> the support of the *Irish Press* was unwavering as successive de Valera governments pursued policies of social conservatism, protectionism, self-sufficiency and neutrality. Since these were the doctrines of Fianna Fáil, so too were they the doctrines of the *Irish Press.*[14]

The *Irish Independent,* meanwhile, had been founded as the organ of one Parnellite faction of the Irish Parliamentary Party in 1891, and in the post-independence era was largely viewed as sympathetic to the Cumann na nGaedheal party and its successor, Fine Gael.[15] The *Irish Times,* too, had long been identified as sharing a certain political inclination, in this case the interests of the Protestant Anglo-Irish Ascendancy. Though the *Irish Times* was beginning to shed this image in the years since independence, in the early 1940s it was still working to re-orient itself towards a wider readership. As its editor, R.M. Smyllie, confessed in the pages of *The Bell,* 'When the British left Ireland in '22, [...] The bottom fell out of the world in which the *Irish Times* previously had existed. Quite frankly, we had been the organ of the British Government. [...] We had now to write for a totally different public'.[16]

Most of the newspapers and periodicals mentioned here would have reached a substantially larger readership than that of *The Bell,* even if O'Faoláin's optimistic estimates were to be believed. Figures show that in the early 1930s, the *Irish Press,* for example, achieved an average daily circulation of 90,000.[17] So, it is not on the basis of numbers that *The Bell's* importance may be argued. In comparison to other periodicals of the day, it was read by only a minority of Irish people, and when we consider that as many as 1,000 copies may have been sent to readers abroad,[18] the number of Irish readers declines still further. But *The Bell* is significant in that it appealed to a broad spectrum of Irish men and women, of different social classes and competing political inclinations, as against the narrowly defined audiences of the other periodicals of the day. And the fact that so many copies were sent overseas meant that *The Bell* could project its version of Irish identity far beyond the country's natural borders, into the hearts and minds of English, American and European readers. In contrast, the only other secular, non-affiliated literary magazine of the mid-century, *Dublin Mag-*

---

14 Mark O'Brien, *De Valera, Fianna Fáil and the* Irish Press (Dublin, 2001), p. 2.   15 Ibid., p. 3.   16 The Bellman, 'Meet R.M. Smyllie', *The Bell* 3:3 (December 1941), p. 185.   17 Mark O'Brien, *De Valera, Fianna Fáil and the* Irish Press (Dublin, 2001), p. 45.   18 McMahon, *Best from* The Bell, p. 11.

azine, was, in Frank Shovlin's description, 'singularly apolitical'.[19] Moreover, its issues of the 1940s were shorter than *The Bell*'s, and appeared only quarterly, so that the body of its work for the period is substantially smaller. Its editor, Seumas O'Sullivan, issued no calls to contributors, and he rarely wrote editorials.[20] Thus the *Dublin Magazine* fits O'Faoláin's contemporary description as an 'exclusively literary' magazine.[21] Each issue began with a number of poems, and long essays and poems in French, without translation, were not uncommon in its pages.[22] Its intended audience seems to have been a highly educated subset of the Irish middle and upper classes.

Though no documentation exists as to the locations or occupations of *Bell* subscribers, anecdotal evidence suggests that they were a varied lot. Fanning notes that *The Bell* 'had an immediate public intellectual impact' and, unlike other Irish literary journals, found an audience that extended 'outside small like-minded cliques'.[23] Conor Cruise O'Brien, who wrote for *The Bell* under the pseudonym 'Donat O'Donnell', described the magazine as a reflection of its readers:

> In its caution, its realism, its profound but ambivalent nationalism, its seizures of stodginess and its bad paper, it reflects the class who write it and read it – teachers, librarians, junior civil servants, the lettered section of the Irish petty bourgeoisie.[24]

But such condescension was not entirely justified. One may point out that the readers O'Brien describes would all have been in positions of influence in the small towns where many of them lived. Dermot Foley, in his essay on *The Bell*'s reception in Ennis, recalls that copies of the magazine were initially passed almost surreptitiously between librarians and teachers in isolated country villages. Features such as 'Mise Eire' eventually came to be read by many others in the area. Foley writes of one evening debate between farm labourers and returned emigrants in a local pub, sparked by the *Bell* article 'Gaelic with the Lid Off', on the subject of Irish-language education.[25] When the bishop of Galway publicly attacked *The Bell* for its criticism of the Church's response to the Mother and Child Scheme in 1951, he recognized that the magazine held sway over a significant sector of the educated reading public.[26] As such it was in a prime position to influence ideas of Irish identity.

19 Frank Shovlin, *The Irish literary periodical, 1923–1958* (Oxford, 2003), p. 43. 20 Ibid., pp 47–8. 21 O'Faoláin, 'A Challenge', *The Bell* 1:5 (February 1941), p. 6. 22 See, for example, D. Merejkovsky, 'L'Avenir du Christianisme', *Dublin Magazine* 14:2 (April–June 1939) and 'Montalembert: Journal de Voyage en Irlande, 1830', *Dublin Magazine* 15:2 (April–June 1940). 23 Bryan Fanning, *The quest for modern Ireland: the battle of ideas, 1912–1986*, p. 217. 24 Donat O'Donnell [Conor Cruise O'Brien], 'Horizon', *The Bell* 11:6 (March 1946), p. 1030. 25 Dermot Foley, 'Monotonously Rings the Little Bell', *Irish University Review* 6:1 (Spring 1976), p. 60. 26 See O'Faoláin, 'The Bishop of

The Bell's initial subtitle, which was carried on the front covers of its first four issues, was 'A Survey of Irish Life', and indeed the magazine's first editorial declared that it would publish writing on a broad range of topics, from all corners of Ireland, inviting its readers to contribute submissions based on their own individual life experiences:

> You who read this know intimately some corner of life that nobody else can know. [. . .] You know a turn of the road, an old gateway somewhere, a well-field, a street-corner, a wood, a handful of quiet life, a triangle of sea and rock, something that means Ireland to you. [. . .] Write about your gateway, your well-field, your street-corner, your girl, your boat-slip, pubs, books, pictures, dogs, horses, river, tractor, anything at all that has a hold on you.[27]

Here O'Faoláin stresses the material surroundings of his readers by asking for concrete depictions of life in contemporary Ireland, rooted in the most mundane details of everyday life. One may also note that the viewpoint sought is a predominantly masculine one; although *The Bell* frequently published articles by women about women's lives, the editors generally failed to challenge the patriarchal structure of mid-twentieth-century society. The new magazine promised to communicate an authentic version of Ireland, undiluted by starry-eyed, romantic nationalism, and therefore, wrote O'Faoláin, it would not follow a predetermined editorial agenda: 'this is not so much a magazine as a bit of Life itself, and we believe in Life, and leave it to Life to shape us after her own image and likeness'.[28] Rather than start by outlining its editorial policy, *The Bell* staked its survival on its commitment to charting the continual maturation of the nation itself: 'how can we have any "policy" other than to stir ourselves to a vivid awareness of what we are doing, what we are becoming, what we are?'[29]

This did not mean, however, that the magazine's editors, as professional writers, would not play a role in guiding and shaping *The Bell*'s development. Throughout its fourteen-year run, *The Bell* would remain open to unsolicited submissions; but from the beginning, the magazine showcased articles by well-known, established Irish authors. All of the first issue's contributors were listed on its front cover, perhaps in imitation of its English counterpart *Horizon,* but perhaps, also, as an attempt to attract readers who might not know the new magazine but would be drawn to buy a copy for the sake of stories and articles by Frank O'Connor, Lennox Robinson, Maurice Walsh, Flann O'Brien, Patrick Kavanagh and Elizabeth Bowen.

Galway and The Bell', *The Bell* 17:6 (September 1951).   27 O'Faoláin, 'This Is Your Magazine', pp 6–7.   28 Ibid., p. 5.   29 Ibid., p. 8.

In his first editorial, O'Faoláin effectively prefigured the aesthetic tensions which would shape the magazine. He stated that the editors' job would be 'to be able to sense the synthetic thing a mile away',[30] and that *The Bell* would aim to favour Truth over Art:

> You will notice that we do not ask, primarily, for perfection in the craft-work; we ask, first and before all, for the thing that lies lurking at the bottom of each man's well, and, if you look through this first number, you will see several things whose merit is not chiefly Art but Truth, but which for that are worth a hundred thousand things that are full of Art but, as for Truth, are as skinny as Famine.[31]

The dichotomization of Art and Truth, though perhaps unnecessarily absolute, would inevitably lead to a sense of internal conflict for O'Faoláin and his fellow editors, and rather quickly too. It would also shape *The Bell*'s form and structure for the course of O'Faoláin's editorship, which spanned the magazine's first eleven volumes, from 1940 to 1946.[32] It is in these early issues that *The Bell*'s dual agenda first emerges: though the magazine declares itself dedicated to representing Irish life, in all its various manifestations, there is clearly a transformational impulse stirring in the breasts of *The Bell*'s editors and writers – a compulsion to instruct the Irish reader, to improve his or her sense of aesthetics, and to refine the raw, native culture he or she may offer, on first invitation, to the magazine.

THE CALL FOR 'ELEGANCE'

The publication of documentary realism, as Wills and Shovlin have noted, was widespread throughout the countries of wartime Europe, and was epitomized in Britain by the documentary journal *Fact*. Wills points out, however, that whereas in Britain such writing was put to the service of utopian socialism, in the Irish context it was intimately connected with the creation of a national identity by 'discovering and documenting modern Ireland'.[33] O'Faoláin and his fellow editors assumed that if they collected and published readers' everyday experiences, a concrete image of contemporary Ireland would emerge. But while issuing a clarion call to *The Bell*'s readers and writers to send in their personal stories may have been revolutionary, it did not necessarily yield satisfactory results. O'Faoláin was to be seen, as early as in the second issue of the magazine, scolding hopeful contributors for submitting 'articles on abstract subjects', and reminding them to write 'from actual experience'.[34]

30 Ibid., p. 7. 31 Ibid., p. 8. 32 See Appendix for a chronological list of *Bell* volumes and editors. 33 Shovlin, *The Irish literary periodical, 1923–1958*, pp 103–4; Wills, *That neutral island*, p. 298. 34 O'Faoláin, 'For the Future', *The Bell*

Yet it is also in *The Bell*'s second issue that O'Faoláin claims to be weary of realism and to pine for beauty, as he explains in the introduction to a collection of observations titled 'The Loveliest Thing I Have Seen: The Artist and the Layman':

> When you have been editing a realistic magazine for a couple of months you cannot help (like Tchekov in provincial Russia) wishing for Turkish slippers and pretty women. So, I thought it might be a good idea to ask twelve artists or so to tell us what is the most lovely thing they have seen in Ireland.[35]

O'Faoláin deliberately includes the reflections of 'a few laymen',[36] including a bookie who recalls the beautiful sight of his horse winning by a neck 'when I had my shirt on her'.[37] The inclusion of such contributors alongside well-known artists such as Jack B. Yeats may be a nod to *The Bell*'s declared mission of democratization, but even the decision to characterize non-artists as 'laymen' suggests the elevation of the artist above the common man, to the status of a sort of cultural priesthood.

The fact that these two editorial notes appear in the same issue, and in only the second issue, of *The Bell* highlights the level of tension produced by the magazine's dual agenda of representation and transformation. Although O'Faoláin had called for factual articles on everyday life throughout Ireland, he and his fellow editors found it difficult to allow mediocre writing to be published in the magazine's pages. In *The Bell*'s third issue, O'Faoláin reiterated the editorial manifesto:

> Let us restate our position. *The Bell* believes that the first thing we must do in Ireland is to see clearly – *voir clair* – to have the facts and understand the picture. This has never been attempted before. When Ireland reveals herself truthfully, and fearlessly, she will be in possession of a solid basis on which to build a superstructure of thought; but not until then.[38]

In other words, the project of authentically representing Irish life would serve as the foundation for debate on the project of cultural transformation, and the latter would not be undertaken until the former had been completed. But this is not quite what occurred. As the months went by, *The Bell*'s efforts towards rep-

1:2 (November 1940), p. 5. 35 O'Faoláin, note preceding 'The Loveliest Thing I Have Seen: The Artist and the Layman', *The Bell* 1:2 (November 1940), p. 40. 36 Ibid., p. 40. 37 A Bookmaker, 'The Loveliest Thing I Have Seen: The Artist and the Layman', p. 43. 38 O'Faoláin, 'Answer to a Criticism', p. 6.

resentation took the shape of articles on the more artistic aspects of native Irish culture, but the magazine's editors did not wait until these first steps had been completed to begin their project of cultural improvement. Instead, they concurrently launched a series of articles that were explicitly designed to transform the state of the arts in Ireland.

O'Faoláin and his fellow editors employed two strategies to elevate the standard of writing published in *The Bell* while remaining true to the magazine's original mission of cultural representation. First, they called for representational articles on the more refined aspects of Irish life, those that might not automatically come to mind in the days of a prevailing image of Ireland as de Valera's rural republic. Second, they launched a series of instructional articles to improve the state of Irish poetry, fiction, and drama. Before *The Bell* began publication, O'Faoláin had privately expressed his concerns to O'Connor: 'Incidentally, there is going to be difficulty in keeping the Bell from being too much I-Lived-in-a-Slum. Gaiety, civilisation, we want that'.[39] In his third editorial, O'Faoláin attempted to describe the type of article he was seeking:

> One might call this Elegance. Of this we have had very little. The reason is probably because the simplicity of our modes of life in Ireland does not immediately suggest elegant subjects. But the subjects *are* there by the score. A perfect furrow at a ploughing match is as artistic an achievement as a perfect poem. There is local craftwork, of which we see excellent examples every year at the Spring Show and the local Shows: rugs, smithwork, pottery, basket-weaving, a perfectly cooked chicken from the bastable, the small garden. *The Bell* would particularly like to encourage articles on these – fine food, fine dress, fine furniture, fine drink, all the things that delight and satisfy the senses, all the lovely things that man makes as against the lovely things that are Nature's free gift to us and for which we deserve no credit.[40]

Here O'Faoláin attempts to draw upon the richness of Irish material culture, in the form of native craftsmanship, in order to bridge the gap between Truth and Art. There never did appear any article about well-cooked chickens. But *The Bell* did endeavour, beginning with its third issue, to expose its readers to articles on more artistic subjects than might be expected in a magazine that had declared itself devoted to documentary writing. Thus in its early days *The Bell* was already beginning to evolve.

39 O'Faoláin, letter to Frank O'Connor, 19 August 1940, Gotlieb Archival Research Center.   40 O'Faoláin, 'Answer to a Criticism', pp 5–6.

It is worth noting that O'Faoláin's editorial, as quoted above, does not call for new topics; it simply asks contributors to approach their subjects from a more critically aesthetic, and not purely representational, stance. Here, as in other areas, O'Faoláin chose to lead by example. In the same issue of *The Bell* in which his statement on 'Elegance' appears, he published an article of his own titled 'Fine Cottage Furniture', in which he praises the aesthetic value added to the design of traditional súgán chairs by a group of students at the Dublin Metropolitan School of Art, under the guidance of designers J.J. O'Connor and James Hicks.[41] The article is accompanied by a full-page glossy black-and-white photograph of four of the chairs, the first such photo plate to be included in *The Bell*.

O'Faoláin's article on new designs for súgán chairs reveals the conflict inherent in *The Bell*'s dual mission of representation and transformation. O'Faoláin consciously chooses a cultural artefact of the most ordinary kind, one that would be familiar to many readers in Ireland, and in fact he extols the traditional súgán chair right from the start for its very ordinariness: 'Its chief merit was that anybody could have made it; that it is comfortable, and flexible; the uneven clay floors and the weight of the bodies of the country-folk demanded this flexibility.'[42] O'Faoláin goes on to explain how the designers of the new chairs have improved on the traditional design, by replacing the straw seat with woven rope, dyed brown or saffron, and by smoothing and shaping the lines of the original chair to make the new version more graceful and light. But O'Faoláin hastens to point out that the new design has been 'realistically planned' in collaboration with country housewives, who asked for the rope seat as a replacement for the traditional straw, which, they complained, bred fleas, and who suggested the elimination of the traditional chair's lower rung, which, they pointed out, made it all too easy for the sitter to scrape mud off the heels of his boots and onto the floor.[43] O'Faoláin admires the designers both for their faithfulness to traditional craft and for their inventiveness in attempting to improve on native customs. 'What we need now', he writes, in a characteristically ambitious phrase, 'is the enlargement of the designs to a further and more sophisticated elaboration, and the publication of many books of designs, not merely for cottage furniture but for urban needs and urban tastes.'[44]

41 O'Faoláin, 'Fine Cottage Furniture', *The Bell* 1:3 (December 1940). *Súgán* is a rope made of straw, and a súgán chair is one in which the seat is of woven straw. O'Faoláin may have had a literary precedent in mind when he chose to write about súgán chairs, in that the first professionally performed play in the Irish language was *Casadh an tSúgán*, or *The twisting of the rope*, by Douglas Hyde, in 1901. (Interestingly, the súgán chair was also the namesake of the Boston-based Súgán Theatre Company, who, from 1992 to 2006, performed plays by contemporary Irish playwrights. The company's directors interpreted the súgán chair as an image associated with the traditional storyteller.)   42 O'Faoláin, 'Fine Cottage Furniture', p. 28.   43 Ibid., pp 29–30.   44 Ibid., p. 30.

What *The Bell* was trying to do for Irish literary culture was not altogether different from what Hicks and O'Connor's furniture design students were trying to do for the súgán chair. O'Faoláin's description of the designers' project could equally have been applied to the agenda of his own magazine. Here is a sentence from the introductory paragraph of 'Fine Cottage Furniture' which resonates with the underlying contradictions in the magazine's declared purpose of representation: 'The experiment of which I am writing has, with great honesty, attempted to create a native tradition in design by going back to the absolutely primitive pieces of the humblest farmhouse kitchen.'[45] O'Faoláin's choice of wording here is telling. His designers are both *creating* a native tradition and *going back* to the primitive pieces of the past. One might ask, then, which is the native tradition: is it the original súgán chair, with its admittedly utilitarian, ungraceful design? Or is it the improved version, made with better materials (native chestnut, for example, whose 'use has been made possible only after years of experiment in seasoning')[46] and a more agreeably aesthetic sense of form? How does one go about the task of consciously *creating* a native tradition? In describing the Hicks and O'Connor chairs, O'Faoláin reveals much about his own aspirations for *The Bell*'s endeavours: the magazine would be representational, to be sure, but it would simultaneously attempt to elevate the aesthetic standard of the entire field of Irish art and literature.

To this end, *The Bell* published several other pieces that fit O'Faoláin's definition of 'Elegance' in native culture. The first of these, 'Make Your Windows Gay' by Norah McGuinness, appeared in the third issue, alongside O'Faoláin's article on súgán chairs and his editorial call for 'Elegance'. McGuinness, who had previously been married to *The Bell*'s second poetry editor Geoffrey Taylor, is introduced to the reader in an editorial note that describes her as 'one of our most interesting painters', and as an artist who had arranged window displays for department stores in Dublin, London, and New York.[47] There is an obvious attempt, both in the editorial introduction and in McGuinness' article, to place Dublin on a level with the two capital cities of the English-speaking commercial world. McGuinness describes store windows on Fifth Avenue that mimic Stravinsky's stage settings, and another New York window designed by surrealist Salvador Dali. 'If I may judge by the interest of passers-by Dublin is just as eager for brightness, good taste, and novelty as any New Yorker',[48] she claims, and lays down a set of rules for Irish shop owners to follow in designing their window displays. She hastens to point out that window dressing is not an exclusively urban art, and offers the example of a country grocer whose displays are always simply but attractively designed.[49]

45 Ibid., p. 28.   46 Ibid., p. 29.   47 Note preceding Norah McGuinness, 'Make Your Windows Gay', *The Bell* 1:3 (December 1940), p. 65.   48 McGuinness, 'Make Your Windows Gay', p. 69.   49 Ibid., p. 68.

In McGuinness' article, as in other *Bell* articles, a stated interest in cultural representation is mixed with the author's impulse to instruct the reader, as when McGuinness scolds Dublin shop owners for not keeping up with seasonal changes:

> When I first came back to Dublin, after some years' absence, I was struck by the little inducement given to me to buy. One day, even the advent of early spring sunshine did not move any shop that I noticed to tell me that a new spring hat *must* be bought at once. I saw hats of brown felt and black felt when I should have been seeing new jaunty spring hats covered with flowers, beckoning me in.[50]

Few *Bell* articles on so-called 'elegant' topics failed to take the opportunity to teach the reader how to direct his or her own efforts at self-improvement. An example is 'Galway Hats', written by O'Faoláin's wife Eileen, which not only celebrates native productivity at the Galway Hat Factory, whose hats were made of felt supplied from Castlebar and trimmed with ribbons from Longford, but also instructs the reader on how a continental 'woman of fashion' gets her hats made bespoke, and critiques the factory's designs by offering the opinions of several prominent 'women of taste' in Dublin society, including ladies with established artistic credentials, such as Elizabeth Bowen, Anne Yeats, and Shelah Richards.[51]

Later articles in the representative but instructive vein were to follow. Musical instrument maker John O'Donoghue contributed an article on the process of constructing fiddles and bagpipes.[52] Artist Anna Sheehy wrote a short-lived series on Irish printmakers, beginning with a linocut of her own and giving instructions on how to produce linocut prints at one's kitchen table, using an old umbrella rib and a spoon.[53] Novelist and *Bell* Editorial Board member Maurice Walsh critiqued the making of Irish whiskey, and, like Eileen O'Faoláin and Norah McGuinness, found himself unable to refrain from suggesting some very specific improvements to the creative process:

> I would like to see our very able distillers more daringly experimental. They make a very fine standard whiskey and are satisfied to stick to that standard come hell or high water. Why not experiment with an occasional run of the still in search of bouquets to please discriminate but varying palates? I often wonder what a Jameson or a Power would taste like if

50 Ibid., pp 68–9. 51 Eileen O'Faoláin, 'Galway Hats', *The Bell* 1:4 (January 1941), pp 68–74. 52 John O'Donoghue, 'Fiddles and Bagpipes', *The Bell* 3:6 (March 1942). 53 Anna Sheehy, 'The Lino Cut', *The Bell* 2:1 (April 1941). See also Sheehy, 'Harry Kernoff, R.H.A.', *The Bell* 2:2 (May 1941); 'Cecil ffrench Salkeld', *The Bell* 2:3 (June 1941); 'Dorothy Blackham', *The Bell* 2:4 (July 1941).

distilled at, say, 40° over-proof, reduced in store to 15° over-proof, and warehoused in a sherry cask for ten years. I suppose I'll never know.[54]

An article by Barney Heron described the artisanal cheese-making enterprise of a Mrs Crichton in County Sligo, whose handcrafted Cheddars and Goudas were attempting to establish a new tradition in Ireland.[55] Heron's article goes further than some of the others in its instructive agenda, in that he not only details Mrs Crichton's cheese-making process, but questions the agricultural policies of the local government, which regulated the selling of milk in Mrs Crichton's creamery district and thus restricted her incoming supply. As Heron argues, 'Mrs Crichton has the right to demand a share [of milk] for her venture. She has this right because from native resources she has created a value – in other words, wealth – where it did not exist before'.[56] These words call to mind Gibbons' insistence on the transformative power of art in society: 'its power to give rise to what was not there before'.[57] One might use Heron's phrase, indeed, to characterize *The Bell*'s project of transformation: using native resources to create cultural value where it did not exist, or was not recognized, before.

INSTRUCTIONAL ARTICLES: 'THE BELFRY', 'NEW WRITERS', AND 'THE COUNTRY THEATRE'

In addition to calling for examples of native 'Elegance', the second strategy employed by *The Bell*'s editors in order to raise the national level of cultural discourse was to introduce a series of instructional features in various aspects of the arts. The first of these, 'The Belfry', began in the magazine's first issue and continued throughout Frank O'Connor's nine-month tenure as *The Bell*'s first Poetry Editor, from October 1940 to June 1941. O'Connor introduced 'The Belfry' as a task he had begrudgingly undertaken at O'Faoláin's behest, and referred to the two writers' earlier days as eager young upstarts: 'The Editor wishes to keep in each number of *The Bell* a few pages for people trying their hand at literature, as he and I once tried it in Cork'.[58] He invited poems from young writers, but warned that his target would be 'the odd young man or woman of talent who really has something to say and can benefit by occasional abuse'.[59] Finally, he reiterated *The Bell*'s editorial call for documentary authenticity by giving this advice to aspiring poets: 'Write briefly; write about things

---

54 Maurice Walsh, 'Whiskey', *The Bell* 2:5 (August 1941), pp 25–6. 55 Barney Heron, 'Irish Cheese: A West of Ireland Venture', *The Bell* 6:2 (May 1943). 56 Heron, p. 126. 57 Gibbons, *Transformations in Irish culture*, p. 8. 58 Frank O'Connor, 'The Belfry', *The Bell* 1:1 (October 1940), p. 92. 59 O'Connor, 'The Belfry', *The Bell* 1:1 (October 1940), p. 92.

you know. Describe some old tramp you have just met; the pattern or races or fair you have been to; some landscape that has moved you. Give us reality, whatever else you give us'.[60]

Over its lifetime as a regular feature, 'The Belfry' featured individual poems by five new poets, and each poem was preceded by a page of bluntly critical commentary by O'Connor. In the middle of the series, O'Connor printed three pages of advice to writers, in which he explained why he had declined to print any of the poems that had been submitted that month. Titled 'To Any Would-Be Writer', the advice printed reveals O'Connor's strongly nationalist views about the purpose of poetry, and about the role of literature in forming a modern Irish identity: 'Poetry is the most national of the arts, and its colouring must be distinctive'.[61] He urges writers hopeful of *Bell* publication to read every book by a modern Irish writer, and reminds them to avoid 'vague romanticism' in favour of portraying the reality of everyday life.[62] Yet even as O'Connor puts forward his own suggestions for aspiring Irish writers, he laments the lack of a national literary movement to encourage the younger generation of poets: 'To all of us on this magazine', he writes, 'the great tragedy of modern Ireland is its stifled talent'.[63]

It seems that there was very little O'Connor liked in the poetry he received for publication in 'The Belfry'. He introduces John Hewitt's poem 'Leaf' with the statement, 'I have selected this poem from a hundred or so of its kind, because it seems to me the most distinguished example of a certain sort of poetry which, personally, I do not like',[64] and proceeds to criticize the poem for following too closely in the tradition of English poets Matthew Arnold and Robert Bridges, and for not being faithful to the Irish use of the English language. 'Leaf' does seem to demonstrate O'Connor's diagnosis, although the lack of regional idiom need not consign it to the literary rubbish heap. In florid anapaestic trimeter the poem compares its speaker's fatigue to the withering of an autumn leaf, and offers an idealized image of nature, as in these lines about pigeons in flight:

> The pigeons, a dozen and two
> take a half mile circle of light:
> they are washed in the green and blue
> and delicate gold of the sky.[65]

Robert Greacen's poem 'The Bird' also comes under criticism from O'Connor, for being 'typical of what one may call Left-Wing verse in Ireland'.[66] O'Con-

---

60 Ibid., p. 94.   61 O'Connor, 'The Belfry: To Any Would-Be Writer', *The Bell* 1:5 (February 1941), p. 88.   62 Ibid. 63 Ibid., p. 87.   64 O'Connor, 'The Belfry: A Matter of Idiom', *The Bell* 1:4 (January 1941), p. 88.   65 John Hewitt, 'Leaf', *The Bell* 1:4 (January 1941), p. 90.   66 O'Connor, 'The Belfry: On Not Being Provincial', *The Bell* 2:2 (May 1941), p. 83.

nor goes on to complain: 'This is what disturbs me about the sort of verse that Mr Greacen writes. It is merely a literary fashion; the fashion is applied direct to the subject regardless of whether or not it fits'.[67] Greacen's poem, however, which uses the metaphor of a black bird for the cruel fact of a family member's death,[68] does not seem particularly leftist or revolutionary, except, perhaps, for the fact that its quatrains are not rhyming or metrical. Its imagery, in fact, recalls the very advice given by O'Connor and O'Faoláin to *Bell* contributors, as it conjures the concrete detail of the relative's body, laid out for visitation:

> I loved the man who lay in the cheap coffin. [...]
> I loved the ploughing of his sun-caught brow,
> and the hay-lines and chicken-feathers in his hair,
> that was hay itself; the strongly cobbled boots [...][69]

It would seem, in this case, that O'Connor is contradicting his own preference for authentic images drawn from rural Irish life. Greacen's use of visual detail such as the chicken feathers caught in the farmer's hair somehow falls short of O'Connor's criteria for Irish poetry.

It is difficult to tell, however, whether the kind of poetry championed by 'The Belfry' as representational Irish verse would be strong enough to withstand criticism on a purely literary basis. O'Connor praises Bryan MacMahon's 'House Sinister' for its sound,[70] and John MacDonagh's 'Maguire' for its Irish 'atmosphere' and 'colouring',[71] but both poems are limited by the rigidity of their highly metrical structure, and both portray a romanticized version of Irish identities – in MacMahon, the 'half-Gael, and half-Gall' inhabitants of a decaying country house,[72] and in MacDonagh, a wild Connacht man whose monologue begins,

> My name is Maguire
> I come out of the West
> Where every dog knows me [...][73]

(It is worth noting that an early version of Patrick Kavanagh's 'A Christmas Childhood', conveying a subtler, more contemporary version of Irish Catholic

67 Ibid. 68 A footnote to 'The Bird' in *Robert Greacen: selected and new poems*, ed. by Jack W. Weaver (Cliffs of Moher, 2006) states: 'The deceased farmer is imagined. The bird is the banshee' (p. 195). 69 Robert Greacen, 'The Bird', *The Bell* 2:2 (May 1941), p. 84. 70 O'Connor, 'The Belfry: A New Poet', *The Bell* 1:2 (November 1940), p. 86. 71 O'Connor, 'The Belfry', *The Bell* 1:3 (December 1940), p. 92. 72 Bryan MacMahon, 'House Sinister', *The Bell* 1:2 (November 1940), p. 88. 73 John MacDonagh, 'Maguire', *The Bell* 1:3 (December 1940), 93. This poem predates Patrick Kavanagh's use of the name 'Maguire' for the protagonist of 'The Great Hunger', an excerpt of which was first published as 'The Old Peasant' in the Irish Number of *Horizon* 5:25 (January 1942).

identity, was first published, without fanfare, in the same issue of *The Bell* as 'Maguire'.) Ironically, the only other poem O'Connor chooses to praise is one not written by an Irish poet. O'Connor called the Welsh poet Cynric Mytton-Davies' 'Salutation from a Darkened World' 'a far finer defence of Irish neutrality than any our propagandists have imagined', but offers only a few lines for *Bell* readers, in which the poet addresses Ireland as an 'Amaranthine queen' whose 'imprisoned stepchildren' wish to recline 'Nepenthean on your welcoming green bosom'.[74] Mytton-Davies' poem 'Leave Trains – Victoria Station' is printed in full, and conjures the image of women bidding farewell to soldiers going to war. In the poem's last line, Mytton-Davies reverts again to classical metaphor: 'Acheron's train bore on their cherished shades'.[75]

O'Faoláin opposed the choice of Mytton-Davies for 'The Belfry' on the grounds that such a choice violated *The Bell*'s nationalist intentions. Privately, he wrote to O'Connor: 'I take the strongest objection to printing a non-Irish writer (of whose merits I have the gravest doubts – to put it very mildly indeed)'.[76] O'Connor had submitted his copy too late, however, to make substitutions, so O'Faoláin appended an editorial note to that month's 'Belfry' confessing that 'we are breaking a fundamental rule' of the series.[77] He furthermore stated a difference of opinion with O'Connor as to the literary value of Mytton-Davies' poetry, and quoted Paul Verlaine's dictum, 'Take eloquence and wring its neck'.[78] Thus the two editors sparred publicly, in print, over their competing tastes in poetry. One is struck by the insensitivity shown to emerging poets in a feature ostensibly designed to encourage them. Indeed, Vivian Mercier later bemoaned the editors' tendency to eschew private channels in favour of advice 'given on the printed page, with the whole of Ireland looking on'.[79]

Perhaps in part because of his editorial differences with O'Connor, O'Faoláin announced his own instructive series focused on short fiction: 'New Writers', which began in *The Bell*'s fifth issue as a monthly feature, but which soon appeared only intermittently, for a total of seven instances between February 1941 and December 1942.[80] In his notes preceding each short story selected for 'New Writers', O'Faoláin is less dogmatic than O'Connor, offering in the series' introduction no advice to aspiring young writers, but only the statement that, of the short stories submitted, 'I will take, always, the one which it is easiest to comment on with clarity: thinking of nothing else but that'.[81] O'Faoláin

74 O'Connor, 'The Belfry: From a Darkened World', *The Bell* 2:1 (April 1941), p. 85.   75 Cynric Mytton-Davies, 'Leave Trains – Victoria Station', *The Bell* 2:1 (April 1941), p. 87.   76 O'Faoláin, undated letter to Frank O'Connor, Gotlieb Archival Research Center.   77 O'Faoláin, editorial note, *The Bell* 2:1 (April 1941), p. 86.   78 Ibid.   79 Mercier, 'Verdict on *The Bell*', p. 158.   80 O'Faoláin was the author in all seven of these instances, with one exception: in *The Bell* 2:1 (April 1941), the 'New Writers' column was written by Elizabeth Bowen, who selected 'Three Talented Children' by Domhnall O'Conaill as that month's featured short story.   81 O'Faoláin, 'New Writers', *The Bell* 1:5 (February 1941), p. 61.

offers his chosen writers advice that is less concrete than O'Connor's. Rather than focusing on sound or word choice, he tells Desmond Clarke to 'preserve some sense of irony' in the treatment of his main characters;[82] he praises David St John because, he says, 'I like cold writing';[83] he applauds Michael O'Beirne for writing that is 'distinguished and aloof'.[84] O'Faoláin's notes are also much more laudatory than O'Connor's, sometimes gushing with praise, as when he claims that 'we have never printed anything more original, fresh, and beautiful in concept and in style than the following excerpt from Michael MacGrian's long piece called *Myself and Some Ducks*'.[85]

Taken together, 'The Belfry' and 'New Writers' highlight *The Bell's* impulse towards transforming the literary landscape of mid-twentieth-century Ireland. In a very direct and often highly critical format, two writers at the forefront of their generation positioned themselves not only as editors but as arbiters of literary taste, upstaging the poems and stories they selected with their own advice, which was often bluntly disparaging. But it was not only in the areas of poetry and fiction that *The Bell* aimed to transform the arts in Ireland. Michael Farrell's series of articles on 'The Country Theatre', perhaps one of the magazine's best-known regular features, soon carved its own niche as a source of advice and instruction for amateur theatre companies across the Irish countryside. Farrell was a neighbour to O'Faoláin in Kilmacanogue, and later wrote the novel *Thy tears might cease*, but appears to have had no theatrical qualifications beyond a critical stance that resembled O'Faoláin's and fit well into *The Bell's* agenda.[86] 'The Country Theatre' began, in accordance with the original spirit of *The Bell*, as a representational project, one in which O'Faoláin commissioned Farrell, as Farrell reported, to 'go forth into the highways and the by-ways, and cast the claw of your eye on one or two little dramatic societies, and bring them back alive'.[87] But it quickly evolved into a platform for transformation, one from which Farrell could project his own ideas about how to produce plays that would raise the standards of amateur theatre and educate the artistic tastes of country audiences.

Amateur dramatics flourished in Ireland during the Emergency, due to a number of factors, including the prominence of the Abbey Theatre as a role model, and the fact that many clergymen encouraged local theatre as an alternative to the questionable morals of the Hollywood cinema.[88] As a nationally distributed magazine, *The Bell* was in a prime position to influence the artistic

82 Ibid. 83 O'Faoláin, 'New Writers', *The Bell* 1:6 (March 1941), p. 67. 84 O'Faoláin, 'New Writers', *The Bell* 3:5 (February 1942), p. 370. 85 O'Faoláin, 'New Writers', *The Bell* 4:4 (July 1942), p. 253. 86 See Martin Lynch, 'Michael Farrell, Carlowman (1899–1962): Writer or "Die, Publish and be damned!"', *Carloviana* 49 (2000). Farrell's wife Frances Cahill ran the Crock of Gold handweavers enterprise, which Farrell later helped manage, and which advertised in later issues of *The Bell*. 87 Michael Farrell, 'The Country Theatre', *The Bell* 1:1 (October 1940), p. 78. 88 Brown, *Ireland*, p. 179.

direction of amateur companies, by establishing in the magazine a regular feature that Farrell described as 'something of a bureau, to which local dramatic
societies will write asking and giving news and information'.[89] From October
1940 to February 1942, Farrell published descriptions of plays, mostly by Irish
authors, that he deemed suitable for rural theatres. Considerations were made
for cast size, set and costume requirements, and crowd-pleasing potential. Perhaps more importantly, Farrell himself toured the countryside in search of successful theatrical companies and published their achievements in the magazine,
often with detailed descriptions of their resources, right down to the measure-
ments of the stage. Dermot Foley, then a member of a rural drama company,
recalls that

> It was exactly what was wanted by people with little or no experience,
> plenty of guts, but no means whatever of assessing their efforts [...]
> To make *The Bell*, or to read of others not much more competent than
> your own crowd who did, was to induce momentary levitation [...] Far-
> rell in his 'Country Theatre' reflected the authority and integrity that
> the magazine enjoyed.[90]

The Bell gave exposure and encouragement to nascent theatre companies, and in so
doing, documented the widespread activity of amateur theatre groups in rural areas.
As a result of the success of 'The Country Theatre' series, O'Farrell was sought
after as an adjudicator for amateur theatre festivals in towns such as Sligo and Dun-
dalk, and he published his thoughts on the performances he judged, as well as on
the developmental trends in rural theatre which he observed at the festivals.[91]

In 'The Country Theatre', as in other areas of *The Bell*, representation was
intertwined with transformation. For example, by offering the details of successful amateur theatre productions, Farrell provided blueprints that aspiring
directors could follow. But he also provided several articles suggesting specific
plays for country audiences, in a clear attempt to raise the artistic aspirations
of rural theatre companies. In his third article, 'Plays for the Country Theatre',
Farrell urges theatre producers to 'remember that when entertainment is
estranged from life it is just *dope*, and that the great period of drama here, and
elsewhere, was when audience and play were one unity'.[92] He offers several suggestions from the annals of Irish drama, including Synge's *Riders to the sea* – to
which Farrell appends his opinion that 'An Irish Theatre which did not try to
do this play would not be worthy of its name'[93] – but also includes Henrik

89 Farrell, 'The Country Theatre', *The Bell* 1:1, p. 78. 90 Foley, 'Monotonously Rings the Little Bell', pp 58–9. 91 Farrell, 'More Country Theatre', *The Bell* 1:4 (January 1941); 'Drama at the Sligo Feis', *The Bell* 2:3 (June 1941). 92 Farrell, 'Plays for the Country Theatre', *The Bell* 1:3 (December 1940), p. 58. 93 Ibid., p. 61.

Ibsen's allegorical morality play *An enemy of the people*, stating that 'a country-town audience which misses the allegory will not, therefore, miss an evening's dramatic fare'.[94] For each play, Farrell includes detailed information on the number of parts for actors and actresses, the sets, costumes, the amateur acting fee, and permit information for Irish and British performances.

Farrell's first list of suggestions was met with a response that he called 'interesting and unsettling'.[95] In keeping with *The Bell*'s policy of editorial honesty, he published the complaints he received, as well as the requests, from amateur dramatic societies:

> First and foremost, they ask for Comedy, which, from inner evidence, seems to mean Farce; next, they want Melodramas or Thrillers; next they want 'good modern plays *not* about Ireland' and they want 'plays with a good many girls' parts.'[96]

To some extent, Farrell obliged, but his second list of suggested plays starts off with five by Irish authors (including Yeats' verse play *The land of heart's desire*, which may not have been perceived as a crowd-pleaser) before indulging his readers' requests with one play each from the genres of farce, thriller, and romantic costume comedy.[97] Subsequent 'Country Theatre' articles offered lists of melodramas and light operas, as Farrell's correspondents had requested.[98] Thus, 'The Country Theatre' series marks *The Bell*'s development as a dialogue between writers and readers, a trend that Farrell himself would later extend under the pseudonym 'Gulliver' for the magazine's series 'The Open Window'.

Farrell also used the platform of his 'Country Theatre' series to criticize the lack of guidance for rural theatre companies offered by Ireland's national theatre, the Abbey, which was sometimes overtly obstructionist to the development of amateur drama in the countryside.[99] One of his earliest articles scorns the Abbey Theatre's decision not to allow 'the valiant and lonely Birr Theatre' in County Offaly permission to perform George Shiels' box office success *The Rugged Path*.[1] In an article on the Louth Drama Festival, he records the passing of a resolution 'deploring the Abbey's monopoly of plays which [...] "works unfairly against amateur companies"'.[2] In a later article, Farrell joins other crit-

94 Ibid. 95 Farrell, 'Plays for the Country Theatre', *The Bell* 2:1 (April 1941), p. 78. 96 Ibid. 97 Ibid. 98 Farrell, 'More Melodrama', *The Bell* 2:2 (May 1941); 'Opera for the Country Theatre', *The Bell* 2:6 (September 1941). 99 See Robert Welch, *The Abbey theatre, 1899–1999: form and pressure* (Oxford, 1999) for a discussion of the Abbey's difficulties during this period. Managing Director F.R. Higgins had died of a heart attack in early 1941, and was replaced by former Minister of Finance Ernest Blythe. Blythe launched a campaign to Gaelicise the Abbey, refusing to employ actors who did not speak Irish, and producing five or six plays in Irish (including an Irish-language pantomime) annually from 1942, which generally proved unpopular with Dublin audiences (pp 141–6). 1 Farrell, 'Plays for the Country Theatre', *The Bell* 1:3, p. 64. 2 Farrell, 'More Country Theatre', pp 85–86.

ical voices of *The Bell* in criticizing the Abbey's overall lack of standards for its own productions,[3] and though he does describe, in one issue, an Abbey training course for country theatre producers and teachers,[4] when it came time to end the 'Country Theatre' series, in February 1942, Farrell did not miss an opportunity to point out the Abbey's lack of connection to amateur theatre across the country. In his valedictory article, Farrell acknowledges the Abbey's role in reviving Irish theatre, and in setting standards for rural theatre companies to follow, but then asserts that 'one may ask right away, that the Abbey must give more, and more idealistic, direction to the countryside'.[5] Thus *The Bell* once again used its status as a nationally respected literary magazine as a platform from which to work for cultural transformation.[6]

CULTURAL COMMENTARY: 'THE BELLMAN' AND 'MISE EIRE'

Perhaps because it was, in O'Faoláin's words, 'the only independent, non-affiliated periodical in the entire country', *The Bell* attempted to fulfil a number of different functions for the Irish reading public.[7] In addition to representational short stories and poetry, and instructional articles on various aspects of the arts, the magazine also instituted several series that can best be categorized as cultural commentary – articles which differed in tone from those discussed above, but which contributed, in their own way, to *The Bell's* mission of elevating the level of cultural discourse in mid-twentieth-century Ireland.

From October 1941 to November 1942, a monthly series of interviews conducted by an anonymous author called 'The Bellman' exposed the foibles and predilections of several of Ireland's leading cultural figures, including writers, editors, actors, businessmen, and senior public officials.[8] In contrast to the lofty, curmudgeonly tone adopted by Frank O'Connor in 'The Belfry', the Bellman comes across as a friendly fellow, disingenuously obsequious to his interviewees, and knowingly sardonic in his commentary. It is intriguing, then, that Holzapfel identifies O'Connor and the Bellman as being one and the same on several occasions, though he speculates, as do other critics, that the playwright Larry Morrow wrote most of the series.[9] Month after month, the Bellman caricatures his interview subjects, describing Rutherford Mayne, for example, as 'the spoiled

---

3 Farrell, 'Drama at the Sligo Feis', *The Bell* 2:3 (June 1941), p. 90. 4 Farrell, 'A Course for Country Producers', *The Bell* 3:1 (October 1941). 5 Farrell, 'The Country Theatre', *The Bell* 3:5 (February 1942), p. 391. 6 See Harmon, *Sean O'Faoláin: a life*, pp 144–7, for more on *The Bell's* criticism of the Abbey, especially Frank O'Connor's review of Louis Lynch D'Alton's play *The money doesn't matter*, which resulted in a case of libel and an expensive settlement for *The Bell* and its printer, J.J. O'Leary. 7 O'Faoláin, 'A Challenge', *The Bell* 1:5 (February 1941), p. 6. 8 The Bellman interviews would briefly reappear in later issues. See *The Bell* 16:1 (April 1948); 16:4 (January 1951); 16:5 (February 1951); 16:6 (March 1951). 9 Holzapfel, p. 1.

Buddha of Ulster, if not of Irish, Drama'[10], and the Church of Ireland arch-bishop of Dublin as a man 'trussed up all the day and half the night in gaiters, apron, the Thirty-Nine Articles *and* the Canons Ecclesiastical'.[11] At the top of one interview, with Film Censor Richard Hayes, an actual caricature is provided, drawn by Seosamh Mac Crosáin.[12] After describing their appearance, dress and mannerisms in a chatty, gossipy tone, the Bellman transcribes conversations in which he cajoles his interview subjects into stating their positions on a variety of issues facing Irish society. For example, he persuades Maurice Walsh, whom he continually quotes as 'the Best-Seller', to comment on the literary Censor-ship, and he asks Denis Guiney, the owner of Clery's Department Store, if he has enough stock to last through the war.[13]

It is the sardonic tone of commentary, such as that found in the Bellman series, which has led critics such as Gerry Smyth to describe *The Bell* as urbane, or even smug, and it is true that some of the Bellman's columns appear today to be overly satirical, and more dated than some of the magazine's other fea-tures. They may have fit better into a humorous publication such as *Dublin Opin-ion*. Nonetheless, the Bellman series of interviews do keep their focus on issues which preoccupied *The Bell* in other areas, especially the construction of con-temporary Irish identity. In nearly every interview, the Bellman asks his subjects to comment on aspects of their work that touch on issues specific to Ireland, asking the theatre producer Christine Longford, for example, to quantify 'the Irish Character' in relation to actors, audiences, and writers, both novelists and dramatists.[14] Even in a feature that could have been printed in the society pages of a middle-class newspaper, *The Bell*'s interest in representing Irish identity comes to the fore.

In the third issue of *The Bell*, published in December 1940, a new feature titled 'Mise Eire' appeared, a collection of quotations from Irish publications, selected by the editors from submissions sent in by *Bell* readers. (The reader who submitted the best quotation each month was rewarded with the prize of a book token.) 'Mise Eire' translates as 'I Am Ireland', and was also used by Patrick Pearse as the title of his 1912 poem about Mother Ireland – a short poem that employed several of the symbolic images which O'Faoláin had declared dead in his first *Bell* editorial. Here the title choice seems to be ironic, in that most of the quotations printed expose petty prejudices and self-con-tradictions. Initially the feature provided a means for *The Bell* to suggest its own version of cultural commentary without delving into explicit political argu-

10 The Bellman, 'Meet Rutherford Mayne', *The Bell* 4:4 (July 1942). 11 The Bellman, 'Meet Dr Barton', *The Bell* 3:5 (February 1942), p. 393. 12 The Bellman, 'Meet Dr Hayes: or The General Censor', *The Bell* 3:2 (November 1941). 13 The Bellman, 'Meet Maurice Walsh', *The Bell* 4:2 (May 1942); 'Meet Denis Guiney', *The Bell* 3:4 (January 1942). 14 The Bellman, 'Meet Christine Longford', *The Bell* 4:5 (August 1942).

ment. It first appeared in the same issue in which O'Faoláin titled his editorial 'Answer to a Criticism':

> Some readers have asked for more 'fight' in *The Bell*. We could fill *The
> Bell* without difficulty with the articles that offer themselves for this
> section, which some may call Controversy, but all of which we reject
> without further consideration. The Editorial Board is adamant on that.
> It is the sort of thing that goes on, and on, night after night, in pubs
> and back-kitchens and front parlours, and never gets anywhere. We call
> it 'Blatherskite.'[15]

The Bell was committed, O'Faoláin reiterated, to representation first, transformation second.[16] As discussed earlier in this chapter, such strict adherence to the separation and sequence of the magazine's dual agenda proved impossible to maintain. A feature such as 'Mise Eire' offered one way around the problem. In its initial form, it served as a collection of humorous quotations from periodicals such as the *Farmers' Gazette* and *Model Housekeeping*, and only gently poked fun at controversial issues such as the literary Censorship, which surfaced, for example, in a quotation introducing the *Irish Rosary's* list of novels by Catholic writers.[17]

Within two months of the feature's first appearance, however, *The Bell's* editors began appending headings to each quotation, suggesting their own interpretations of current events. Foley recalls that 'In country places especially, those clever titles at the head of each extract exposed the nonsense even more clearly for those of us who did not always recognize the humbug and pomposities we lived with'.[18] After six months, the editors clarified their representational intentions for 'Mise Eire', advising readers that 'Good critical snippets on Irish life are what we want rather than howlers, bulls, misprints, or inane idiocies'.[19] Foley writes that the feature was widely read and discussed in rural areas. He himself was struck by one quotation sent in by

> some woman from a townland beyond Lahinch that I had never heard
> of before [...] Ever afterwards there was a picture in my mind of a
> woman up there moving round a dark kitchen or feeding hens at the
> door, hearing all day and every day the thunder of the ocean against the
> Moher cliffs a few fields away, and thrown on the dresser, perhaps, her
> copy of *The Bell*.[20]

15 O'Faoláin, 'Answer to a Criticism', p. 6.   16 Ibid.   17 'Mise Eire', *The Bell* 1:3 (December 1940).   18 Foley, 'Monotonously Rings the Little Bell', p. 57.   19 Editorial note, 'Mise Eire', *The Bell* 2:3 (June 1941), p. 47.   20 Foley, 'Monotonously Rings the Little Bell', p. 56.

The provenance of readers' submissions for 'Mise Eire' reflects the wide-ranging appeal of *The Bell*, and reinforces the series' title in that its sources were not limited to Dublin publications. The 'Mise Eire' for April 1941, for example, features excerpts from the *Munster Express*, the *Drogheda Independent*, and a Limerick football programme, as well as from three Dublin newspapers.[21] Submissions in Irish were not uncommon.[22]

'Mise Eire' appeared monthly from December 1940 to July 1941, then disappeared from *The Bell*'s pages for over a year. When it resurfaced, in November 1942, an introductory editorial note stated, more pointedly than in previous issues, its intended mission as a piece of cultural commentary: 'We will publish this feature occasionally, again offering a Book-Token valued 7s. 6d. for the best entry. The extracts should suggest a social comment, not consist of mere misprints or personal inanities.'[23] The timing of the reappearance of 'Mise Eire' hints at a particular interest on the part of *Bell* editors to extend their criticism of the Board of Literary Censors, which had recently banned Kate O'Brien's novel *The land of spices* and had triggered a series of hearings in the Seanad in November and December 1942. In fact the 'Mise Eire' printed in January 1943 ran to two pages, the first seven quotations being taken directly from Senators participating in the hearings, preceded by self-consciously ironic headings such as 'Kehoe Contra Mundum', 'O'Donovan Contra Mundum', '"Nothing Smutty, Sir?"' and 'The Last Straw'.[24] As such it complemented O'Faoláin's editorial in the same issue, 'The Senate and Censorship',[25] at a time when the magazine was moving away from a purely representational mission and beginning to engage in direct commentary on the political and cultural controversies of contemporary Ireland. As the next section will show, such editorial juxtapositions were far from uncommon in *The Bell*.

GALWAY HATS AND SLUM PENNIES: EDITORIAL JUXTAPOSITIONS

'First of all, let us see how *The Bell* is shaping out', began O'Faoláin's third *Bell* editorial. 'As far as one can see, our contributors are organising the magazine into a few main sections, which are apparent and defined enough'.[26] Clearly, O'Faoláin intended to preserve the idea that *The Bell* was following the policy he laid out in his first editorial, and that the editors had left it to Life itself to

21 'Mise Eire', *The Bell* 2:1 (April 1941), p. 45. 22 See, for example, 'Mise Eire', *The Bell* 2:3 (June 1941), p. 47. 23 Editorial note, 'Mise Eire', *The Bell* 5:2 (November 1942), p. 109. 24 'Mise Eire', *The Bell* 5:4 (January 1943), pp 299–300. 25 O'Faoláin, 'The Senate and Censorship', *The Bell* 5:4 (January 1943). 26 O'Faoláin, 'Answer to a Criticism', p. 5.

shape the magazine according to the sort of contributions submitted by writers from across Ireland. If *The Bell* were a purely representational magazine, it
might indeed have become something of a haphazard anthology, a collection
of bits and bobs from any Irish writers who felt they had authentic experiences
to express. But O'Faoláin's statement that the contributors were organizing the
magazine is highly disingenuous. While it is true that the call for representational writing had led to compilations of short, largely autobiographical articles – some as short as three pages, many devoid of narrative or reflection – it
is also evident that the editors of the magazine paid careful attention to the juxtaposition of articles, and that it was they who were structuring the magazine,
often placing articles beside one another in such a way as to provoke the reader
to reflect on the multifariousness of life in contemporary Ireland.

An early example appears just a few pages after O'Faoláin's disingenuous
remark, in the third issue of the magazine, when Peadar O'Donnell's impression-
istic short story 'Why Blame the Sea-Gulls?' is juxtaposed with Arland Ussher's
translation of an Irish-language poem by Tomás Ó Muirthe, of West Waterford,
under the title 'Caoine' ('Lament'). In his short story, O'Donnell describes the discovery of a drifting cargo ship, from the point of view of an islander off the west
coast of Ireland. The narrator and his fellow islanders, initially excited by the
prospect of recovering timber from the unmanned ship, are horrified to discover
a cluster of gulls shrieking over the body of a dead sailor, floating nearby. They
pull the body into a boat, bring it ashore, lay it on an old door and light a lamp
to stay with the body all night before burying it the next morning. The story is a
chilling reminder of the war in which Ireland was an unwilling observer, as the
islanders discover when they try to return to their customary habits:

> But the war had struck us its blow. No man now stands on the cliff-top
> and looks out, without dread, over the wide wastes of the bay for sign
> of things floating. For now and then we see that cluster of sea-gulls.
> And underneath, that darkness bobbing. It is getting so that we throw
> stones at sea-gulls whenever we see them, we who looked at sea-gulls as
> part of the joy of the day. And yet, why blame the sea-gulls? What of
> the lights that had gone out before ever they picked the eyes out of that
> up-tilted head [...] Now you know our misery, those young faces with
> empty eye-sockets, up-tilted and sea-gulls screaming.[27]

O Muirthe's poem 'Caoine', which follows O'Donnell's story, laments the death
of Josie, a clever, generous, able, country wife, who managed her house and pro-

27 Peadar O'Donnell, 'Why Blame the Sea-Gulls?', *The Bell* 1:3 (December 1940), p. 9.

vided for her husband. *The Bell* printed an English translation, by permission of An Gúm, from the book *Cainnt an tSean-Shoighail.*[28]

The pairing of these two laments, or keens, one for an unknown sailor, in English, and one for a peasant wife, in Irish, can hardly be accidental. In printing the two pieces side by side, *The Bell* connects a husband's highly personal grief for his beloved wife to an island community's collective grief for an anonymous young man who has fallen victim to war. The fact that both deaths are observed in accordance with native traditions – for the sailor, an all-night wake, and for the wife, a keen in the Irish language – connects the loss of an Irish woman to the loss of a man whose nationality remains unknown. It should also be noted that 'Caoine' is followed by three love poems translated from the Irish by Frank O'Connor, yet another example of juxtaposition in terms of both language and subject matter.

Other examples of editorial juxtaposition point out the diversity of circumstances faced by Irish women and men in their daily routines. A striking example of editorial arrangement appears in *The Bell*'s fourth issue, when Eileen O'Faoláin's article on 'Galway Hats', described earlier in this chapter, is followed directly by 'Slum Pennies', a documentary article in which an unnamed narrator details the tricks she must play in order to feed, clothe and house her family of seven on twenty-three shillings a week relief. Thus, just a few pages after Eileen O'Faoláin's description of 'the hats one dreams about',[29] comes the 'Slum Pennies' narrator's account of her elaborate system of borrowing from agents and money-lenders as she plays one debt off another. When one reads of her lying to the St Vincent de Paul Society visitor about going to Mass, in order to cadge 'half a dozen dockets for a daily loaf of bread',[30] it is difficult to imagine that she goes to bed dreaming of hats. Again, the juxtaposition of these two articles can surely not be accidental. Placed side by side, they reveal the wide disparity of wealth and poverty as they were experienced by women in Ireland in 1941.

A third example of this type of juxtaposition occurs in February 1944, when Eily O'Horan's short story 'Optimists', which describes Paddy and Róisín, a young couple separated by the exigencies of wartime – he working in England and she tending her sick mother and two siblings in Dublin – is followed by an article on yacht racing in Dublin Bay. Paddy describes to Róisin his near death in a bombing attack, then says bitterly, 'But sure if I did get hit, isn't a quick death preferable to a long-drawn-out affair such as I'd have at home here

28 Tomás Ó Muirthe, 'Caoine', trans. by Arland Ussher, *The Bell* 1:3 (December 1940). Note that 'Caoine' was published in Irish in *Ireland To-Day* 2:6 (June 1937), pp 41–2, and in that version 'Josie' was named as 'Siobhán'. See also Ussher's note on Ó Muirthe in *Ireland To-Day* 2:11 (November 1937), p. 45. 29 Eileen O'Faoláin, 'Galway Hats', p. 68. 30 'Slum Pennies', *The Bell* 1:4 (January 1941), p. 77.

– unemployment, and labour queues, and misery – for the likes of me, anyway?'[31]
Paddy speaks for those who have been forced into economic migration and
resent Ireland's incapacity to offer them full employment. It is unsettling, then,
to read the words of the author 'Naneen', only a few pages afterward, describing the revival of yacht racing in Dublin Bay, and dismissing the war as if it were
only a minor obstacle to the pleasures of the yachting class: 'When the "emergency" has been fought and won, sailing will surely continue to flourish'.[32] The
two very different encounters with war described in these two articles give the
lie to any perception of uniformity in the Irish experience of the Emergency
era. The technique of juxtaposing articles drawn from a diversity of Irish experience allowed *The Bell*'s editors to move beyond simple representation as they
sought to widen the spectrum of Irish identity. By using juxtaposition to bring
together articles written from disparate points of view, O'Faoláin and his fellow
editors could exercise their influence while appearing to take a passive role.

Another form of juxtaposition was the frequent publication of articles in the
body of the magazine which reflected themes introduced by O'Faoláin in his
opening editorial commentary. Malcolm Ballin points out an example in the January 1942 issue of *The Bell*, as O'Faoláin's editorial lamenting the low level of contributions to a memorial fund for the poet F.R. Higgins is juxtaposed with articles on the literary censorship, and with poems by new Irish poets, giving an
overall impression of a vital literary tradition besieged by public neglect.[33] Similarly, in December 1943, O'Faoláin's editorial 'Past Tense', stressing the importance
of confronting the 'wounded past',[34] is followed by an article on 'History in Our
Schools', in which a history teacher expresses her views on how and what to teach
children, aiming for a balance between Irish, European and English history.[35] And
in December 1944, O'Faoláin's editorial on 'The Gaelic Cult', which warns that
the myth of Irish Gaelic purity resembles 'the National Socialist mythology of
the Pure Aryan'[36] is echoed in his short story 'The Man Who Invented Sin', which
describes a local curate's tirade against a group of young people – including the
layman narrator as well as some young nuns and monks, who have spent a
summer in the Gaeltacht learning Irish – when they are caught singing songs
together late into the night.[37] Both pieces describe the danger posed by those who
would recast the iconic figure of the Gael as a puritanical killjoy. Thus, by juxtaposing his opening commentaries with stories and articles that connected to his
themes, O'Faoláin was able strategically to reinforce his editorial arguments.

31 Eily O'Horan, 'Optimists', *The Bell* 7:5 (February 1944), p. 412.   32 'Naneen', 'Yacht Racing in Dublin Bay', *The
Bell* 7:5 (February 1944), pp 423–4.   33 Ballin, 'Transitions in Irish Miscellanies', p. 30.   34 O'Faoláin, 'Past Tense',
The Bell 7:3 (December 1943), p. 186.   35 Eileen F. Webster, 'History in Our Schools', *The Bell* 7:3 (December 1943).
36 O'Faoláin, 'The Gaelic Cult', *The Bell* 9:3 (December 1944), p. 187.   37 O'Faoláin, 'The Man Who Invented Sin',
The Bell 9:3 (December 1944).

SPECIAL ISSUES

Eventually, *The Bell*'s editors opted for a more overt form of influence over the contents of the magazine. With the introduction of the first 'Ulster Number' in July 1941, *The Bell* initiated an occasional series of special issues, which appeared throughout O'Faoláin's editorship, from 1940 to 1946. The 'Special Short Story Number' of October 1942 was expressly intended to showcase a literary genre. The 'Summer Number', in August 1944, included Irish celebrities' reminiscences of summer holidays, and a commentary on the state of Irish tourist hotels. And the four International Numbers published during the Second World War invited articles on non-Irish subjects.

The first of *The Bell*'s special issues were the 'Ulster Numbers' that appeared in July 1941 and July–August 1942, and although much of the content of these issues will be discussed in Chapter Four, it is worth noting here their position in relation to the magazine's stated editorial policy of representation.[38] As Editor, O'Faoláin apparently felt he needed to explain that *The Bell* was not entering into political discussion over the future of Partition, which was then only twenty years old. Rather, he wrote that he and his fellow editors had observed a divergence of expression between the manuscripts they received from either side of the border, and they wanted to lend a platform to a collection of voices from the North, which might not normally be heard in the South:

> One wishes, therefore, that this Ulster issue could be merely a little part of a constant interchange of ideas between our people – between the common people on both sides; not for political or commercial reasons but for those purely human reasons which are so much more likely to create a real and fruitful affiliation.[39]

Notice that O'Faoláin keeps *The Bell*'s focus squarely on the 'common people', those whose lives are best expressed through the communication of their daily experiences. As he stresses in the concluding paragraph of his editorial for the 1941 Ulster Number, 'there is nothing in all this which conflicts with the pattern of *The Bell*'.[40]

In the second Ulster Number, which appeared in July and August 1942, O'Faoláin asserted – as he had in his first *Bell* editorial – that the magazine would emphasize the experience of ordinary citizens as a way of counterbal-

38 For the second Ulster Number, in July 1942, *The Bell* received so many contributions that the editors decided to publish half of the material the following month, i.e., August 1942.   39 O'Faoláin, 'Ulster', *The Bell* 2:4 (July 1941), p. 10.   40 Ibid., p. 11.

ancing the symbolic forces conventionally perceived to be at work in Irish, and in this case Northern Irish, society:

> The important thing is that so long as the gantries go on producing writers like these in this and the next issue the victory is not with the brutality of nineteenth century industrialism, non-conformity, the kirk, the lodges, the bosses, but with the fine and intelligent humanity of the natural, wide-awake Ulsterman.[41]

For *The Bell*, 'the natural, wide-awake Ulsterman' was more important than the leaders of the churches, lodges, or industries that were seen to dominate life in Northern Ireland. By giving voice to ordinary citizens, the Ulster Numbers could attempt to influence southern Irish readers' perceptions of their fellow countrymen across the border.

The Ulster Numbers of 1941 and 1942 both appeared in July, a month chosen for its significance in the Northern Irish calendar, which marks the Twelfth of July as the annual celebration of King William's victory in the Battle of the Boyne.[42] In 1943, however, *The Bell* began a new series of special issues, the International Numbers, and the Ulster Numbers were unceremoniously discontinued. The International Numbers were a direct reaction to the isolation imposed by de Valera's vision of self-sufficiency and complicated by Ireland's neutrality in the Second World War. For O'Faoláin, the Irish idea of independence, which had glowed so brightly for his own generation, had metamorphosed into a stultifying insularity: 'Self-reliance has taken on the astonishing implication of estrangement from the world. We have become, that is to say, alienated from Europe'.[43] The sense of isolation was bolstered by the Irish government's strict adherence to its declaration of neutrality, which extended to the banning of any commentary on the war, including radio reports and newsreels (which were invariably produced in Britain or America) that might favour combatants on one side or the other. The Irish government's policy of censoring war news was strictly enforced, and was based on concerns that any journalistic slant might influence the Irish public to side with either Allied or Axis forces.[44]

The International Numbers, therefore, contrast with the Ulster Numbers, in that they represent a true break with *The Bell's* initial editorial policy. O'Faoláin admitted as much in his editorial introducing the first International Number in March 1943: 'So, in this little magazine, which has persistently devoted itself

41 O'Faoláin, 'An Ulster Issue', *The Bell* 4:4 (July 1942), p. 231.   42 Editorial note, *The Bell* 2:3 (June 1941), p. 60.   43 O'Faoláin, 'Ireland and the Modern World', *The Bell* 5:6 (March 1943), p. 423.   44 See Wills, *That neutral island*, pp 244–7. Wartime censorship is further discussed in Chapter Five.

to the cultivation of our own garden, we here take a peep and a smell at some other gardens.'[45] The first two International Numbers provided a sampling of articles on topics as wide-ranging as café conversation in France and social unity in India; the third debated whether Ireland should join the British Commonwealth of Nations, and presented a symposium on post-war plans for peace; and the fourth, published at the tail end of the war and of wartime censorship, presented a mix of articles, some focused on Ireland and some on the United States of America.

Although Wills has, not unfairly, criticized the first International Number for portraying an idealized, pre-war version of European culture,[46] it must be conceded that the series did attempt to provide Irish readers with a more varied picture of the world outside Ireland than that which they received from the mainstream domestic media. It should also be noted that the logistics of wartime cross-Channel communication posed a formidable obstacle to *The Bell's* efforts to obtain timely articles by writers from outside Ireland. As discussed in Chapter One, the first International Number actually took the place of a proposed English Number, whose publication was prevented by 'war-time difficulties'.[47] An announcement preceding the first International Number promised contributions on France, Russia, Germany, England, Italy, America, Ireland, Spain and Norway, but when the issue appeared, it featured only authors from Ireland, England and the US, although some of them did write on topics drawn from France, Russia, Germany and Italy. The third International Number was eventually published after nine months of repeated editorial notices, assuring that it would appear in April, then May, then, finally, in September 1944;[48] and the fourth International Number was promised in July 1945, but only 'if the mails arrive in time'.[49] The end of the series coincided with the end of the war; presumably, once the Emergency-era censorship was lifted, it was less necessary for *The Bell* to direct its efforts towards special issues on international topics, for the magazine would now be free to publish commentary that touched directly on post-war world politics.

Having begun, then, with a declared policy of documentary representation, *The Bell* had gradually moved into the realm of cultural and political commentary. As O'Faoláin and his fellow editors had discovered, the task of representation was not divorced from questions of interpretation. While O'Faoláin insisted, in his third editorial, that *The Bell's* first mission was only to 'see clearly — *voir clair'*,[50] the truth was that the magazine was inclined towards

45 O'Faoláin, 'Ireland and the Modern World', p. 427. 46 Wills, *That neutral island*, p. 294. 47 Editorial note, *The Bell*, 5:5 (February 1943), p. 342. 48 Editorial notes, *The Bell* 7:3 (December 1943), p. 200; 7:5 (February 1944), p. 441; 7:6 (March 1944), p. 495; 8:4 (July 1944), p. 317; 8:5 (August 1944), p. 421. 49 Editorial note, *The Bell* 10:3 (June 1945), p. 220. 50 O'Faoláin, 'Answer to a Criticism', p. 6; 'This Is Your Magazine', p. 7.

the active transformation of perceived notions of Irish identity almost from its very beginning. Over the latter years of its publication, as shifts in the editorial staff brought about changes in its editorial mission, *The Bell* would continue to evolve towards more direct forms of commentary on Irish literature, politics and culture.

CHAPTER THREE

The evolution of *The Bell*

In November 1944, four years into *The Bell's* publication, O'Faoláin deemed the magazine ready to move beyond representation and into the sphere of explicit critical commentary, because, he wrote, 'this is the stage in the development of a periodical when, at last, what is commonly called a policy may at last begin to emerge'.[1] The magazine, in other words, had remained faithful to its original, documentary agenda, and the second, transformational phase of its mission could now begin. Of course, the fact of O'Faoláin's declaration, dramatized by his perhaps unconscious repetition of the phrase 'at last', only thinly masks the reality that *The Bell* had been engaged for some time in the construction of its own version of Irish identity, as the editor himself acknowledged: 'For, although we set out mainly to *describe* – each man his own corner of life, what is that but to write a form of History?'[2] In describing and documenting Irish life, the editors had implicitly begun to work towards transformation of the very definition of what it meant to be Irish. The evolution of the magazine, however, is marked by a growing sense of distance from the day-to-day experiences of ordinary Irish men and women, and the development of *The Bell's* role as an instrument of direct criticism, both cultural and political.

In the course of its evolution, *The Bell* encountered formidable financial and political obstacles to its continued survival. O'Faoláin resigned as editor in 1946, to be replaced by Peadar O'Donnell, and the magazine's political agenda shifted to the left, only to be balanced by a sway towards conservatism in its criticism of poetry and the arts, which was most evident in its traditionalist response to the emergence of modernism in Irish poetry. This chapter will chart the forces, both external and internal, which guided *The Bell's* development, and will describe the magazine's response to the fluctuations in its domestic and international markets during the late 1940s and early 50s. Even as *The Bell* faced its own challenges, its project of representing Irish identity gradually expanded further into the sphere of cultural commentary, and its editors and contributors worked towards the transformation of the cultural and economic climate for Irish poets and writers.

1 O'Faoláin, 'On Editing a Magazine', p. 98. 2 Ibid.

MATERIAL OBSTACLES AND FINANCIAL DIFFICULTIES

The early years of the Second World War were not a propitious time to start a new magazine. As *The Bell* progressed beyond its first year of publication, its editors were faced with acute shortages in paper and ink that were a direct result of battlefield developments. The German invasion of Norway in early 1940 had diminished the British supply of wood pulp by 80 per cent, and Irish paper supplies were similarly curtailed. O'Faoláin noted in his autobiography that 'We were lucky to get any [paper] from a Britain so hardpressed that its own publications soon dwindled every year in number, size and quality'.[3] In Britain, the paper shortage was so severe that the government made it illegal to start a new periodical after May 1940.[4] In Ireland, the Minister for Industry and Commerce, Seán Lemass, ordered that 'No person shall [...] destroy, place in a refuse bin or otherwise discard any waste paper' so that all supplies could be saved for recycling.[5]

Coming onto the market in October 1940, *The Bell* was able to publish all twelve issues of its first two volumes on heavy white paper stock, but beginning with the third volume, in October 1941, the paper quality was noticeably diminished, and printing runs were smaller than the magazine's readership might have warranted. An editorial note in May 1941, warned of potential difficulties and advised readers to act accordingly:

> At the present moment we are turning away readers. We cannot get enough paper to print all the copies we could sell. Yet, in some shops, copies remain unsold while in others there are disappointed customers. Help us to fight the paper shortage by asking your newsagent to keep a copy for you each month. *After May if you do not do this you may have difficulty in getting your* BELL.[6]

A second note, in June 1941, repeated the warnings:

> Owing to paper shortage we cannot print enough copies. April was sold out. May was probably sold out — we have not our final returns yet. All we ask you to do is to choose one newsagent, go to him and say: — '*Would you please keep me a* BELL *each month?*' That will help to defeat the Paper Shortage.[7]

---

3 O'Faoláin, *Vive Moi!*, ed. Julia O'Faolain (London, 1993), p. 315.   4 Michael Shelden, *Friends of promise: Cyril Connolly and the world of* Horizon (London, 1990), p. 48.   5 Oireachtas Eireann, Emergency Powers (Waste Paper) Order, 1942, signed Seán F. Lemass, p. 2. I am grateful to Frank Reynolds of the University of Ulster library for helping me to obtain copies of this order along with the Emergency Powers (Paper) (No. 1) Order, 1941 and Emergency Powers (Waste Paper Prices) Order, 1944.   6 Editorial note, *The Bell* 2:2 (May 1941), p. 64.   7 Editorial note, *The Bell* 2:3 (June 1941), p. 60.

The quality of the paper used during the war years prompted one critic to joke, as O'Faoláin later reported in his autobiography, that *The Bell* was 'the only magazine in the world printed on lavatory paper with ink made of soot'.[8] *The Bell's* supply of recycled paper occasionally revealed the phantom print from pulped-down pages used to make it, and many of the issues produced during the war years are now in such a state of decomposition that merely turning the pages causes them to crumble.

In addition to issues of quality, however, *The Bell* still faced cutbacks in the quantity of paper available. In September 1942, the editorial board signed over their shares in the magazine to the businessman Eamonn Martin, who was a friend of Peadar O'Donnell, in exchange for £360 cash, which was needed to buy advance paper supplies.[9] In February 1943, the magazine's editors announced that they had made significant layout changes in order to cope with the ongoing paper shortage:

> We would like to draw our readers' attention to the fact that we are now giving them an increased amount of words per copy. The print-space has been lengthened on each page, all possible blanks are eliminated, and in *The Open Window* and *Eureka* [both regular features] we have crammed twice the matter into half the space. We hope that the typographical appearance of the magazine is not unduly blemished thereby, but in war times, when even Utility Clothes are on the way, the æsthetics of printing have to yield something to circumstances.[10]

The new printing layout meant that articles and stories no longer started at the top of a page; even poems were forced into awkward configurations, sometimes printed with the first stanzas on the bottom of one page, the middle stanzas on a page of their own, and the final stanzas on the top of a third. Regular features 'The Open Window' and the shorter-lived 'Eureka' were laid out in dual columns of eight-point print. Page counts dropped from an average of ninety-five pages in each of the six issues in Volume One (1940–1), to eighty-five pages in Volume Five (1942–3).

Anecdotal evidence supports the idea that *The Bell* was nonetheless a popular success. O'Faoláin claimed in his second editorial that 'Only once before, so far as I know, has a paper sold out in Dublin on the first day of publication and that was *The Nation*. There could not be a better augury'.[11] It is revealed in a later editorial note that the initial printing order was for 5,000 copies, and that by

8 O'Faoláin, *Vive Moi!*, p. 315. 9 O'Faoláin, letter to Frank O'Connor, 19 September 1942, Gotlieb Archival Research Center. 10 'Announcements', *The Bell* 5:5 (February 1943), p. 342. 11 O'Faoláin, 'For the Future', *The Bell* 1:2 (November 1940), p. 5.

the magazine's second year that number had been increased to 5,500.[12] In July 1941, the magazine ran a full-page 'Memo for Businessmen' thanking its original advertisers for their support 'at a very difficult period' and encouraging more firms to enlist: 'We are glad to be able to say to advertisers generally that *The Bell* has reached a stage where Good Will Advertising in *The Bell* is just Good Advertising.'[13] Indeed, *The Bell* was fortunate to have a few faithful advertisers who bought space in every single issue, chief among them Pye Radio, whose adverts covered nearly every back cover of the magazine (and whose Irish principal, J.P. Digby, also contributed articles on inland fisheries), and Kilkenny Woollen Mills who, like Pye, could be counted on for a large advertisement in every number of *The Bell*.[14]

High sales numbers, however, could not fully insulate the magazine from the turbulence of the wartime marketplace. In spite of the support of its most faithful advertisers and readers, *The Bell* continued to encounter financial difficulties. In January 1942, the newsstand and subscription price was increased from 1s. to 1s. 6d., a change that the editors attempted to announce in a humorous vein: 'HENCEFORTH THE BELL WILL COST YOU – THE PRICE OF A PACKET OF CIGARETTES / MOST PEOPLE WOULD PREFER THE CIGARETTES BUT – THANK YOU!'[15] The resulting decline in circulation numbers, however, was anything but funny: sales of the magazine fell immediately, by nearly twenty-five per cent. In his editorial marking the second anniversary of the magazine's publication, O'Faoláin faced the crisis head-on. He attributed the price hike to increased costs and 'inevitably contracting advertising' in the midst of wartime, and went to great lengths to reference the prices and page counts of other Irish periodicals in comparison to *The Bell*: 'We merely indicate that in charging one-and-sixpence we came tardily into line with every similar contemporary periodical in respect of price', he points out. 'Nevertheless when we did so our sales dropped by almost a fourth'.[16]

In a clever move, O'Faolain re-interpreted the magazine's original mission, and appealed directly to *The Bell*'s readers for help: 'We said in our first number that we feel this magazine to be your magazine, not ours. It is in that spirit of common ownership that we put the situation before you'.[17] Among his suggestions were that each reader should sell (not lend, he stressed) his copy of *The Bell* to a friend when he had finished with it, as a way of restoring circulation numbers to their previous levels: 'We are confident that once it gets into the hands of a potential reader he will want to go on reading it'.[18] Another suggestion was that readers should give *Bell* subscriptions as Christmas presents, to

12 'Memo for Businessmen', *The Bell* 2:4 (July 1941), p. 54.   13 Ibid.   14 See Rudi Holzapfel, *An index of contributors to* The Bell (Blackrock, 1970), p. 3.   15 Inside cover, *The Bell* 3:4 (January 1942).   16 O'Faoláin, 'Third Year', *The Bell* 5:1 (October 1942), p. 1.   17 Ibid., p. 2.   18 Ibid.

friends both at home and abroad. In fact the *Bell* tradition of sending a Christmas card from the Cuala Press with every gift subscription was initiated by O'Faoláin as an attempt to boost circulation. The first card, printed for Christmas 1942, was a reproduction of 'Evening Star'; in later years, *Bell* Christmas cards included reproductions of Anna Sheehy's linocut print 'Sisters of Charity', a photograph of an old woman minding a market stall at Carraroe Races, and a drawing by Jack B. Yeats, reproduced alongside the text of 'The Connaught Toast', a blessing that one imagines might have been as popular with Irish Americans then as it is now: 'Health and long life to you, The woman of your choice to you, Land without rent to you, And death in Erin'.[19]

The appeal for overseas subscribers was not new. Evidence suggests that much of *The Bell*'s reading base was located outside of Ireland, a fact which is important to keep in mind when considering the magazine's intended audiences and its impact on conceptions of Irish identity. Sean McMahon estimates that the normal monthly print run was approximately 3,000 copies, of which 1,000 – a significant proportion – were sold abroad.[20] As early as its sixth issue, in March 1941, *The Bell*'s pages included response slips that listed subscription rates in American currency as well as Irish: three months for 3*s.* or $1.00, six months for 6*s.* or $2.00, and twelve months for 12*s.* or $4.00.[21] (In promoting American subscriptions, *The Bell* was not alone; the *Dublin Magazine* advertised its own subscription scheme in *The Bell*, with an American annual rate of $3.00.)[22] In January 1942, an editorial note suggested: 'Give *The Bell* as your New Year's Gift to your friends abroad. Nine shillings, post free, for six months'.[23] The first letter to the Editor from an American reader appeared in June 1944, when a subscriber in Brookline, Massachusetts responded to the article 'Insanity in Ireland'.[24] Nor was America the only destination for overseas copies of *The Bell*. Michael Farrell, in his column 'The Open Window' for August 1945, refers to the large number of letters received from soldiers on the battle front, and in a 1947 column, he notes the provenance of readers' replies to one of his poetry translation contests: 'There were 52 entries, Ireland providing 34, England 10, US 3, Scotland 2, France 2, Switzerland 1'.[25] One Christmas appeal for gift subscriptions, in December 1943, informs readers that '*The Bell* now goes into many parts of the world, including belligerent zones'.[26] Indeed, the letters that *The Bell*

19 *The Bell* 9:1 (October 1944), inside back cover; 16:2 (November 1950), p. 64: 11:2 (November 1945), inside back cover. 20 McMahon, *Best from* The Bell, p. 11. O'Faoláin's initial budget, which he sent to O'Connor in an undated letter now kept in the Gotlieb Archival Research Center, estimates a print run of 2,000 copies per month. 21 Subscription slip from *The Bell* 1:6 (March 1941). 22 Advertisement for the *Dublin Magazine*, *The Bell* 4:4 (July 1942), inside cover page (unnumbered). 23 Editorial note, *The Bell* 3:4 (January 1942), p. 253. 24 Bernardine Truden, letter on 'Insanity in Ireland', in 'Public Opinion', *The Bell* 8:3 (June 1944). 25 'The Open Window, A Monthly Perambulation Conducted by Gulliver', *The Bell* 10:5 (August 1945), p. 461; *The Bell* 13:6 (March 1947), p. 80. 26 Editorial note, *The Bell* 7:3 (December 1943), p. 259.

received from Irish soldiers serving in the British army soon drew the attention
of Emergency-era censors, who refused to allow Farrell to publish them.

The end of the war did not bring an end to *The Bell's* financial straits, and
the editors employed only limited strategies in their attempts to address the
problems. In December 1947, O'Donnell wrote a full-page editorial appealing
to readers to help increase the magazine's circulation, once again, by giving
Christmas gift subscriptions. O'Donnell estimated that with 1,000 additional
subscribers the magazine could secure its continued publication, at least in the
short term. Two factors were cited for *The Bell's* continuing struggles: the
increased cost of printing, which 'puts the life of this magazine in jeopardy',
and new restrictions on the importation of magazines into Britain.[27] The British
Board of Trade had banned large-scale imports of publications, but allowed
mail order subscriptions to continue, as O'Donnell informed *Bell* readers. British
and Irish trade agreements (and disagreements) had long been an obstacle for
The Bell. Although the magazine was only a small player in the international marketplace, it often fell victim to the vicissitudes of trade negotiations between
the newly independent Irish government and its British counterpart, the former
colonial authority. It seems possible that restrictions on money transfers may
have interfered with *The Bell's* earliest efforts to expand its subscriber base in
England. In November 1940, George Bernard Shaw, then aged eighty-four and
resident in Hertfordshire, cited such restrictions in a hand-written postcard
which was stamped 'PASSED BY CENSOR' and addressed to O'Faoláin:

> I should very willingly subscribe to The Bell for the period of my expec-
> tation of life – say thirty shillings non-returnable in case The Bell
> should cease to ring within that period – but the British Government
> will not permit me to export money to Eire without an investigation
> of my purposes and motives for which I cannot spare the time. Will
> you therefore put me on the free list as a fellow journalist and distin-
> guished Eirishman [*sic*], and pray that you may presently be rewarded
> by Providence.[28]

It may be an acknowledgment of the difficulties of the Emergency period that
the aging Shaw believed he would outlive the upstart new magazine. Indeed, the
increased pressure brought to bear by British Board of Trade restrictions on the
importation of Irish books would eventually play a major role in *The Bell's* suspension of publication in April 1948.[29]

27 Peadar O'Donnell, 'To Our Readers', *The Bell* 15:3 (December 1947), p. 1.   28 George Bernard Shaw, postcard to
Sean O'Faoláin, dated 3 November 1940, John J. Burns Library, Boston College.   29 *The Bell* resumed publication
in November 1950, the same month Shaw died, and continued to appear monthly until December 1954.

CRITICAL DISTANCE AND THE WRITER-READER DIALOGUE

While *The Bell* weathered the external challenges of production in wartime, the internal changes to the magazine were just as significant. Over the later years of O'Faoláin's editorship, *The Bell's* commitment to documentary writing faded, and an increased concern with cultural and political criticism emerged. As early as in the magazine's third year of publication, the tone of some representational articles seems removed from the tactile experiences of the people they describe. First-person monologues decline in number, in favour of third-person accounts whose authors sometimes aim to be clever; for example, the author of 'A Day in the Life of a Dublin Mechanic', though he uses the pseudonym 'Night-Shift', writes from an observer's point of view when he describes a typical mechanic's morning tea break:

> Having, as we have seen, missed his breakfast, our friend hastens to repair the omission. From eight to eight-thirty every morning in every garage or workshop in Dublin, every gas-ring (until recently) was occupied in boiling billy-cans of water. Here is the recipe for making mechanics' tea pre-war: — When the water boils, without removing the can from the gas, and without lowering the gas, put in about twice as much tea as mother puts in at home, and follow this with about half-a-pound of sugar, and follow this with a bottle of milk. Give another ten minutes with the gas at full strength, and then pour it into a cup that has been cleaned twice since Christmas. If not strong enough, curse the apprentice.[30]

The first *Bell* documentary pieces had represented the efforts of writers struggling to find their voice, and the resulting articles were a little rough around the edges. In later issues the voice is more confident, more aware of an editorial presence, but also more removed from the grittier details of experience.

Whereas earlier *Bell* articles took their titles directly from their narrators' perspectives – 'I Live in a Slum' or 'Two Years in a Sanatorium', for example – later articles such as 'Crime in Dublin' suggest a broader view of experience and a more highly trained critical eye. 'Crime Reporter', for example, describes a woman whose Corporation home was attacked by her neighbours after she inherited two thousand pounds:

> Following upon this tentative approach, the request was made more directly by a deputation carrying implements in their hands. But the

30 Night-Shift, 'A Day in the Life of a Dublin Mechanic', *The Bell* 5:3 (December 1942), p. 233.

good lady's generous impulses had become so atrophied by the sudden
acquisition of wealth that she steadfastly declined to share her good
fortune. The room in which she lived with her family was promptly
wrecked by the deputation, perhaps with some idea of facilitating her
removal.[31]

The inflated vocabulary and flippant tone of the author's account add fuel to
the fire of those critics who would call *The Bell* smug and condescending. But
they also reveal the growing distance between the magazine's initial declarations
of commitment to representational writing and its evolving interest in critical
commentary.

One aspect of *The Bell* in which the trend towards cultural criticism can be
most clearly traced is in Michael Farrell's re-assignment away from the 'Country Theatre' series to become the author of a new monthly feature, 'The Open
Window'. O'Faoláin briefly introduced the new feature in December 1943, as 'a
new monthly Magazine Section of eight pages: a "Liberty Hall" where personal
opinion will have full scope and the Editor abdicates (growling impotently)'.[32]
The feature was subtitled 'A Monthly Perambulation Conducted by Gulliver',
and though Michael Farrell has been universally identified as the author,[33] his
name was never revealed in the pages of the magazine. The pseudonym Gulliver
adroitly makes reference to the Anglo-Irish writer Jonathan Swift and the intellectual curiosity of the Enlightenment era, and also suggests that the author of
'The Open Window' stands among his fellow Irishmen like a giant among Lil-
liputians, with a far-reaching worldview and a marked advantage in critical distance. ('In Lilliput' was the title of O'Faoláin's first published short story, which
appeared in the *Irish Statesman* in 1926.)[34] 'The Open Window' took another
Anglo-Irish, Enlightenment-era writer as its inspiration, and was always printed
under the epigraph 'This is Liberty Hall, gentlemen; you may do as you please
here' – a quotation from Oliver Goldsmith's play *She stoops to conquer.*

In 'The Open Window' Farrell was free to discuss any topic that interested
him, within the bounds of the wartime censorship. The feature appeared monthly,
with very few omissions, from January 1944 until the suspension of publication
in April 1948, and occasionally reappeared, half a dozen times, before the magazine went out of print in 1954.[35] In both its content and its interaction with *Bell*
readers, 'The Open Window' represents a step towards the magazine's critical
maturity. Farrell metaphorically opened a window onto the world outside Ireland, and focused his critical musings on American and European writers such

31 Crime Reporter, 'Crime in Dublin (2)', *The Bell* 5:4 (January 1943), p. 301.   32 'Announcements', *The Bell* 5:3 (December 1943), p. 246.   33 See Holzapfel, *An index of contributors* and McMahon, *Best from* The Bell.   34 See Shovlin, p.
28.   35 See Holzapfel, *An index of contributors*, p. 24.

as Walt Whitman and Ivan Turgenev. He offered *Bell* readers book tokens in exchange for interesting quotations and contributions, and advised that 'Paragraphs about Irishmen abroad, or about Irish influences abroad, interest him particularly.'[36] He regularly set contests for translating poetry from French into English, and published the winners, who were rewarded with book token prizes. One long-running debate between readers sought to establish the identity of James Whistler's model 'Jo', and the nature of her Irish connections.[37] Another reader discussion grew out of Gulliver's competition for 'the best list of 10 guests to be invited to your party and for the best list of 12 books which might help a stranger to know and understand Ireland.'[38] Suggestions for party guests included Jane Austen, Confucius, and Constance Markievicz, among others.

In continuing the dialogue with readers that he began in his 'Country Theatre' series, Farrell both sheds light on the social class and education of *The Bell's* readership, and reveals an intriguing aspect of literary magazines as opposed to other forms of literature. In contrast to novels or poems, periodicals are uniquely placed to incorporate the voice of the reader within the text itself. Even drama, though it depends on audience reaction, cannot bring the viewer onto the stage in the same way that a magazine can. As discussed in my Introduction, Beetham's work towards a theory of the periodical suggests the need for further consideration of the periodical as an 'open' form, one that 'involves [readers] not just in the production of their own individual readings but actually in the development of the text'.[39] Farrell was perhaps *The Bell's* most ardent practitioner of the writer-reader dialogue, but the magazine as a whole was always participatory, whether in O'Faoláin's repeated calls for contributions, in O'Connor's criticism of hopeful young poets, or in the heated political debates that filled the 'Public Opinion' pages of later issues of *The Bell*.

One particular example of *The Bell's* commitment to maintaining dialogue with its readers is the report on a reader survey published after Vivian Mercier's pointed 'Verdict on *The Bell*' of May 1945. Although Mercier had praised *The Bell* for its factual articles, he criticized the editors for being overbearing towards new writers and for their 'over-pessimism' in the area of cultural and political commentary.[40] Conor Cruise O'Brien, writing as 'Donat O'Donnell', had added a 'Rider to the Verdict' which mocked *The Bell's* preference for documentary realism in parodic titles of upcoming *Bell* features, among them 'Crubeens v. Boxty: A Symposium' and 'Why I am a Tánaiste' by Seán T. O'Ceallaigh.[41] O'Faoláin responded, in the same issue, with a 'Speech from the Dock' in which he blamed

36 Editorial note, *The Bell* 6:4 (July 1943), p. 337.   37 See, for example, 'The Open Window', *The Bell* 9:6 (March 1945), 543–551.   38 Farrell, 'The Open Window: A Monthly Perambulation Conducted by Gulliver', *The Bell* 12:1 (April 1946), p. 85.   39 Beetham, 'Towards a Theory of the Periodical', pp 26–7.   40 Mercier, 'Verdict on *The Bell*', p. 164.   41 Donat O'Donnell, 'A Rider to the Verdict', *The Bell* 10:2 (May 1945), pp 164–5.

his overbearing style as an editor on the fact that 'most Irish free-lance journalists are as lazy as sin', and claimed that 'What you get in *The Bell* is the result
of a stern application of high standards'.[42] He closed, however, by asking readers to respond to a questionnaire that asked them, among other questions, to
rank their preferences among seven categories of regular features. As in his first
editorial, O'Faoláin appealed to readers to take ownership of *The Bell*: 'Help us
to make the magazine a still better magazine, and still better value for your
shilling and sixpence'.[43]

In the results, which were published two months later, readers ranked editorials on world politics and on local affairs first and second, with Farrell's 'The
Open Window' column finishing third; it was noted that 'His main support
comes from the provinces'.[44] Responses to open-ended questions such as 'Have
we enough creative work, e.g. short-stories, or are we too factual?' and 'Are we
too heavy, or too light and trivial?'[45] were varied, but overall, the anonymous
compiler Scrutator (presumably O'Faoláin) reported that 'the general *Bell* public
do not want a literary magazine', and that there was 'a murmur of approval' for
The Bell's frequent attempts to 'point a telescope on the busy coasts of Europe
and the New World'.[46] Interestingly, Scrutator also reported that 'Opinions
clashed with an angrier ring in the *Poetry* section than in any other'.[47] Still, as the
next section will show, the magazine's editors remained determined to maintain
dialogue with their readers and contributors, and frequently encouraged the representation of conflicting points of view, as was the case in debates over the
magazine's stance towards contemporary poetry.

POETRY AND LITERARY CRITICISM: THE DEBATE
OVER MODERNISM

One side effect of the effort made by *The Bell*'s editors to define and establish a
national identity, ironically, was that it effectively closed off an engagement with
the internationalized aesthetics of modernism, especially in poetry. While much
of *The Bell*'s energy was directed towards concerns that resemble those of twentieth-century modernist artists and writers – addressing fragmentation in conflicting experiences of modern life, incorporating the multifarious voices of
contemporary culture into the discussion of national identity – the magazine
was largely conservative when it came to the newer forms of art and literature
that were generating controversy in Europe and America. For Geoffrey Taylor,

---

42 O'Faoláin, 'Speech from the Dock', *The Bell* 10:2 (May 1945), pp 166–7.   43 Ibid., p. 167.   44 Scrutator, 'Verdict on "The Bell"', *The Bell* 10:5 (August 1945), pp 431–2.   45 'Bell' Questionnaire, *The Bell* 10:2 (May 1945), p. 187.
46 Scrutator, 'Verdict on "The Bell"', p. 435.   47 Ibid., p. 433.

who took over the position of *Bell* Poetry Editor from Frank O'Connor in July 1941, contemporary debates about the use of poetic form were far more interesting than nationalism. In his four-and-half-year tenure as Poetry Editor, he brought the debate over modernist technique to the forefront of *The Bell*'s literary criticism, consistently arguing that poets should pay attention to the representational 'sense' of their work rather than to what he labelled abstract or experimental 'nonsense'.[48] Overall, Taylor valued the traditional aesthetics of the poetry he published more than its investment in expressing contemporary national identity, a bias which soon led him into conflict with some of Ireland's younger generation of poets. Interestingly, in keeping with *The Bell*'s commitment to writer-reader dialogue and to the representation of multiple perspectives, Taylor and O'Faoláin went to great lengths to include the ensuing debates over modernism in Irish poetry within the pages of the magazine itself.

Taylor was less concerned with the expression of Irish identity through poetry than was his predecessor, but he saw that by re-publishing eighteenth- and nineteenth-century Irish and Anglo-Irish poetry in *The Bell*, he could advocate for the expanded inclusion of poetic verse from the Enlightenment and Victorian eras within the canon of national literature. Among his first *Bell* contributions were literary criticism of nineteenth-century poets Thomas Caulfield Irwin, William Allingham – he claimed to have borrowed Allingham's books from John Betjeman, who was then stationed in Dublin as the British press attaché[49] – and Aubrey De Vere, who, Taylor argued, 'should stand in the company of Ferguson and of Mangan'.[50] In March 1942, he listed a dozen nineteenth- and early twentieth-century poets whom he believed had been undeservedly omitted from the 1924 anthology *Golden treasury of Irish verse*, edited by Lennox Robinson, with whom he had worked in the formation of the Carnegie libraries,[51] and he expressed the hope that they would be 'reconsidered by some future compiler'.[52]

In an effort to establish a sense of continuity between Irish poetry of the past and of the present, Taylor initiated, in May 1943, a series of six features entitled 'Time and Poetry', in which he printed poems by contemporary Irish poets side by side with some of his favourites from earlier eras and invited critical comparison. O'Faoláin introduced the series with a note that acknowledged Taylor's commitment to his editorial duties but conceded the reading public's lukewarm reception of most of the poetry published in literary magazines:

48 Geoffrey Taylor, 'Sense and Nonsense in Poetry', *The Bell* 7:2 (November 1943),   49 Taylor, 'A Neglected Irish Poet', *The Bell* 3:4 (January 1942); 'William Allingham', *The Bell* 4:2 (May 1942), p. 144.   50 Taylor, 'Aubrey De Vere', *The Bell* 4:3 (June 1942), p. 204.   51 Terence Brown, 'Geoffrey Taylor: A Portrait' in *Ireland's literature: selected essays*, (Gigginstown, 1988), p. 143.   52 Taylor, 'Notes Toward an Anthology', *The Bell* 3:6 (March 1942), p. 450.

> Nobody but the Editor of this magazine knows with what devotion poetry has been treated here by Mr. Geoffrey Taylor, who has for two years, now, selected every month two poems out of countless manuscripts. For all that, we both feel that the public's scepticism is deeply-rooted and we have agreed that the only way to re-establish magazine-poetry is to pay it the honour of an utterly severe test which readers will themselves help to apply.[53]

O'Faoláin explained that *The Bell* would henceforth publish only one contemporary poem each month, and would print alongside it, for the reader's comparison, 'an unfamiliar poem which has yet passed the test of the most severe of all critics, the only absolutely reliable critic there is – to wit, Time'.[54] O'Faoláin does not defend the apparently contradictory position that a poem might be simultaneously unfamiliar and time-tested; it would seem that he adopted, wholesale, Taylor's belief in the importance of championing minor poets whose names and works have been lost to history.

Contrary to its stated goal, the 'Time and Poetry' series seems intent not on challenging new poets to rise to established standards, but on raising the profile of minor poets both past and present. The first 'Time and Poetry' offers an eighteenth-century poem by Isaac Bickerstaffe, a playwright brought to Taylor's attention by Lennox Robinson, alongside the poem 'Servant Boy' by D.J. O'Sullivan, a poet, short story writer and Donegal lighthouse keeper who had been introduced to *Bell* readers in O'Faoláin's 'New Writers' column one year earlier.[55] Subsequent 'Time and Poetry' features printed John Hewitt alongside Thomas Caulfield Irwin, Sean Jennett alongside Edward Dowden, Maurice James Craig alongside William Wilkins, Valentin Iremonger alongside James Ward, and Patric Stevenson alongside Sir Richard Steele. Among the poets chosen to represent the time-tested standards of the eighteenth and nineteenth centuries, very few would be familiar to non-specialist readers. Indeed, in the case of James Ward, a section of whose 1717 poem 'Phoenix Park' is paired with Iremonger's 'Poem' about a young friend's death, Taylor admits his own lack of knowledge about the earlier poet: 'The poem which we print this month to contrast with 1943 is by an Irishman about whom I have discovered nothing'.[56] Terence Brown has compared Taylor's dedication to unearthing the work of minor poets to his tireless efforts to encourage new writers during his time as a magazine poetry editor: 'It is a sense that without a rich compost of minor verse a culture will not nourish the earth in which large talents can flourish'.[57] Taylor's belief in the

53 Editorial note, 'Time and Poetry', *The Bell* 6:2 (May 1943), p. 162.   54 Ibid., p. 162.   55 'Time and Poetry', *The Bell* 6:2 (May 1943), p. 163; see also 'New Writers', *The Bell* 4:1 (April 1942).   56 Taylor, editorial note, *The Bell* 7:1 (October 1943), p. 40.   57 Brown, 'Geoffrey Taylor: A Portrait', p. 147.

importance of minor poets may help to explain some of the choices he made in selecting poetry for *The Bell*. With the exception of a few poets such as John Hewitt and Patrick Kavanagh, most of the poetry published under Taylor's editorship is the work of obscure new writers, and most of the poems have faded from popular memory.

In June 1943, Taylor wrote an appreciation of nineteenth-century poet John Francis O'Donnell which reveals much about his poetic priorities, and which brought him into conflict with Belfast poet Roy McFadden. Under the title 'The Best "Nation" Poet', Taylor extols O'Donnell's sense of loyalty to his poetic instincts, and his preference for nature imagery over patriotic verse:

> Another thing that strikes one is that O'Donnell, almost alone among the 'Nation' poets, disregarded Thomas Davis' injunction not to 'live influenced by wind and sun and tree' but 'by the passion and deeds of the Past.' Not but that O'Donnell was intensely a patriot; and he could invoke the passions and deeds of the past with considerable effect [...] But by and large it was precisely in wind and sun and tree that O'Donnell lived, and it is by their influence on him that his poetry now lives.[58]

As Taylor states here, he selects John Francis O'Donnell as the best poet writing in *The Nation* precisely because he is the only poet who chose to ignore *The Nation*'s declared philosophy. Accordingly, much of the poetry Taylor chose for *The Bell* was studiously unengaged with the social context of mid-twentieth-century Ireland, as McFadden, an attorney who would later become founding editor of the Northern Irish poetry magazine *Rann*, pointed out in a *Bell* article titled 'Poetry in Ireland':

> I am aware that Mr John Hewitt has written some charming poetry in the English pastoral tradition – a form greatly favoured by *The Bell* – but I cannot help feeling that literature should be the expression of new experience. I would like to see a sincere interpretation of life in the drab city of Belfast, with its dogma and its patient hates; for our industrialism differs in many ways from English industrialism and offers something new to the imaginative writer.[59]

McFadden takes the opportunity, in his article, to name Robert Greacen as a fellow practitioner of the new kind of poetry he favours, and to consign W.R. Rodgers, along with Hewitt, to the category of poets too preoccupied with poetic

58 Taylor, 'The Best "Nation" Poet', *The Bell* 6:3 (June 1943), p. 238. 59 Roy McFadden and Geoffrey Taylor, 'Poetry in Ireland: A Discussion', *The Bell* 6:4 (July 1943), p. 345.

form to express contemporary Irish consciousness. *The Bell* printed McFadden's submission in the form of a dialogue, giving him the left-hand column of four-and-a-half pages, and allowed Geoffrey Taylor to respond, point by point, in the right-hand column. The resulting article was subtitled 'A Discussion', but it more closely resembles a manifesto by McFadden, accompanied by a defence from Taylor. As such, Taylor gets to have the last word: 'It may be politically necessary that a would-be independent State should develop a "national" poetry. [...] In the meantime (and always) Poetry is more important than politics'.[60]

McFadden's manifesto sparked a firestorm of debate about the definition of poetry, and highlighted the tensions between Ireland's older generation of traditionalists and the younger cohort of modernist, or 'abstract' poets. The popular novelist Ethel Mannin, who had been a friend and lover to W.B. Yeats, was quick to respond to McFadden with a letter in the following month's *Bell* in which she condemned the work of the young poet and his peers:

> As Gertrude Stein might say, 'A poet is a poet is a poet.' And a poem is a poem is a poem – or *not.* In the case of Mr McFadden and his friends mostly not. Unless there is a new meaning to the word nowadays; unless prose chopped up into lines, and prose as obscure as possible at that, and as straining after effect, is what the bright young things, for whom the early thirties are already 'history and old times', understand by poetry. Some of us are simple, and like our poetry to be intelligible, to have music, to have form, to have metre; what we understand by poetry is Shakespeare, Shelley, Keats; some of us contend that the last of the great modern poets died with Yeats and Chesterton.[61]

Mannin goes on to cite Chesterton's satirical poem 'To a Modern Poet' as 'the last word on the Modern (so-called) Poets'[62] – but her words would not be the last. McFadden responded in the following issue of *The Bell* with an accusation that Mannin lacked a basic knowledge of contemporary verse, and that her attack had been based on her misunderstanding of 'a vague something called modern poetry'. McFadden challenged Mannin's assumption that modern poets never used conventional metre, and criticized her dismissal of contemporary poets in favour of the English Romantics, who, McFadden pointed out, were not widely embraced in their own day.[63]

In November 1943, Taylor and O'Faoláin jumped into the fray, co-author-ing an article titled 'Sense and Nonsense in Poetry' that took up the debate

60 Taylor, 'Poetry in Ireland: A Discussion', p. 346.   61 Ethel Mannin, letter in 'Public Opinion', *The Bell* 6:5 (August 1943), p. 445.   62 Ibid., p. 445.   63 Roy McFadden, 'Public Opinion: Poetry in Ireland', *The Bell* 6:6 (August 1943), p. 534.

between the traditionalists and modernists in the form of a two-column discussion similar in format to McFadden's initial submission on the topic. This
time, Taylor took the first speaking part, laying out his definitions of poetry
and explaining his choice of Nick Nicholls' poem 'The Bone and the Flower'
for that month's *Bell*, while O'Faoláin offered a running commentary on Taylor's
argument and formulated his own objections. 'The Bone and the Flower', an
expressive but highly abstract dialogue between a rose and a bone, had apparently incited a disagreement between the two editors; Taylor was inclined to
publish it, arguing that he enjoyed the poem's 'nonsense', which he defined as
its 'aura of association', as much as he valued its 'sense', or literal meaning.[64]
Taylor goes so far as to compare the poem to Eliot's 'The Waste Land', which,
he notes, 'in our day [...] has been accepted, with or without the Notes, as an
important poem'.[65] He ends his half of the article with a statement of his 'belief
that Poetry and Language are not coincident and that Poetry *may* transcend Language in the Editorial usage of that word'.[66] This last sentence would seem to
indicate that Taylor has been at least somewhat persuaded by modernism to
accept poems that veer from the traditionally accepted forms of literal communication. He adds in a postscript, however, that he is more inclined to
Nicholls' poem than he might have been to other modernist poets because
Nicholls 'submits to the elementary discipline of rhyme and metre'.[67] Thus
Taylor confirms that he remains a formal traditionalist, a position borne out
by his choice of poetry for *The Bell*, which rarely published poems written in free
verse.

    O'Faoláin, on the other hand, remained a poetic traditionalist in every sense
of the word, and his contribution of comments to Taylor's essay on 'Sense and
Nonsense' demonstrates his intention to stay closely involved in the Poetry
Editor's selection of poems for *The Bell*:

> My sympathy is with the Poetry Editor. On one side of him are the rev-
> olutionary poets (if they *are* revolutionary, and not just too proud or care-
> less to be clear), and on the other a doubtless conservative Editor, who
> – for all its faults, which are legion – believes, even still, in Tradition.[68]

O'Faoláin dismisses the modernist poets as a group because of their opacity,
and, like Mannin, refers to Yeats as the traditional standard bearer: 'Yeats' explanation for the modern poets was that they are so bored that they have to whip

---

64 Taylor, 'Sense and Nonsense in Poetry', p. 158. 65 Ibid., p. 162. In an earlier review of Nicholls' published poetry, Taylor had written: 'A good many of Mr Nicholls' poems belong to the *Finnegans Wake* kind – that is to say, in my opinion, they are not poems at all' (*The Bell* 4:5 (August 1942), p. 379). 66 Ibid., p. 163. 67 Ibid., p. 167. 68 O'Faolain, 'Sense and Nonsense in Poetry', p. 162.

their temperaments with artifice'.[69] Despite his statement that 'the Poetry Editor is the Poetry Editor and his final word is final',[70] O'Faoláin admits that if Taylor were to have presented him with the manuscript of 'The Waste Land', he would have protested against its publication. (He adds, for good measure, that he would also have fought against *Finnegans Wake* if he had been given the editorial opportunity.)[71] Not long before, he had written to O'Connor that he had been reading Antonio Fogazzaro's banned novel *The Saint*: 'I'm being steeped in the Modernist thing. It's terrifying'.[72]

Modernism was still a new phenomenon in the early 1940s, one with which even educated Irish readers may have been unfamiliar. Elizabeth Bowen, for example, writing in *The Bell* in March 1941, reflected on the recent death of James Joyce and the puzzled reception that critics were still giving *Ulysses* and *Finnegans Wake*: '*Was* the man kidding? What was he getting at? Had he, for the last twenty years and more, been leading young intellectuals up the garden path?'[73] Bowen noted with chagrin that most Irish readers had been denied access to *Ulysses*, due to the literary Censorship: 'Passages of it – notably the Dublin Bay sequence at the beginning – are so beautiful, and so in every sense inoffensive, that I wish they could be extracted from the rest of the book and made available to the public in Ireland'.[74] The fact that the book's sale was banned in Ireland also meant that Irish readers had been largely unable to assess Joyce's literary technique, and so remained unaware of modernist trends in literature long after some of their European counterparts. Carol Taaffe has noted that 'modernism hardly penetrated the arts in Ireland until 1943's Exhibition of Living Art'[75] – an exhibition that was allotted less than one page of commentary in *The Bell* by the critic Arthur Power, himself a friend of Joyce's in Paris.[76]

In the two decades after independence, the aesthetics of modernism and of Irish nationalism often came into conflict. Many modernists challenged the idea that art depends on representation, an approach which, in itself, conflicted with *The Bell*'s declared agenda and its editors' belief that in documenting the details of contemporary Irish life they could shape a new national identity. For examples of modernism in Irish poetry, it is necessary to examine smaller publications such as the five poetry quartos edited by Jonathan Hanaghan and published by the Runa Press in 1943–44, which, like *The Bell*, issued a call to 'Irishmen and Irishwomen' interested in an 'Irish literary renaissance'. [77] Hanaghan promised prospective subscribers to the quartos that they would 'hear

69 Ibid., p. 159. 70 Ibid., p. 162. 71 Ibid., p. 161. 72 O'Faoláin, letter to Frank O'Connor, 19 September 1942, Gotlieb Archival Research Center. 73 Elizabeth Bowen, 'James Joyce', *The Bell* 1:6 (March 1941), p. 44. 74 Bowen, 'James Joyce', p. 47. 75 Carol Taaffe, 'Coloured Balloons: Frank O'Connor on Irish Modernism' in Hilary Lennon (ed.), *Frank O'Connor: critical essays* (Dublin, 2007), p. 209. 76 Arthur Power, 'The Exhibition of Living Art', *The Bell* 7:1 (October 1943). 77 Advertisement included in Quarto 2, *Bannered Spears*, ed. by Jonathan Hanaghan (Dublin, July 1943).

the music of the new age' and 'catch the spirit of Europe in strife for beauty and life, often hurt by bitterness and pain'.[78] Whereas O'Faoláin declared *The Bell* to be openly biased in favour of Irish poets and writers, Hanaghan emphasized his contributors' wide-ranging origins, and unabashedly looked abroad for inspiration. Poets in these slim volumes included Sir Herbert Read and Henry Treece, both influential figures in the British Apocalyptic movement, of which Dylan Thomas was also an early proponent. In contrast, very little of the poetry published in *The Bell* demonstrates an engagement with the preoccupations of modernist writers who were then at work in Europe and America.

The Bell was not alone in its hesitation to embrace modernist poetry. Although critics such as Paige Reynolds have begun to argue that the nationalist Irish Revival was not in fact antithetical to the modernist movement, it remains the case that many writers found themselves placed into one camp or the other.[79] Until recently, for example, there has been a persistent reluctance to include modernist poets in the canon of Irish literature, as demonstrated by the frequent omission of such poets as Brian Coffey, Denis Devlin, Thomas Mac-Greevy and George Reavey from anthologies of twentieth-century Irish poetry. For example, Patricia Coughlan and Alex Davis, editors of a volume of critical essays on modernism and Ireland, note that the work of these poets

> has tended to be viewed, in the main, as of minor import beside the achievements of Kavanagh and Clarke, thus showing the greater ease of the critical establishment with work which can be more readily accommodated under the rubric of a more literalist and self-proclaimed Irishness.[80]

Similarly, Gerald Dawe writes that mid-century modernist poets such as Coffey, Devlin, and Thomas Kinsella worked in 'exile' from the accepted canon of Irish poetry, noting that 'Conservatism is one of the most significant features of the Irish poetic inheritance.'[81]

Against such a background, *The Bell*'s choice of Nick Nicholls' poem 'The Bone and the Flower' as the focal point for a discussion about modernist poetry serves to demonstrate the extent to which both Taylor and O'Faoláin were outside the debate over modernism, much as Roy McFadden had accused Ethel Mannin of being out of touch. As Taylor notes in the first lines of 'Sense and Nonsense', his choice of poems had already attracted 'complaints about the

78 Ibid.   79 Paige Reynolds, *Modernism, drama, and the audience for Irish spectacle* (Cambridge, 2007).   80 Patricia Coughlan and Alex Davis, 'Introduction' to *Modernism and Ireland: the poetry of the 1930s* (Cork, 1995), pp 7–8.   81 Gerald Dawe, 'An Absence of Influence: Three Modernist Poets' in Terence Brown and Nicholas Grene (eds), *Tradition and influence in Anglo-Irish poetry* (London, 1989), p. 120.

apparently unadventurous attitude of *The Bell* to poetry'; McFadden's critique
was 'only one instance of many'.[82] 'The Bone and the Flower' was perhaps chosen
as a partial remedy to the magazine's traditionalism – but the poem itself is less
representative of the modernist aesthetic than of a Neo-Romantic tendency
towards abstraction. In rhyming, metrical verse, grouped into numbered sections of two or three stanzas, Nicholls creates a repetitive, incantatory dialogue
between two objects whose symbolism is unexplained. The poem's mystical,
dreamlike imagery may owe more to Yeats' early 'Rose' poems of the nineteenth
century than to a twentieth-century modernist agenda:

> Dark dark dark the power
> Of unwieldy magnificence in the breath
> Dark dark dark the hour
> Of the intractable and encoiléd breath!
>
> Dark dark dark the flower's entanglements
> The virulent rose, the flagellant power
> Dark the hour of the flower's entanglements
> The sibilant rose, the insinuate power![83]

Nicholls had published a chapbook in 1942, and his poems were included in the
Runa Press quartos, alongside those of Henry Treece. Nicholls published several other poems in *The Bell* between 1943 and 1953, all of which reflect his pre-
occupation with symbolic imagery. In a critique of the British Apocalyptic poets,
Arthur Salmon describes their work as 'another manifestation of the nineteenth-
century Romantic tradition' and includes Neo-Romanticism as an outgrowth
of their movement.[84] Nicholls' work would seem to fit the Neo-Romantic
model, both for its introspective tone and its elevation of visual imagery, which
suggests connections to Pound and his fellow Imagists – though it seems likely
that Pound would have decried Nicholls' insistence on decorative language and
abstraction.

Like most of its Irish literary periodical predecessors, *The Bell* never fully
embraced the modernist movement that was stirring discussion in English and
American literary circles. Instead, the magazine was content to publish an eclec-
tic range of traditional poetry, both old and new. O'Faoláin declared himself
satisfied 'that we have a Poetry Editor of the widest wave-length. For he fights
to the end for the most esoteric poetry, and in practice prints every type, from
Mr Nicholls to the most classic eighteenth century versifiers'.[85] It may have been

82 Taylor, 'Sense and Nonsense in Poetry', p. 156.   83 Nick Nicholls, 'The Bone and the Flower', *The Bell* 7:2
(November 1943), p. 165.   84 Arthur Edward Salmon, *Poets of the apocalypse* (Boston, 1983), p. 5.   85 O'Faoláin, 'Sense

more accurate, however, to say that Taylor preferred the eighteenth- and nine-teenth-century poets he championed, and published those contemporary poets whose work most closely reflected his own traditional poetic values.

This is not to say that *The Bell* did not publish good contemporary poetry. In fact, both Patrick Kavanagh and John Hewitt owed much of their early pub-lishing careers to the magazine's acceptance of their work, including some of their best-known and most enduring poems. Antoinette Quinn, whose biogra-phy of Kavanagh 'chronicles his twenty-year search for a well-paid job', among other topics, devotes an entire chapter to *The Bell's* support for his early work.[86] Quinn describes at length his relationship to O'Faoláin and O'Connor, 'the two Corkmen who were teaching him "to be wise"', as he wrote in a discarded draft of his poem 'To a Child'.[87] Quinn also provides a detailed discussion of Kavanagh's published work in *The Bell*.[88] His novel *Tarry Flynn* was serialized almost in entirety in the pages of the magazine, accompanied by an editorial note that described him as 'the outstanding Irish novelist to-day; the most authentic voice rural Ireland has yet achieved'.[89] Peadar O'Donnell arranged to print a 'Bellman' interview with Kavanagh to coincide with the novel's publica-tion by the Pilot Press,[90] and in that interview Kavanagh declared that his only publicity agents had been O'Connor and O'Faoláin.[91]

Both Kavanagh and Hewitt benefited from *Bell* editors' generous assign-ments of writing work: Hewitt contributed book reviews, as did Kavanagh, who also published critical essays in the magazine. After being introduced as a new writer in O'Connor's 'Belfry' series, Hewitt published 'The Hired Lad's Farewell' and numerous other poems in *The Bell*, including 'The Colony', which appeared in the same issue as Kavanagh's essay 'A Goat Tethered Outside the Bailey', con-taining the poem 'Kerr's Ass'.[92] In December 1941, Geoffrey Taylor wrote an early critique of Hewitt's poetry, both published and unpublished, and lamented the lack of a collection in book format. Characteristically, Taylor placed Hewitt in the tradition of seventeenth- and eighteenth-century English nature poetry, charting his influences through Edward Thomas to Robert Frost and William Wordsworth.[93] For Taylor, traditionalist poetry would always set the standard by which new work was assessed.

and Nonsense in Poetry', p. 169. **86** Antoinette Quinn, *Patrick Kavanagh: a biography* (Dublin, 2001), p. x. **87** Ibid., p. 146. **88** See Quinn, *Patrick Kavanagh*, Chapter 9, 'Bell-*Lettres*', pp 146–64. **89** Patrick Kavanagh, 'Three Glimpses of Life', *The Bell* 8:4 (July 1944); 'Tarry Flynn', *The Bell* 14:2 (May 1947); *The Bell* 14:3 (June 1947); *The Bell* 14:4 (July 1947); *The Bell* 14:6 (September 1947). **90** Quinn, *Patrick Kavanagh*, p. 264. **91** The Bellman, 'Meet Patrick Kavanagh', *The Bell* 16:1 (April 1948), p. 10. **92** John Hewitt, 'The Hired Lad's Farewell', *The Bell* 3:3 (December 1941); 'The Colony', *The Bell* 18:11 (Summer, 1953); Patrick Kavanagh, 'A Goat Tethered Outside the Bailey', *The Bell* 18:11 (Summer, 1953). Shovlin (p. 144) notes that 'Kerr's Ass' was first published in Kavanagh's 'Diary' for *Envoy* magazine in Octo-ber 1950. **93** Taylor, 'The Poetry of John Hewitt', *The Bell* 3:3 (December 1941), p. 230.

THE BELL AND IRISH PUBLISHING

Hewitt and Kavanagh were only two of the many poets whose work *The Bell* encouraged. During Taylor's poetry editorship, *The Bell* took a strong interest in supporting the work of young Irish poets and actively promoted their publication. Both O'Faoláin and his successor, Peadar O'Donnell, took issue with the wider economic and cultural conditions that hampered the publication of Irish writers in the mid-twentieth century. In one of his early editorials, O'Faoláin lamented the lack of wartime publishing avenues, given the loss of access to English and American markets. Irish neutrality had proved a stumbling block for readers in Allied countries, O'Faoláin noted, and not only for economic reasons: 'In that field which was once wide open to us we now find a very chilly welcome indeed'.[94] Rather than blame English and American readers, O'Faoláin turned his critique to recent trends in Irish publishing, and lamented the fact of Irish dependence on overseas printers, publishers and markets over the preceding thirty years: 'In fine we have had for all this period no financial responsibility whatsoever for our own literature or our own writers'.[95] An important first step, he proposed, was an increase in public support for literary periodicals such as *The Bell*. O'Faoláin praised the private donors and advertisers who had helped bring the magazine into existence and had established it as a paying forum for Irish writers during the lean times of the Emergency era. But he also pointed out that additional support was needed to maintain the greater Irish periodical market, and he named several competing magazines (including the *Standard* and the *Dublin Magazine*) as potential recipients of funds. O'Faoláin suggested that the Irish government consider subsidizing Irish writers in an initiative similar to the American government's National Recovery Act, part of which provided paid work for writers and artists during the Depression of the 1930s. Finally, he invoked a rural metaphor to foretell the consequences of ignoring the crisis in Irish publishing: 'If something on these, or some such lines, is not done, Irish literature will go "back" like a field that has been salvaged from the gorse by hard work and is finally allowed to go barren'.[96]

O'Faoláin revisited the question of Irish publishing in later editorials focusing on the book industry and on book reviewing in the Irish press, and in every instance he attempted to bring a broad perspective to bear on the issue. In his editorial 'Books in the Country', published in March 1942, O'Faoláin suggested improvements in the County Library system to bring more high-quality books to rural readers. He urged the provincial and daily newspapers to improve their standard of criticism, and he named the only publication whose work he found

94 O'Faoláin, 'Dare We Suppress That Irish Voice?', *The Bell* 3:3 (December 1941), p. 171.   95 Ibid.   96 Ibid., p. 174.

satisfactory (the *Irish Times*) and those who needed to step up their book reviewing (the *Irish Press, Cork Examiner,* and *Irish Independent*):

> Some provincial papers do good work [...] But we beg them all to do
> much more – to carry reading-lists, to have a regular book-column, to
> be alive to this most important part of our whole national education.[97]

In light of the impoverished critical landscape O'Faoláin describes, the importance of *The Bell*'s regular publication of book reviews, with an emphasis on
books from Irish writers and publishers, becomes even more apparent. Indeed,
as O'Faoláin implies above, *The Bell*'s book review section, of which he himself
would become editor after stepping down from the chair of the magazine, was
seen as part of its project of 'national education' to raise the level of Irish literary standards and tastes, very much in line with its earlier series of instructional articles for young poets and short story writers. Soon after 'Books in the
Country' appeared, *The Bell* began publishing lists of the best-selling books, gath-
ered from booksellers across Ireland, perhaps in an effort to fill the gap
O'Faoláin had noticed among the provincial and daily press.[98]

For O'Faoláin, the paucity of government support for the Irish publishing
industry would continue to be a sticking point in the development of a national
literature. In his editorial 'Books and a Live People', which appeared in May
1943, he compared the Irish book publishing industry to those in other European countries with similarly small populations. Armed, as always, with financial figures and statistics (including a half-page chart on book production in
Sweden from 1932 to 1938, obtained from the Swedish Consulate), O'Faoláin
debunked the idea that the Irish reading public was too small to rival neighbouring Britain in its capacity to publish native books. He noted the historical
tendency of Irish writers to circumvent the lack of domestic publishers by sending their work, and sometimes by relocating themselves, to England, and stated
that 'Literature will not, I repeat, suffer if we do nothing. Our writers will not
expire. They will export'.[99] The loss, in O'Faoláin's view, was a national one, and
upon it impinged the viability of Irish literary culture: 'The richness or poverty
of life is involved'.[1]

Eventually *The Bell* took matters into its own hands. Whereas in its earliest
issues the magazine had invited individual poems and short stories from new

---

97 O'Faoláin, 'Books in the Country', *The Bell* 3:6 (March 1942), p. 409. 98 See, for example, 'The Best Selling
Books', *The Bell* 6:1 (April 1943); 'The Best Selling Books', *The Bell* 6:4 (July 1943). The difficulties of wartime trade
limited book sales as well. In December 1944, 'Best-Selling Books' includes the following explanation from one
bookseller for low sales numbers: 'no stock of anything worth while', *The Bell* 9:3 (December 1944), p. 259. 99
O'Faoláin, 'Books and a Live People', *The Bell* 6:2 (May 1943), p. 97. 1 Ibid., p. 92.

Irish writers, as it grew into maturity, *The Bell* took a more activist stance towards promoting the publication of new Irish literature. One avenue taken was the sponsorship of literary competitions. In September 1942, *The Bell* published the winners of a short story competition organized by the Friends of the Irish Academy of Letters in connection with the Book Fair of 1942. Judges Lennox Robinson, Lynn Doyle and Professor H.O. White chose two stories which were noticeably different in both style and content from those normally published in *The Bell*, and which had little to do with interpreting Irish identity. 'Wise Man's Son', by Terence de Vere White, used a potboiler plot, with shifting points of view, to tell the story of Cornelius Pat, a boy whose father, as Cornelius Pat discovers years later, has poisoned his mother. The second place winner, 'Her Only Son', by Ulick Burke, presents the point of view of an old woman whose son is facing trial and sentencing to the County Asylum.[2] One year later, in August 1943, *The Bell* sponsored a playwriting competition over which it maintained greater editorial influence, with both O'Faoláin and O'Donnell among the six judges. The contest was for 'plays with a social angle', in keeping with *The Bell*'s representational agenda, and the winning play was to be awarded fifteen guineas and production by the New Theatre Group in Dublin.[3] The winner, *Clever Lad, Eh?* by Nora O'Hare (whose name was printed in *The Bell* only as 'Mrs O'Hare'), was one of three finalists, all of which, the editors noted, dealt with life in Northern Ireland.[4]

A second avenue for the promotion of Irish writers was *The Bell*'s publication, in 1944, of its own poetry anthology, edited by Geoffrey Taylor. Taylor carried *The Bell*'s commitment to improving the Irish artistic environment to its next logical stage of development when he edited *Irish poems of to-day*, which contained twenty-five poems by eighteen poets, all originally published in *The Bell* during its first three-and-a-half years of publication. Taylor's direct engagement with the publishing marketplace marked a new departure for *The Bell*. The anthology was first issued by the magazine's Dublin publisher, Cahill & Co., Ltd, and reprinted by London publisher Secker and Warburg. The jacket text of the London edition describes *Irish poems of to-day* as a successor to Lennox Robinson's 1924 Irish poetry anthology, and Taylor's introduction makes it clear that he intends his book to provide 'a small, nearly representative, sample of the valid contemporary English poetry by Irish writers'.[5] Taylor notes the omission of established poets Robert Graves, Louis MacNeice, and Austin Clarke, but points out that *The Bell*'s editorial policy had led to a focus on young or little-

2 Terence de Vere White, 'Wise Man's Son', *The Bell* 4:6 (September 1942); Ulick Burke, 'Her Only Son', *The Bell* 5:1 (October 1942). 3 Editorial note, *The Bell* 6:5 (August 1943), pp 437–8. 4 Editorial note, *The Bell* 8:1 (April 1944), p. 81. The large number of submissions from Northern Ireland was noted in the poetry section of *The Bell* as well (see pp 132–3). 5 Taylor, 'Editor's Note', *Irish poems of to-day* (London, 1944), p. 3.

known poets. Accordingly, the anthology includes three poems each by John Hewitt and W.R. Rodgers, as well as Nick Nicholls' 'The Bone and the Flower' and Roy McFadden's 'Plaint of the Working Man'. Even Robert Greacen's 'The Bird', which Frank O'Connor had so cuttingly disparaged, wins a place in Taylor's book. (One poem of Patrick Kavanagh's is included in the original anthology, but he is, curiously, excluded from the London edition.)

The anthology, overall, reflects *The Bell*'s lack of a defined agenda with regard to poetry, and Taylor's selection of poems gives the impression that mid-twentieth-century Irish poets drew on a mixture of traditional and modern influences. Experimental poetry is absent, although many poems do employ blank verse instead of rhyme. Several poems describe rural Irish landscapes, and some are elegies for dead or dying farmers or childhood friends. Only two poems confront the contemporary reality of the Second World War: Freda Laughton's 'The Bombed House' and McFadden's 'Plaint of the Working Man', which describes the modest lives of the working class and asks, 'Why should the bomb stalk us who are unworthy of notice [...] What are we to the fat old men who rule us?'.[6] Contemporary critics received *Irish poems of to-day* as a commentary on the transitional state of poetry in 1940s Ireland. One review, published in the pages of *The Bell* itself, called the mixture of poetic trends 'a trifle bewildering' and ascribed the anthology's eclecticism to the fact that it was 'reflecting the chaos of the times'.[7]

Austin Clarke, in an *Irish Times* review of the anthology titled 'Wanted – A Tradition', noted the general sense of apathy against which contemporary Irish poets had to struggle, and connected the lack of Irish publishing opportunities to the sense of uncertainty among young Irish poets: 'In the book shops these young writers have found, not Irish poetry, but the innumerable Faber books of contemporary English and American verse, all uniform and spick-and-span in appearance'.[8] Clarke applauded *The Bell* for taking the initiative in publishing its own anthology, and excused the limitations of its selection of poems and poets as being chosen from a relatively short time period in *The Bell*'s publication history. He concluded that if Taylor had been able to include longer poems such as Kavanagh's 'The Great Hunger' (then available to Irish readers only in what Clarke deemed 'an expensive, semi-private edition' published by the Cuala Press) and Robert Farren's 'The First Exile', as well as some of the work of Padraic Fallon, then the strength of contemporary Irish poetry would not be in doubt.[9] In a later column for the *Irish Times*, Clarke scolded O'Faoláin for lamenting the decline of Irish poetry and 'appoint[ing] himself as the Banshee

6 Roy McFadden, 'Plaint of the Working-Men', in *Irish poems of to-day*, p. 29.   7 Sam Harrison, review of *Irish Poems of Today*, *The Bell* 8:5 (August 1944), p. 452.   8 Austin Clarke, 'Wanted – A Tradition' [review of *Irish poems of to-day*], *Irish Times*, 13 May 1944, p. 2.   9 Ibid.

of the Irish poetic movement'; he was joined in this playful attack on O'Faoláin
by fellow poets Valentin Iremonger, Robert Greacen, and Robert Farren.[10] At
the end of 1944, the *Irish Times* published its own anthology of poetry from its
pages, edited by Donagh MacDonagh and roughly three times the length of the
Bell anthology.[11] And in 1949, Faber brought out a comparatively large anthology of contemporary Irish poetry, which included over one hundred poems by
thirty-four poets and was edited by Greacen and Iremonger, both of whom had
been published in *Irish poems of to-day*.[12]

   Despite its limited resources, *The Bell* did what it could to advance the publication of Irish writers; and the promotional ethos extended beyond the material
pages of the magazine. Besides the literary contests and Taylor's anthology, *The Bell*
frequently engaged in the endorsement of fellow literary magazines, whether by
carrying advertisements for *Horizon* or by announcing the publication of regional
magazines such as *Wales* and the Scottish *New Alliance*.[13] These last two were praised
as being similar in sensibility to *The Bell*, with *Wales* being noted for its openness to
publishing foreign writers alongside native ones, and the *New Alliance* being
described as 'Nationalist in outlook, and mainly literary'.[14] *The Bell* went so far as
to stock the *New Alliance* in its offices, and offered copies to readers in exchange for
seven penny stamps.[15] Furthermore, *The Bell* was an early advertising venue for the
Irish writers' union, the Writers, Artists, Actors and Musicians Association, or
WAAMA, of which O'Faoláin was President from its founding in 1941, and whose
self-proclaimed seriousness Flann O'Brien, writing as Myles na gCopaleen, mer-
cilessly mocked in a series of 'Cruiskeen Lawn' columns in the *Irish Times*.[16] Despite
its unwieldy name, WAAMA successfully advocated for increases in pay for writers, especially those working for Radio Éireann – an issue O'Faoláin had raised in
his first *Bell* editorial on the need for state support of Irish writers.[17] O'Faoláin
succeeded in getting the *Irish Times* to cover many of WAAMA's activities, including a 1942 'WAAMA Week' and a literary magazine, *Puck's Fare*, which included
WAAMA members' illustrations, poems, stories, and critical articles.[18] Even while
The Bell faced its own financial struggles, O'Faoláin continually spoke out for better
conditions and pay for his fellow writers. This campaign would continue after
Peadar O'Donnell took over *The Bell's* editorship.

---

10 Austin Clarke, 'A Vision of Glendalough', *Irish Times* 19 April 1946, p. 4.   11 *Poems from Ireland*, ed. by Donagh
MacDonagh (Dublin, 1944).   12 *Contemporary Irish poetry*, ed. by Robert Greacen and Valentin Iremonger (London,
1949).   13 See *The Bell* 5:2 (November 1942), p. 156; 7:2 (November 1943), p. 155; 2:2 (May 1941), p. 72.   14 Nigel
Heseltine, 'Welsh Writing To-Day', *The Bell* 6:5 (August 1943), p. 414; Editorial note, *The Bell* 2:2 (May 1941), p. 72.
15 Editorial note, *The Bell* 2:2 (May 1941), p. 72.   16 See Myles na Gopaleen [Flann O'Brien], 'Waama, etc.' in *The
best of Myles*, ed. by Kevin O Nolan (New York, 1983).   17 *The Bell* 4:3 (June 1942), p. 227; 4:4 (July 1942), inside
cover page, unnumbered; O'Faoláin, 'Dare We Suppress That Irish Voice?', p. 175; see also Harmon, *Seán O'Faoláin:
a life*, p. 154.   18 See, for example, 'WAAMA First General Meeting', *Irish Times* 15 September 1941; 'WAAMA Week',
Irish Times 19 May 1942; 'WAAMA Critic of Radio Eireann', *Irish Times* 4 December 1944.

EDITORIAL STAFF CHANGES

In his editorial 'Signing Off', in April 1946, O'Faoláin announced his resignation as Editor of *The Bell* and the appointment of his successor, Peadar O'Donnell, who had been a member of the Editorial Board from the start and had also served as business manager. O'Faoláin's work over the magazine's first five-and-a-half years had been, as Maurice Harmon has described it, difficult and draining. He had experienced frustration in his efforts to secure financial support for *The Bell* from the Irish government, and he had neglected his own fiction writing because of the enormous time pressures inherent in editing a monthly magazine.[19] In his farewell editorial, O'Faoláin recalled the magazine's original appeal for authentic representation, and expressed his disappointment at not having inspired a higher standard of literary output from young Irish writers:

> All I can say is that our pages were and are open to all men of good-will, and that we have worked hard and will keep on working hard to lure every writer to speak through these pages to Ireland. Besides, it is one thing to have a noble vision of life to come and another to have to handle what does come.[20]

O'Faoláin blamed much of *The Bell*'s shortcomings on the straitened circumstances of life in contemporary Ireland, and wondered rhetorically whether the magazine's increasing tendency to engage in political and cultural commentary had sapped some of the strength from its literary ambitions. As he formally retired from the Editor's chair, he regretted that *The Bell* had not printed 'more articles on literature, and on aesthetics, and technique', and he hoped that the end of the war would bring more contributions from overseas, as an antidote to the parochialism and isolation of the Emergency era.[21] Indeed, in the final sentences of his valediction, O'Faoláin seems unable to resist the temptation to set an agenda for his successor, and hints that the magazine will be measured by its success in carrying on its original Editor's vision.

Whether O'Donnell followed in O'Faoláin's footsteps has been the subject of limited debate. Other than a few brief statements from commentators on *The Bell*, O'Donnell's editorship of the magazine has been largely unexamined. Shovlin provides a rare discussion of O'Donnell's tenure, and accurately describes the second editor's predilection for overt political argument. Rather than turning away from political commentary, O'Donnell extended O'Faoláin's initial steps into this area, and indeed occasionally went farther than O'Faoláin

19 Harmon, *Sean O'Faoláin: a life*, pp 147–150. 20 O'Faoláin, 'Signing Off', *The Bell* 11:6 (April 1946), p. 2. 21 Ibid., p. 4.

would likely have deemed acceptable. Shovlin points out the importance of O'Donnell's Republican-socialist political background to his editorial agenda, and states that 'When O'Donnell took over, certain issues surrounding the national question came more to the forefront. Sympathy was expressed for IRA objectives, and partition came under increased scrutiny.'[22] While O'Faoláin's editorials had been lengthy, energetic discussions of cultural and political issues such as the Censorship and post-war international relations, O'Donnell preferred short, direct attacks on specific government policies such as the continued internment of IRA volunteers.[23] Val Mulkerns notes that

> O'Faoláin had sometimes been in danger of filling a whole issue with what he wanted to say, and to this day, those editorials make marvelous reading. Peadar's were brief, staccato, sometimes baffling in syntax, and greatly in need of the actual physical presence that would have given them impact at, say, a public meeting.[24]

Indeed, O'Donnell's writing in his editorials is mechanically simple, and he displays few of the linguistic flourishes in which O'Faoláin regularly indulged.

O'Donnell's political tendencies were also apparent in his choice of material for *The Bell*. A new openness about IRA operations marked articles by Francis Stuart about Frank Ryan, who had collaborated with the German navy in an attempt to sabotage the Irish Free State in 1940, and articles by Stephen Hayes, the former IRA chief-of-staff who had been arrested and imprisoned by Northern IRA operatives in 1941, before escaping and surrendering to the Garda Siochána.[25] One article described the IRA raid on Magazine Fort in Phoenix Park on Christmas Eve, 1939; another two-article series chronicled the involvement of the Irish Republican Brotherhood in a Chicago murder in the late nineteenth century.[26] Socialism and trade unionism were two other recurring themes. Beginning with his first issue as Editor, in which an article on William Thompson, 'the first Irish socialist', appeared, O'Donnell consistently published articles that were sympathetic to socialist ideology.[27] Trade union actions such as the primary schoolteachers' strike in 1945–6 were another of O'Donnell's pet concerns, and were given increased space in *The Bell* after he took over the Editor's chair.[28]

22 Shovlin, p. 115. 23 See, for example, 'Liberty Ltd', *The Bell* 12:4 (July 1946); 'Tourists' Guide to Irish Politics', *The Bell* 14:5 (August 1947). 24 Val Mulkerns, '"Did You Once See Shelley Plain?": Dublin, *The Bell*, the Fifties', *New Hibernia Review* 10:3 (Autumn, 2006), p. 10. 25 Francis Stuart, 'Frank Ryan in Germany', *The Bell* 16:2 (November 1950) and 16:3 (December 1950); Stephen Hayes, 'My Strange Story', *The Bell* 17:4 (July 1951) and 17:5 (August 1951). 26 'The Capture of the Magazine Fort', signed 'I Was There', *The Bell* 17:12 (March 1952); Michael J. Lennon, 'The Murder of Doctor Cronin', *The Bell* 18:1 (April 1952) and 18:2 (May 1952). 27 Patrick K. Lynch, 'William Thompson of Cork', *The Bell* 12:1 (April 1946), p. 34. 28 O'Donnell, 'Teachers Vote Strike', *The Bell* 11:2 (Novem-

In his editorials, O'Donnell called repeatedly on Irish writers to involve themselves in the political controversies of the time, in a much more pointed manner than had O'Faoláin. In one of his earliest editorials, O'Donnell used the metaphor of the writer or artist as tradesman, working with his community in the same way that a tradesman might work 'in the materials that excite his mind'.[29] O'Donnell's editorials were often more abstract than O'Faoláin's, and he frequently linked *The Bell*'s policy of representation directly to movements for social change. For him, the writer was inextricably connected to the community, so that the representation of individual experience became part of the greater work of giving voice to the people as a whole: 'He [the artist] is the aspect of the imagination of the people which speaks to them through a representation of their own experiences'.[30] A true accounting of Irish life, O'Donnell argued, would dispel the myths that were shrouding the real difficulties of making a living in post-war Ireland. If writers joined the effort to reveal and interpret the problems of the rural economy, for example, the result might be a movement to improve the wages and standard of living of farmers and farm labourers, which might in turn stem the flow of emigration.[31]

O'Donnell also called on Irish writers to confront the myths about Ireland circulating through post-war Britain and the rest of the world. He argued that writers could play a crucial role in rehabilitating the position of Ireland in the world after years of silence due to wartime neutrality, and he recalled an image used by Arthur Griffith when he suggested that writers begin to address

> the paper wall with which all subject nations are surrounded; on the inside is written what their enemies would have them believe of themselves, to their demoralisation, and on the outside what they would have the world believe of them, to their isolation.[32]

O'Donnell believed that one beginning would be to connect the story of the Irish independence movement with revolutionary movements in other countries, and proposed that to this end, 'a group of our young writers' might work on editing a new anthology of revolutionary literature.[33] He worried about the British and American perception that Ireland had declared neutrality because of pro-Fascist sentiment, and argued that young Irish writers needed to band together to combat the idea that Ireland was a backward-looking nation. O'Donnell repeatedly expressed frustration at the state of 'bewilderment into which

ber 1945); 'Grand-Children of the Insurrection', *The Bell* 12:5 (August 1946). 29 O'Donnell, 'Under the Writer's Torch', *The Bell* 12:6 (September 1946), p. 462. 30 O'Donnell, 'Under the Writer's Torch', p. 462. 31 O'Donnell, 'At the Sign of the Donkey Cart', *The Bell* 12:2 (May 1946). 32 O'Donnell, 'Facts and Fairies', *The Bell* 13:1 (October 1946), p. 1. 33 Ibid.

Irish writers have temporarily fallen'.[34] In his editorials he tried to rouse his fellow writers to 'overcome their lack of cohesion, and come out of retirement'.[35] It was his feeling that young writers, in particular, could lead the way in shaking off the cultural isolation imposed by wartime restrictions on communications and intercultural exchange: 'a sense of kinship with the world needs cultivating in Ireland to-day'.[36]

Given O'Donnell's exhortations to Irish writers to engage directly in political argument, it seems ironic that under his editorship *The Bell*'s contents would be re-oriented towards longer pieces of fiction and literary commentary. The fact that both O'Faoláin and O'Donnell refer, in their valedictory and salutatory editorials, to *The Bell*'s original ambition to be 'A Magazine of Creative Fiction',[37] a legend used only on its letterhead to contributors and correspondents, and not as 'A Survey of Irish Life', which had been printed as the subtitle of its first four issues, signals an ambivalence, even at the editorial level, about the magazine's original purposes – and it also demonstrates the difficulty of *The Bell*'s attempt to juggle multiple roles in a society underserved by native publications. If measured by the former slogan, *The Bell* might, as O'Faoláin implied, be deemed a failure; but the latter slogan more accurately describes the magazine's representational mission, and suggests a broad understanding of Irish experience as an expression of contemporary national identity.[38] In later years, *The Bell* would carry the subtitle 'A Magazine of Ireland To-Day'[39] – perhaps a more bland statement of its existence, but nonetheless an assertion of its focus on representing Irish life in the present, not in an idealized past.

Under O'Donnell's editorship, *The Bell* devoted an increasing proportion of its pages to long pieces of fiction and to criticism of current literature, as well as of contemporary music and art. Long stories by established writers such as Mary Lavin and O'Faoláin took up twenty pages or more, whereas in earlier issues, most short stories had run three to five pages, and had often been contributed by unknown writers.[40] In contrast, more than one quarter of the issue for December 1946 was taken up by Liam O'Flaherty's short story 'Two Lovely Beasts', and nearly the same proportion of the issue for April 1947 was given over to his story 'The Beggars'.[41] While this pattern might suggest that *The Bell* had finally fulfilled its aspirations to be 'A Magazine of Creative Fiction', a closer

34 Ibid., p. 5. 35 O'Donnell, 'Liberty Ltd', *The Bell* 12:4 (July 1946), p. 280. 36 O'Donnell, 'A Word to Young Writers', *The Bell* 13:4 (January 1947), p. 4. See also pp 144–5 on foreign journalists' perceptions of Irish neutrality. 37 O'Faoláin, 'Signing Off', p. 1; Peadar O'Donnell, 'Signing On', *The Bell* 12:1 (April 1946), p. 5. 38 Mercier remarked on the disparity between the two slogans in his 'Verdict on *The Bell*', p. 158. 39 This slogan first appeared on the cover of *The Bell* 16:2 (November 1950), the first number issued after a two-and-half year hiatus in publication. 40 Mary Lavin, 'A Story with a Pattern', *The Bell* 12:5 (August 1946); O'Faoláin, 'The Silence of the Valley', *The Bell* 12:6 (September 1946). 41 Liam O'Flaherty, 'Two Lovely Beasts', *The Bell* 13:3 (December 1946); 'The Beggars', *The Bell* 13:6 (March 1947).

look at the context in which these long pieces of fiction were published reveals a magazine lagging in energy, lamenting the impoverished state of Irish litera-ture and Irish publishing, and the consequent apathy of Irish writers. Against such a background, the publication of long stories by well-known fiction writ-ers seems an attempt at compensation for the lack of a more vibrant well of new material from which to draw. In an apologetic editorial, printed only months before *The Bell's* eventual demise, O'Donnell acknowledged the maga-zine's change in focus:

> Good writing is never irrelevant to the circumstances of ordinary living, and good creative or interpretative writing tells us more in the end about ourselves than even the most excellent and the most honest documen-tary journalism. There is room, or course, for both; and we hope that there will always be room for both within the covers of *The Bell*.[42]

The tone of this statement implies that O'Donnell was aware that *The Bell* had lost its original spark; his use of the double negative seeds doubt that 'good' cre-ative writing can be as relevant as superlative documentary writing – the kind of writing which *The Bell* had first aimed to publish when it began.

When O'Donnell did publish documentary articles, he made it clear that he interpreted the task of representation as being in service to sociological study, rather than to the exploration of national identity. In his first issue as Editor, the first of three new articles by the ex-convict 'D83222' opened with an author's note that described a conversation with O'Donnell in which he urged the former banker and embezzler to tell the story of his criminal life: 'and here and there let us all have a look at the bankers of Ireland, at the lean men on overdrafts, and the fat depositors'.[43] The importance of the individual has faded, and a new emphasis on whole social classes rises to the fore, as in an article on pawnshops which is written not by an actual slum dweller, as would have been the case in earlier issues of *The Bell*, but by a reporter who invents the character of Mary McGinty, an imaginary woman described as 'rep-resentative of her kind' as she goes about the business of pawning her husband's Sunday suit every Monday morning.[44]

O'Faoláin, meanwhile, did not go gently into that good night of editorial oblivion; he continued to contribute articles and short stories, and remained an important influence on the content of *The Bell*. Upon retiring from the position of Editor, he agreed to edit the book review section of the magazine, and con-

---

42 O'Donnell, 'Changing the Content', *The Bell* 19:4 (March 1954), p. 5.   43 D83222, 'There but for the Grace of God …', *The Bell* 12:1 (April 1946), p. 23.   44 Martin Dalton, 'Monday is Pawnday', *The Bell* 14:5 (August 1947), p. 49.

tinued to do so for one full year. He gradually increased the space devoted to book reviews, and changed the name of his section to 'People and Books' beginning in December 1946, which gave him the freedom to write opinion pieces that were not strictly tied to particular texts: for example, his discussion of Flaubert's potential significance for Irish writers.[45] Thus O'Faoláin retained his prerogative to write commentary during a time when O'Donnell opted, with increasing frequency, to forego the privilege of writing an opening editorial for the magazine. When O'Faoláin disagreed with O'Donnell's editorials, he did so publicly, in the pages of *The Bell* itself, writing indignant letters to the editor about 'your magazine', or going so far as to usurp the opening editorial column, as when he criticized O'Donnell's comments on the Jewish-Arab conflict in Palestine.[46] It may have been their disagreement over Palestine that caused O'Faoláin to resign as book review editor: the row had been ignited by O'Faoláin's decision to publish Elizabeth Monroe's review of Arthur Koestler's *Thieves in the night*, which included her strongly worded critique of Jewish actions in the region, and Harmon records O'Faoláin's disgust at O'Donnell's reaction, which argued for the accommodation of Jewish settlement in Palestine.[47] In any case, O'Faoláin resigned his position the following month, and O'Donnell promptly replaced him with his former IRA colleague Ernie O'Malley, whose first name is listed in his *Bell* contributions as the Gaelicized 'Earnán'. O'Faoláin, however, continued to contribute occasional short stories and articles to *The Bell*, most notably his commentaries on the Mother and Child Scheme crisis in 1951, and on the growing tendency towards anti-Americanism that he sensed in postwar Irish society.[48]

O'Malley had been incarcerated with O'Donnell during the Civil War, and the two had first discussed the possibility of working together on a monthly periodical while they were recovering from a forty-one-day hunger strike in 1923.[49] Shovlin speculates that it may have been O'Malley's connections that secured Louis MacNeice as *The Bell*'s Poetry Editor when Geoffrey Taylor resigned; MacNeice, though by then well established in London, had become friends with O'Malley, and had stayed in O'Malley's house in Co. Mayo during the summer of 1945.[50] The exact details of MacNeice's appointment as Poetry Editor, however, remain unknown. His formal involvement with the magazine pre-dates O'Malley's, and according to his biographer Jon Stallworthy, he was resident in England during the period from December 1945 to May 1947, when

45 O'Faoláin, 'People and Books: The Irish Conscience?', *The Bell* 13:3 (December 1946).   46 O'Faoláin, 'Foreign Commentary', *The Bell* 13:3 (December 1946), p. 62; 'Public Opinion: Pro-Soviet', *The Bell* 13:5 (February 1947); 'Palestine', *The Bell* 14:2 (May 1947).   47 Harmon, *Seán O'Faoláin: a life*, pp 148–9.   48 O'Faoláin, 'The Dáil and the Bishops', *The Bell* 17:3 (June 1951); 'Autoantiamericanism', *The Bell* 16:6 (March 1951). See also pp 156–8.   49 Shovlin, *The Irish literary periodical*, p. 120.   50 Ibid., p. 121–2; Jon Stallworthy, *Louis MacNeice* (London, 1995), p. 335.

he was listed in *The Bell* as Poetry Editor.[51] Jonathan Allison's collection of Mac-Neice's letters makes no mention of *The Bell*, but shows that MacNeice was in Rome in May 1947 and then travelled extensively as a BBC correspondent in India and Pakistan after their partition in August 1947,[52] which presumably ended his work for the magazine.

As Poetry Editor of *The Bell*, MacNeice took a much less activist role than had Geoffrey Taylor. He wrote no commentary articles or reviews, and seems to have been inclined to publish mainly his friends and other poets whose out-look resembled his own. In the eighteen months that he served as Poetry Editor, *The Bell* published poems by Charles Madge and Cecil Day-Lewis, both of whom were part of MacNeice's circle in London, and by W.R. Rodgers, with whom MacNeice worked in the BBC.[53] Few of the poems chosen by MacNeice dealt with Irish topics, except for those by Bruce Williamson, the *Irish Times* lit-erary editor, and by Geoffrey Taylor, which expressed a sense of loss on the demise of the Anglo-Irish Ascendancy.[54] (One other exception, Kavanagh's poem 'Jim Larkin', also appeared during MacNeice's editorship.)[55] Other poems chosen by MacNeice took up classical themes, such as Valentin Iremonger's 'Hector' and Michael Gregory's 'Poem Atmospherical', which told of a weary Aeolus.[56] MacNeice published four of his own poems in *The Bell* during his time as Poetry Editor; these would be his only contributions during the entire run of the mag-azine.[57] In June 1947, his name is no longer listed on the masthead, although there does appear a critical study of his work, by Valentin Iremonger.[58] After-ward, poetry continues to appear in *The Bell*, but the magazine apparently oper-ated without a designated Poetry Editor for the final ten months before publi-cation was suspended in April 1948.

HALT IN PUBLICATION, 1948, AND REVIVAL, 1950

In January 1948, a series of articles appeared in *The Bell* which concerned them-selves with the impact of recent British Board of Trade restrictions on the importation of Irish books into Britain. Notices to Importers Numbers 225

---

51 Stallworthy, *Louis MacNeice*, pp 343–53.   52 Louis MacNeice, *Letters of Louis MacNeice*, ed. by Jonathan Allison (London, 2010).   53 Charles Madge, 'Regents' Park, I' and 'Regents' Park, II', *The Bell* 12:6 (September 1946); Cecil Day-Lewis, 'Married Dialogue', *The Bell* 13:5 (February 1947); W.R. Rodgers, 'From *Europa*', *The Bell* 11:6 (March 1946); 'Song', *The Bell* 12:5 (August 1946).   54 Bruce Williamson, 'Afternoon in Anglo-Ireland', *The Bell* 12:2 (May 1946); Geoffrey Taylor, 'Country House, Clontarf', *The Bell* 13:5 (March 1947).   55 Patrick Kavanagh, 'Jim Larkin', *The Bell* 13:6 (March 1947).   56 Valentin Iremonger, 'Hector', *The Bell* 13:1 (October 1946); Michael Gregory, 'Poem Atmospherical', *The Bell* 13:1 (October 1946).   57 Louis MacNeice, 'Enfant Terrible' and 'Aubade for Infants', *The Bell* 11:5 (February 1946); 'Carol' and 'Hands and Eyes', *The Bell* 13:3 (December 1946).   58 Valentin Iremonger, 'Louis MacNeice: A First Study', *The Bell* 14:3 (June 1947).

and 261 limited the importation of most foreign books to pre-war levels, and required booksellers to provide documentation to prove that their current imports did not exceed the total value of their imports for the year ending 31 August 1939.[59] Five of the six Irish publishers who contributed their reactions to the Board of Trade position forecast doom for the Irish publishing industry, which, one publisher noted, sold as much as 87 per cent of its books to readers in Britain.[60] It was noted that the restrictions included sales of both trade and text books to Northern Ireland, which was 'a particularly bitter blow from a Nationalistic aspect'.[61] In April 1948, the Dublin-based Talbot Press ran an ad in *The Bell* which reminded readers that 'Although there are restrictions on bulk imports of books into Great Britain and Northern Ireland, your Bookseller can send single copies to any address.'[62] However, the burden of paperwork created by the Board of Trade and the fact that inflation had pushed 1948 prices well beyond those of 1939 meant that few British booksellers would be motivated to continue importing quantities of Irish books. As one publisher put it, 'The British Board of Trade restriction on book imports is the most crippling blow the Irish publishing trade could have received'.[63] Another was more severe: 'The "restriction" incidentally amounts to a complete embargo'.[64] Only Martin J. McManus of the Parkside Press disagreed, choosing to characterize the new restrictions as 'a blessing in disguise', one which he hoped would force Irish publishers to free themselves from their dependency on British markets, and develop their customer base among the Irish reading public.[65] Such a proposal, however, may have been wishful thinking.

The Bell was similarly affected by the British Board of Trade restrictions, and soon found itself cut off from a significant share of its paying readers. The magazine had previously announced changes to its printing schedule in order to accommodate the number of copies being produced for export to the US, and had even foregone time-sensitive features such as theatre reviews and foreign commentary in order to meet shipping deadlines.[66] When its British market was threatened, *The Bell* turned for help to American benefactors, who had recently accounted for an increase in the magazine's overseas subscriptions.[67] The American government, O'Donnell wrote, was also directly to blame for the British cutback on imports, having issued trade directives as part of its loan programme to Britain under the Marshall Plan.[68] In April 1948, O'Don-

59 Browne and Nolan in 'Irish Publishers Answer Two Questions', *The Bell* 15:4 (January 1948), p. 3.   60 Maurice Fridberg in 'Irish Publishers Answer Two Questions', p. 8.   61 Talbot Press in 'Irish Publishers Answer Two Questions', p. 10.   62 Talbot Press, advertising in *The Bell* 16:1 (April 1948), p. 68.   63 Metropolitan Publishing Co. Ltd in 'Irish Publishers Answer Two Questions', p. 7.   64 Maurice Fridberg in 'Irish Publishers Answer Two Questions', p. 8.   65 Martin J. McManus, 'Publishing in Ireland', *The Bell* 15:4 (January 1948), p. 69.   66 Editorial note, *The Bell* 13:5 (February 1947), p. 82.   67 O'Donnell, 'Exiles', *The Bell* 13:5 (February 1947), p. 4.   68 O'Donnell, '*The Bell* Suspends Publication', *The Bell* 16:1 (April 1948).

nell described his intentions to tour several American cities, with the encouragement of Irish-American friends, to seek out subscriptions and possible advertising revenue for *The Bell.* But the trip was not to be. O'Donnell was denied an entry visa to the United States on the grounds of his Communist sympathies and his pre-war anti-fascist activities in Germany, and despite appeals to four American Senators to intervene, he was forced to cancel his travel plans.[69] O'Donnell's account of the incident reversed *The Bell's* standard metaphor of Ireland as an infant nation: instead, referring to the large number of Irish descendants in America, O'Donnell compared the Irish-American relationship to that between a parent and child, noting that 'the United States for the moment is in short pants' but that its 'tantrum' must be tolerated because 'there is so much of ourselves in its people'.[70]

As a result, O'Donnell announced that *The Bell* would temporarily suspend publication, and that he hoped it would return by that autumn.[71] In fact, the magazine did not reappear until November 1950, a hiatus of two-and-a-half years.[72] During this time *The Bell* was absent from any discussion of political developments such as the declaration of the Republic of Ireland in December 1948. Despite his bitterness about the circumstances leading to the shutdown, O'Donnell ended his suspension notice with a statement that the break 'could be very useful' to a reassessment of *The Bell's* editorial mission: 'I have been of opinion [*sic*] that the original impulse in *The Bell* has exhausted itself, and that if we are to serve any real purpose we must move closer to the problems of the moment – domestic and international'.[73] O'Donnell's statement reinforces the impression that he had grown weary of documentary writing, of which the magazine had been publishing less and less over the first two years of his editorship.

As Shovlin has noted, when *The Bell* resumed publication in late 1950 it did indeed take up the discussion of several 'problems of the moment', most notably the Mother and Child Scheme proposed by Dr Noel Browne in 1951.[74] However, an examination of O'Donnell's first editorial after the break in publication suggests that the magazine had taken on so many purposes as to result in a diffusion of editorial energy. In contrast to his previous editorial, O'Donnell declared upon *The Bell's* return that the magazine would maintain 'the same recognisable gait' with which it had set out in 1940, and that it would convey 'a fair sample of the variety of Irish life' through the work of 'a few established writers'.[75] In addition,

---

69 Ibid. 70 Ibid., p. 3. 71 Ibid., p. 4. The American magazine *Time* picked up the story and ran it under the headline 'A Bell for O'Donnell' on 14 June 1948. *Time* reported that New York's United Irish Counties Association was attempting to intervene with the U.S. government on O'Donnell's behalf, but their efforts were apparently unsuccessful. 72 Shovlin notes that British Board of Trade restrictions on the import of publications had been lifted in April 1950 (p. 134). 73 O'Donnell, '*The Bell* Suspends Publication', p. 4. 74 Shovlin, *The Irish literary periodical*, pp 125–7. 75 O'Donnell, 'A Recognisable Gait of Going', *The Bell* 16:2 (November 1950), p. 5.

O'Donnell wrote, *The Bell* would continue its sense of 'obligation to new writers fumbling for their technique and searching for their public'.[76] Finally, O'Donnell hoped that the magazine would become 'a social influence of considerable usefulness', and that contributing writers would 'report on special aspects of life' in contemporary Ireland.[77] One may turn for comparison to *Horizon*, which had declared only one purpose, to provide a platform for English writers during the war (favouring established writers over unknowns) and which had closed up shop in January 1950. *The Bell*, on the other hand, having missed two-and-a-half years of Irish political and cultural life, struggled to balance multiple missions in a new decade. Though there are several individual pieces published in *The Bell*'s final years which merit a closer look, the magazine as a whole never regained the integrity of purpose which had marked its initial setting out.

The sense of conflict between *The Bell*'s multiple agendas is clearly defined and discussed in a symposium on 'The Young Writer' which appeared in the magazine in late 1951. O'Donnell commissioned Associate Editor Anthony Cronin to open the discussion as a referendum on the state of Irish writing, and on *The Bell*'s current format and its future. The young writers surveyed were bluntly critical in their responses. The most strident was John Montague, who accused *The Bell* of having allowed social and political commentary to overshadow its commitment to literary writing:

> What I am trying to show is that literature has suffered by having to appear beside this work of mainly social emphasis and reference, that the young writers nurtured by *The Bell* have tended towards a uniform pattern, perhaps more harmful than helpful in any final analysis.[78]

Valentin Iremonger concurred, and protested against what he saw as two schools of established Irish writers: those who favoured sociological writing, and those who favoured writing in the revivalist mode of the early twentieth century. 'Neither group seems to be interested in the young writer as writer only, as endeavouring to formulate and answer the fundamental questions that present themselves to all humanity'.[79] The young writers surveyed by *The Bell* wanted to transcend nationalism and representational writing, in favour of topics and styles that responded to influences from outside Ireland as well as within.

In the four years following the break in publication, *The Bell* increased the print space devoted to cultural commentary – not only literary, but dramatic and musical criticism as well. Book reviews remained a constant feature, with Hubert Butler serving as editor of the review section from May 1951 to March

76 Ibid. 77 Ibid., pp 6, 7. 78 John Montague in 'The Young Writer', *The Bell* 17:7 (October 1951), p. 6. 79 Valentin Iremonger in 'The Young Writer', p. 15.

1952, an appointment he later remembered with gratitude to *The Bell*'s editors.[80] John Montague contributed several theatre reviews, as did Val Mulkerns. For a time, *The Bell* took up the issue of classical music in Ireland, focusing a number of articles on the need for development in musical education and support for performance musicians. A leading force in this area was Samuel Beckett's first cousin John Beckett, who was then only in his mid-twenties and was keenly interested in the future of music in Ireland. He was named as Music Editor in May 1951, and continued to serve in that role until July 1952. Many of the articles he wrote and edited offer parallels between the challenges confronted by Irish writers and Irish musicians; in a series of articles on the need for a concert hall in Dublin, for example, it is argued that 'The task facing Irish musicians to-day is nothing less than the gradual building up of a vital tradition in teaching, performing and composing'.[81] Thus *The Bell* continued to offer its pages to the discussion of Irish cultural development, and the need for new traditions in every area of the arts.

Beginning in mid-1953, the book review editor was named as Val Mulkerns, a young novelist who became *The Bell*'s only female Associate Editor when Cronin left for London in mid-1952, though the masthead never listed her in this position. 'I didn't feel good about that at all', Mulkerns recalls. 'I spoke to Peadar [O'Donnell] about it. He said, we'll come to that later. Peadar was as old-fashioned about that as anybody'.[82] Mulkerns stayed on as Associate Editor after her marriage in 1953 to the writer Maurice Kennedy, but convention dictated that she step down when her first child, Maev, was born in 1954: 'I was working as long as I was let. There was no question of my staying on after the baby was born'. By that time, Cronin had returned, and he reassumed the position of Associate Editor until *The Bell* ceased publication in December 1954. In an excerpt from her unpublished memoir, Mulkerns writes vividly of one of O'Donnell's schemes to raise money for *The Bell* by selling advertising space on litter bins that he had purchased for the streets of Dublin.[83] Both she and Cronin describe O'Donnell as affable but disorganized, and largely uninvolved in the day-to-day running of the magazine. Though Mulkerns says of O'Donnell, 'You couldn't help liking him', both she and Cronin also recall their disagreements with him over editorial decisions. Cronin says of O'Donnell, 'We worked in partnership, not always in harmony'.[84]

Publishing continued to be a major concern for *Bell* editors and writers in the final years of the magazine, but there were so many demands, from so many different quarters, that without government intervention, all that could be done

80 Hubert Butler, '*The Bell*: An Anglo-Irish View', *Irish University Review* 6:1 (Spring 1976). 81 Patrick Delany, 'A Concert Hall for Dublin?', *The Bell* 17:10 (January 1952), p. 8. 82 Mulkerns interview. 83 Val Mulkerns, '"Did You Once See Shelley Plain?"', p. 11. 84 Anthony Cronin, interview, 3 November 2008.

was to re-hash discussions of the problem. In 1947, Valentin Iremonger had raised the issue of poetry publishing in a slap at Irish publishers who, he wrote, favoured older poets writing in the established Irish mode: such poems 'have nothing new whatsoever to communicate and nothing profound to say, and as I have said, do not contribute to the current of contemporary poetry here'.[85] In 1952, John Hewitt raised a similar issue in lamenting the lack of government support for publishers willing to print contemporary poetry.[86] O'Donnell continued to re-examine and re-assess the role of *The Bell* in publishing younger writers, but he also recognized that the problem was much larger than any question of the role that could be played by a monthly magazine, as indicated by the title of one of his editorials on the topic: 'And Again, Publishing in Ireland'.[87] O'Donnell acknowledged the argument that *The Bell* had been weakened by attempting the 'dual role' of publishing literary writing side by side with political and cultural commentary, and he expressed the hope that new periodicals would arise to take on a share of the burden.[88] Meanwhile, *The Bell* soldiered on, shifting to quarterly publication for nine months in 1953, but eventually returning to its standard monthly, multi-purpose format.

As Associate Editor, Cronin attempted to find a new direction for the magazine in its final months. He, too, expressed frustration with the state of Irish writing and publishing in the 1950s, and suggested that *The Bell* might experiment with other forms of publication in an effort to revive the literary culture:

> We may occasionally bring out a paper-backed book and circulate it instead of an issue of the magazine. We may devote entire issues of the magazine to a single writer or a single work. Whatever sort of experiment in terms of publication on our part will best serve to get the patient up and about again we will anyway try.[89]

In August 1954, the first of such experiments was undertaken: a volume of five short stories by James Plunkett, titled *The eagles and the trumpets* and published as Volume 19, Number 9 of *The Bell*. Cronin explained that its appearance was due to the editors' 'belief that the actual publication of books in Ireland is certainly a more necessary and may even be a more rewarding activity than the keeping open of a clearing house for short-stories, poems, and essays in periodical literature'.[90] Such a statement would seem to indicate that the magazine was on the verge of abandoning its original mission, and even its origi-

85 Valentin Iremonger, 'Poets and Their Publishers', *The Bell* 14:1 (April 1947), p. 79. 86 John Hewitt, review of *New poems, 1952: A PEN anthology*, *The Bell* 18:6 (November 1952). 87 O'Donnell, 'And Again, Publishing in Ireland', *The Bell* 18:10 (March 1953). 88 Ibid., p. 582. 89 Anthony Cronin, 'This Time, This Place', *The Bell* 19:8 (July 1954), p. 7. 90 Cronin, 'Preface', *The Bell* 19:9 (August 1954), p. 7.

nal format, in favour of throwing its whole support behind the publication of young Irish writers.

But there would be no subsequent experiments for *The Bell*. The next issue appeared two months late, without explanation, in November 1954, and it carried the standard holiday advertisement encouraging readers to purchase gift subscriptions for Christmas or New Year. The issue for December of that year, however, would be the last of the magazine's fourteen-year run. There have been various theories proposed to explain *The Bell's* demise. Holzapfel suggests that O'Donnell's 'punchy left-wingism' caused a decline in Irish readership;[91] Furze counters with the assertion that the overall quality of the magazine, both in terms of content and production, had fallen to unsustainable levels.[92] Shovlin notes only that *The Bell* had come to 'a quiet end',[93] and even Hubert Butler, who was well acquainted with the magazine in the early 1950s, would later write, 'I never learnt why *The Bell* died'.[94] Cronin declines to offer a definitive explanation, saying only: 'I think Peadar was a bit fed up. It was a constant struggle to keep it alive. I think I was a bit relieved'.[95] In the absence of archival materials relating to the magazine's publication, we may have to be satisfied with ambiguity.

91 Holzapfel, *An index of contributors to* The Bell, p. 3.   92 Richard A. Furze, 'A Desirable Vision of Life: A Study of *The Bell*, 1940–1954' (PhD thesis, UCD, 1974), pp 43–4.   93 Shovlin, *The Irish literary periodical*, p. 130.   94 Butler, '*The Bell*: An Anglo-Irish View', pp 71–2.   95 Cronin interview.

CHAPTER FOUR

Representations of Irish identity in *The Bell*

On St Patrick's Day, 1943, Taoiseach Eamon de Valera gave voice to his vision of an ideal Ireland in a national radio address which has since become one of his best-known speeches:

> The ideal Ireland that we would have, the Ireland that we dreamed of, would be the home of a people who valued material wealth only as a basis for right living, of a people who, satisfied with frugal comfort, devoted their leisure to the things of the spirit; a land whose country-side would be bright with cosy homesteads, whose fields and villages would be joyous with the sounds of industry, with the romping of sturdy children, the contests of athletic youths, and the laughter of happy maidens; whose firesides would be forums for the wisdom of serene old age: the home, in short, of a people living the life that God desires that men should live.[1]

In recent years the significance of de Valera's ideal version of Ireland has been much debated. Both Wills and Brown discuss its implications for economic self-sufficiency and political independence.[2] Kiberd calls de Valera's happy maidens 'a pastoral figment of the late-Victorian imagination'.[3] Gearóid Ó Crualaoich points out that while de Valera's vision was explicitly formulated as a dream, his ideology was built upon 'an essentially static conception of a "truly Irish" way of life', one that narrowly defined Irish identity as rural and rooted in folkloric tradition.[4] Ó Crualaoich goes on to discuss the anthropological model of the peasant society, and its use as a stereotype by de Valera and his Fianna Fáil con-temporaries. Diarmaid Ferriter, on the other hand, warns against characteriz-ing the era of the 1930s and 40s by the measure of de Valera's personal influ-ence, asserting that the idealization of rural Ireland is most appropriately seen as a continuation of republican aspirations of the 1920s.[5]

The government's commitment to the ideal of a Catholic, Gaelic, self-suf-ficient rural republic, however, went beyond speechmaking. While opinions may

---

1 Eamon de Valera, 'Address by Mr de Valera, 17 March 1943', RTÉ Archives. 2 Wills, *That neutral island*, p. 333; Brown, *Ireland*, pp 145–6. 3 Kiberd, *Inventing Ireland*, pp 182–3. 4 Gearóid Ó Crualaoich, 'The Primacy of Form: A "Folk Ideology" in de Valera's Politics', John P. O'Carroll and John A. Murphy in (eds), *De Valera and his times* (Cork, 1983), pp 47–9. 5 Ibid., p. 374.

vary as to the extent of de Valera's conservative influence, one area in which politics and culture undoubtedly intersected is in the work of the Board of Literary Censors. In the letter of the law, the Censorship was empowered to ban any
literature, including both books and periodicals, which it determined to be 'in
its general tendency indecent or obscene', or which advocated or explained meth-
ods of contraception or abortion.[6] In practice, as O'Faoláin wrote at the time,
its decisions often reflected a desire to shield 'the plain people of Ireland' from
any mention of sex, and to preserve a sense of Irish identity in keeping with
traditional religious beliefs.[7] O'Faoláin commented wryly that while patriots
such as Wolfe Tone, Daniel O'Connell and James Connolly had stirringly called
on 'the People' of Ireland, their use of the word had been undercut by Irish Senators' repeated insertion of the belittling adjective 'plain' when arguing in defence
of the Censorship. And he noted with bitter irony that the real-life Irish characters of one book, *The Tailor and Ansty*, were condemned as 'apparently too plain',
since the record of their fireside conversations was banned by the Censorship
as indecent.[8] Indeed, although the Censorship had been created to guard against
the importation of obscene publications from abroad, many of the authors
whose books were censored were in fact Irish writers whose work was well
respected in England and America, including Kate O'Brien, Frank O'Connor,
Liam O'Flaherty and O'Faoláin himself, whose books *Midsummer Night madness*
and *Bird alone* had been banned in 1932 and 1936, respectively.[9] As O'Faoláin stated
in *The Bell*, the 'alleged native instincts about literature' which the Censorship
was meant to 'codify' were thus proven not to be inherently native after all.[10] The
fact that Irish writers so often fell afoul of the Censorship's standards suggested
that those standards were in themselves arbitrary and artificially constructed.

Michael Adams' *Censorship: the Irish experience*, written in the late 1960s, while
the Censorship was still active, remains the most detailed account of the formulation of the Censorship of Publications Act and the public reaction to its
implementation. Adams' study usefully documents the journalistic atmosphere
of Dublin in the 1930s, when conservative religious publications such as the *Irish
Rosary*, the *Catholic Mind* and the *Catholic Bulletin* (what Val Mulkerns calls 'Holy
Joe magazines'), dominated the periodical landscape.[11] Such magazines consistently voiced support for the Censorship, sometimes even complaining that it
did not go far enough. Adams also describes in detail *The Bell's* campaign of
opposition to the Censorship in the early 1940s, when O'Faoláin and other *Bell*
editors and contributors objected vehemently to the censorship of *The Tailor and*

6 Oireachtas Eireann, Censorship of Publications Act, 1929. 7 O'Faoláin, 'The Plain People of Ireland', *The Bell*
7:1 (October 1943), p. 1. 8 Ibid., p. 5. 9 Harmon, *Sean O'Faolain: a life*, pp 97–109. 10 O'Faoláin, 'Standards and
Taste', *The Bell* 2:3 (June 1941), p. 7. 11 Adams, *Censorship*, pp 15–17, 65–8; Mulkerns interview.

Ansty and Kate O'Brien's novel *The land of spices*, which was banned in its entirety because of one sentence in which the protagonist sees her father 'in the embrace of love' with another man.[12] The controversy over the banning of these two books, as well as another, *Laws of life*, which dealt with the 'safe period' method of birth control and had been approved by the Catholic archbishop of Westminster, eventually resulted in a heated debate in the Seanad in late 1942 over whether to adopt a motion of no confidence in the Board of Literary Censors. By that date, an estimated 1,600 books, many of them by well-known authors from Ireland, England and America, had been banned from sale or distribution in Ireland on the grounds of moral indecency. Both *The Bell* and the *Irish Times* had printed numerous editorials and letters advocating reform, while the *Irish Independent* and the *Irish Press* vociferously defended the Board. After four days of debate, the Seanad voted almost unanimously to reject the motion, and the Censorship was allowed to continue.[13]

De Valera's conservative influence extended to other areas of Irish life as well. Throughout the 1930s, his Fianna Fáil government had been engaged in the erection of high tariff walls to protect Irish markets from British agricultural imports, a policy which was reciprocated by the British government, resulting in an economic war between the two countries, and a necessary reliance within Ireland upon goods from native producers.[14] Despite their negative impact for many traditional export businesses, such as brewing, biscuit-making and cattle farming, the public response to these protectionist strategies was generally positive. De Valera's ideology of self-sufficiency extended beyond economic policy, and formed the basis of popular thought in many areas of Irish culture. For example, the cultivation of national distinctiveness often meant the adulation of Irish peasantry. Ferriter quotes Father John Hayes, an organizer of Catholic parish councils, as stating that 'Rural Ireland is real Ireland and rural Ireland is Ireland true to Christ'.[15] The conflation of rural life, Catholicism, and the Irish language with an ineffably 'real' sense of Irish identity was a common feature both of popular conceptions of Ireland as well as of official definitions of Irish identity. The 1937 constitution, ratified by Dáil Eireann, recognized the 'special position' of the Catholic Church as 'the guardian of the Faith professed by the great majority' of Irish citizens,[16] and it named Irish as the national language, to be privileged over English in state communications.[17]

But there is a danger, in the drive to develop national identity, of slipping into narrow definitions of religious and ethnic purity, and this was a danger of

12 Kate O'Brien, *The land of spices* (London, 1941), p. 175. 13 Adams, *Censorship*, pp 81–95. The powers of the Board of Literary Censors were later weakened by the introduction of an appeal process in 1946. 14 See Brown, *Ireland*, pp 131–46. 15 Ferriter, *Transformation*, p. 376. 16 *Bunreacht na hEireann (Constitution of Ireland)* (Dublin, 1937), p. 144. 17 Ibid., p. 6.

which *The Bell*'s editors were well aware. O'Faoláin himself had written a laudatory biography of de Valera in 1933, but had since become highly critical of the
Taoiseach's 'constant appeals to peasant fears, to peasant pietism, to the peasant sense of self-preservation, and all ending in a half-baked sort of civilisation
which, taken all over, is of a tawdriness a hundred miles away from our days of
vision.'[18] It may be useful to note that Franz Fanon, too, commented on the
ultra-nationalism of newly independent people, using the Ivory Coast as an
example, when foreigners were driven from Ivorian society with the explicit con-
sent of the native government: 'From nationalism we have passed to ultra-nationalism, to chauvinism, and finally to racism.'[19] It was a core mission of *The Bell* to
fight against the homogenization of what it meant to be Irish.

Fanon describes the process by which colonized peoples undergo the 'emaci-
ation' of national culture, after centuries of exploitation: 'Little movement can be
discerned in such remnants of culture; there is no real creativity and no overflow-
ing life'.[20] In O'Faoláin's view, the past was not to be ignored, but the next phase
of Irish history would have to begin from a new starting point. Twenty-five years
after the Easter Rising, O'Faoláin voiced an ambivalence towards the past which
he characterized as a necessary product of modernity. In words that prefigure
Bhabha's articulation of hybridity, he described the conflict between traditional
and experimental modes of expression as a source of creativity: 'From that struggle between the Traditional and the Individual, there must come a new thing'.[21] It
was essential that the struggle be allowed to continue, and that Irish intellectual
life not be allowed to slide into simplistic formulations of national culture.

In Irish political and cultural life, *Bell* editors saw ominous signs of the
development of what O'Faoláin called 'monomania'.[22] The Censorship was one
example; the Gaelic League's insistence on cultural unity was another; and when,
in 1943, an education professor was denied appointment at University College,
Dublin, because of his inadequate knowledge of the Irish language, O'Faoláin
denounced the decision as an attempt by hyper-nationalists to control Irish intellectual life: 'The truth, as our eyes can show us, is, that nowhere to-day, neither
here nor elsewhere, and never again, can there be a National Culture as those
people understand it'.[23] In response to what they saw as a growing tendency
towards narrow-minded definitions of Irishness in popular and political debates,
Bell editors commissioned two groups of articles that explicitly examined the
diversity inherent in Irish culture: the Five Strains symposium, which explored

18 O'Faoláin, 'Principles of Propaganda', *The Bell* 10:3 (June 1945), pp 194–205, at p. 205. See Harmon, *O'Faoláin: a
critical introduction* (pp. 32–46) for a discussion of the evolution of O'Faoláin's views on de Valera. 19 Fanon, *The
wretched of the earth*, p. 125. 20 Ibid., p. 191. 21 O'Faoláin, '1916–1941: Tradition and Creation', *The Bell* 2:1 (April 1941),
p. 6. 22 O'Faoláin, 'The Gaelic League', *The Bell* 4:2 (May 1942), p. 86. 23 O'Faoláin, 'On State Control', *The Bell*
6:1 (April 1943), p. 3.

the legacies of the past, and the 'Credo' series, which described religious diversity in the present.

The Five Strains Symposium appeared in *The Bell* in September 1941, the final issue of the magazine's first year of publication. The editors recruited five historians to name the influences of five different cultural heritages on present-day Irish life: the Gaelic influence, the Classical influence, the Norman stream, the Anglo-Irish strain, and the English strain. (One month later, a discussion of the Scottish strain was appended to the symposium.) The editorial note which headed the symposium contained a statement of the importance of re-inventing native culture as well as a pointed reference to those who would prefer to focus only on Gaelic traditions:

> In the business of building up a native mode of life agreeable to the natural genius of our people we are always searching, consciously or unconsciously, for a guiding line [...] and perhaps the only line acknowledged on all sides is the Gaelic one. This interesting symposium enlarges that rather elementary picture. Yet, we *have* been considerably influenced by the English tradition [...] and there have been several other strains – the Norman strain, the Classical strain, and that mixed strain which we call Anglo-Irish. They have all gone to the building of this Ireland. This symposium should serve to remind us of the danger of oversimplifying history.[24]

O'Faoláin frequently stressed the importance of complexity, in contrast to what he saw as a fixation, common to both de Valera and the Gaelic League of the 1930s and 40s, on oversimplifying Irish identity: 'it has been the mark of the Gael ever since we have known him that he cannot abide a complex pattern'.[25]

In addition to the complexity of Irish cultural heritages, *The Bell* also examined religious diversity. One year after de Valera's St Patrick's Day radio speech, the 'Credo' series began: a sequence of articles written by individual members of six religious denominations in contemporary Ireland. Over several months, *The Bell* printed articles titled 'What It Means to Be a Presbyterian', 'Why I Am "Church of Ireland"', 'What It Means to Be a Catholic', 'What It Means to Be a Unitarian', 'What It Means to be a Quaker', and finally, in June 1945, after the end of the war and the end of war censorship, 'What It Means to be a Jew', A.J. Leventhal's poignant memoir of growing up in the Jewish community of Dublin's Oakfield Place, and his description of the movement to establish a Jewish homeland in what was then Palestine.[26] It is surely not an accident that

24 Editorial note preceding 'The Five Strains: A Symposium', *The Bell* 2:6 (September 1941), p. 13. 25 O'Faoláin, 'The Gaelic and the Good', *The Bell* 3:2 (November 1941), p. 102. 26 Violet Disney, 'Why I am "Church of Ire-

the article on Catholicism is tucked away in the middle of this series, flanked by articles on Protestant churches whose congregations were much smaller in number. It would seem that *The Bell*'s editors intended to send a message, both to readers and to the powers that be, that the non-Catholic religions of Ireland should not be relegated to second-best status. By focusing on individual accounts of each faith, the 'Credo' series not only remained true to *The Bell*'s commitment to documentary representation, it also emphasized the importance of individual identity over definitions of Irishness formulated by the government or by the majority. Leventhal's account of the street taunts sung by warring Christian and Jewish children in the streets of Dublin, for example, serves to illustrate his recollection that as a child his identity was tied up entirely in his religion, and that the neighbouring children were seen not as Irish, but only as *goyim* [gentiles]. It might also be noted that Leventhal's description of Jewish and Christian children throwing stones at one another in the streets of Dublin paints a striking contrast to de Valera's imagined landscape of cosy cottages and happy maidens.

RURAL AND URBAN REALITIES

From its inception, *The Bell* printed short stories drawn from rural Irish life, and very few presented an idealized view of the Irish peasantry. Most took a sympathetic stance towards their subject, and several addressed head-on the difficulties of making a living as a farmer in de Valera's Ireland. Desmond Clarke's short story 'Flight', for example, which appeared in the fifth issue of *The Bell*, portrays the economic hardships faced by Manny Cranmer, a newly-wed farmer, and describes his weekly journey, by foot or bicycle, to nearby Galway, where he has a second job, working six days a week to build a new hat factory – possibly based on the Modes Modernes factory, which Eileen O'Faoláin had described in her *Bell* article 'Galway Hats' the previous month. Wistfully, Manny reflects on government policies favouring tillage over cattle raising, and tells his young wife, Bridget, that they may have to sell their land and move to Dublin or England:

> A neat stone cottage and five acres of rocky ground had no market value now. There was no money in land, no money to buy or keep it, no money to be made out of it. That was not always so; time was when

land"', *The Bell* 8:5 (August 1944); T.W.T. Dillon, 'What It Means to Be a Catholic', *The Bell* 9:1 (October 1944); Revd E. Savell Hicks, 'What It Means to Be a Unitarian', *The Bell* 9:2 (November 1944); Stella M.B. Webb, 'What It Means to Be a Quaker', *The Bell* 9:3 (December 1944); A.J. Leventhal, 'What It Means to Be a Jew', *The Bell* 10:3 (December 1945).

a calf each year helped to pay all charges and left a bit over, but now
the government was slaughtering calves [...] It was all some new-fan-
gled idea. People were told, too, to grow wheat but you couldn't grow
wheat in Connemara, so the people were just leaving the land, getting
work where they could.[27]

'Flight' ends when the hat factory is completed, and Manny is made redundant.
He tells Bridget, tersely, that he has made up his mind to sell the farm and seek
work in England; she 'caught the sigh in his voice, deep and low like the distant
murmur of the brown stream below Faughnarua which she might never hear
again'.[28] The emotional undertones of Manny and Bridget's predicament expose
the contradiction in government policies aimed at self-sufficiency; and *The Bell*'s
editorial decision to run the story after Eileen O'Faoláin's highly complimen-
tary article on the hat factory's promotion of native industry demonstrates the
magazine's commitment to portraying multiple aspects of rural experience, using
various literary forms.

The *Bell*'s articles and short stories on rural Ireland express a diversity of
experiences and personalities, suggesting a wide range of individual differences
beneath the exterior appearance of homogeneity. True to his original policy of
representation, Sean O'Faoláin declared that 'as for definitions, we consider
abstract terms (as, for example, 'Nationalism') unhelpful since they only come
to life when they take concrete form'.[29] For example, an essay on 'Pattern Day'
describes the details of a local rural tradition, the pilgrimage to St Mullin's Well
in Co. Carlow, but does not shy away from the combination of old and new elements in parishioners' celebrations, as when children wear 'little paper hats of
American sailor fashion' and young men and women take part in 'modern danc-
ing' as well as Irish dances: 'Up on the green again the old world contains yet
contrasts to the new, tradition accepting, as it has always done, the fashions and
foibles of the moment'.[30] Faithfulness to tradition did not necessarily require
the rejection of modernity; when traditions were strong enough, they could
accommodate new elements without losing their inherent character.

But the nature of Irish identity was still under debate. One of *The Bell*'s most
dispiriting moments came about when it championed the publication of *The
Tailor and Ansty*, a collection of anecdotes documenting the lives and translated
sayings of the Gaelic-speaking Tim Buckley and his wife Anastasia, who lived
in a traditional cottage near Gougane Barra in West Cork and were well known
to local residents as well as to seasonal visitors such as Sean O'Faoláin and Frank

---

27 Desmond Clarke, 'Flight', *The Bell* 1:5 (February 1941), p. 57. 28 Ibid., p. 60. 29 O'Faoláin, 'Beginnings and
Blind Alleys', *The Bell* 3:1 (October 1941), p. 1. 30 Patricia Hutchins, 'Pattern Day', *The Bell* 3:2 (November 1941), p.
138.

O'Connor. The first of three excerpts was published in *The Bell* in February 1941, heralded by O'Faoláin with a special note of introduction: 'I believe that it is in the nature of a minor literary discovery, to rank in its way with *Island Man*, or *Twenty Years A-Growing*' – two Irish-language texts that had become part of the canon of traditional Irish literature.[31] The Tailor and his wife lived in a four-room whitewashed cottage, heated only by a turf fire, 'the heart of the house', which the Tailor tended around the clock in the manner of 'a delicate art':

> He takes great delight in astonishing you with his skill and will let the fire die down until Ansty is almost speechless with wrath and you, the spectator, imagine that at last the fire must be relit and the hearth desecrated with a match.[32]

The Tailor's attention to his hearth represents a native intelligence and an example of the kind of 'elegance' for which O'Faoláin had called in his third editorial.[33] The Tailor's lifestyle, which rejects even matches as a modern intrusion, was viewed by O'Faoláin and O'Connor as part of the 'traditional world' of rural Ireland, and his far-ranging talk – which was peppered with jokes about 'going to bed' – made him resemble 'a sort of rural Dr Johnson' in O'Connor's eyes.[34]

The Censorship Board saw it differently. In 1942, *The Tailor and Ansty* was banned for being 'in its general tendency indecent', a decision deplored by O'Faoláin for its narrow-mindedness. *The Bell* had already begun to fight against the Censorship after the banning of Kate O'Brien's novel *The land of spices* in 1941; but the banning of *The Tailor and Ansty* seemed especially damaging in that it depended upon a puritanical ideal of rural Irish identity which, according to O'Faoláin, did not exist in real life. In an earlier editorial, he had commented that 'Our ancient literature is far from fastidious. Our conversation is racy and homely'.[35] Moreover, he argued, since the building up of native traditions was still a work in progress, there could be as yet no single definition of Irish identity: 'The danger, at this stage, is to define at all'.[36] Indeed, those who tried to force their definitions of Irishness on the rest of the public were perilously close to suggesting a 'Master Type', a phrase O'Faoláin used twice in his editorial on *The Tailor and Ansty*'s banning, and with which he pointedly implied a similarity to the racial programme of Nazi Germany.[37]

O'Faoláin and his fellow editors acknowledged the importance of rural life to Irish identity; in one editorial, O'Faoláin argued that 'there *is* a visible and

31 O'Faoláin, 'A Challenge', p. 6.   32 Eric Cross, 'The Tailor on the Cleverness of Animals', *The Bell* 1:6 (March 1941), p. 31.   33 O'Faoláin, 'Answer to a Criticism'.   34 Frank O'Connor, Foreword to *The Tailor and Ansty* by Eric Cross (London, 1942), pp 5–6.   35 O'Faoláin, 'Our Nasty Novelists', *The Bell* 2:5 (August 1941), p. 12.   36 O'Faoláin, 'That Typical Irishman', *The Bell* 5:2 (November 1942), p. 82.   37 Ibid., pp 79–80.

sensible pattern of Irish life, rooted (where most things are rooted) in the earth'.[38] But *The Bell* remained committed to authentic representations of rural life as well as of the economic and social challenges faced by rural Irish men and women. Migration and emigration, in particular, were recurring themes, as seen in short stories such as 'Flight', which took internal migration as their starting point, as characters left rural communities and sought work in the cities of Dublin, Galway and Cork. Peadar O'Donnell contributed several articles on the realities of seasonal migration in northwest Donegal, in which he described the necessity for small farmers to travel to industrial cities in Scotland and England in order to supplement their farming income and 'keep a grip' on their land holdings.[39] The farmer who tended his livestock in summer was the same man who drove lorries and laboured on building sites in Glasgow or Birmingham in winter. Thus the dichotomy between rural and urban was not absolute. The line between country and city was often crossed and re-crossed by young men and women obeying the need for work and wages. In this way the migrant inhabited a transitional space, similar to the interstitial space Bhabha describes as existing between the colonial past and post-colonial present: 'The "past-present" becomes part of the necessity, not the nostalgia, of living'.[40]

O'Faoláin addresses the transitional identity of rural migrants to Irish cities in a short story entitled 'The Sugawn Chair', which appeared in *The Bell* in December 1947. Most critical assessments of the story focus on its usefulness to understanding O'Faoláin's childhood,[41] but it may also be read as a representation of the unsettling shift of identity experienced by those who moved from the Irish countryside into urban areas. The narrator of the story recalls the memory of an annual gift from his mother's childhood home on the farm, a sack of apples and potatoes sent as 'a sort of diplomatic messenger between the fields and the city'.[42] Every year, the narrator reports, his mother would open the sack with a mixture of joy and sorrow, and would always 'boast about the good thing it is to have a "back" – meaning the land, and relatives on the land, so much more solid and permanent than this changing, alien, flickering life of the city'.[43] One evening, inspired by the delivery of the sack of apples and potatoes, the narrator's father brings down from the attic an old súgán chair, which stands ever afterward in the living room, a reminder of country life, amid the plush upholstered furniture and all the ornaments of the narrator's middle-class urban home.

'The Sugawn Chair' echoes O'Faoláin's earlier article on 'Fine Cottage Furniture' when the narrator explains why his father prefers the súgán chair to the

---

38 O'Faoláin, 'All Things Considered – I', *The Bell* 11:2 (November 1945), p. 651.   39 Peadar O'Donnell, 'Migration is a Way of Keeping a Grip', *The Bell* 3:2 (November 1941).   40 Homi K. Bhabha, *The location of culture* (London, 1994), p. 7.   41 See, for example, Harmon, *Seán O'Faoláin: a life*, p. 18.   42 O'Faoláin, 'The Sugawn Chair', *The Bell* 15:3 (December 1947), p. 22.   43 Ibid., p. 22.

other stuffed armchairs and sofas: 'After all, the great pleasure of a sugawn chair is that it *gives* with you and there is something solid to put your heels on'.[44] Here the chair symbolizes the family's rural heritage, and one can note the story's repetition of the word 'solid' in describing a sense of place that provides both a solid back and a solid identity to stand on. But the chair becomes a symbol of what has been lost when one day the seat of it collapses, and the narrator's father is totally unable, even with the help of two friends from the country, to weave a replacement seat from a bundle of straw. 'As I crept after him', the narrator remembers, 'I knew in my heart that they were three impostors'.[45]

Using fiction as his vehicle, O'Faoláin here expresses the complexity of the identity shift faced by some who left rural life behind and moved into the cities. As such he both complicates and transforms the idea of rural Irish identity. The súgán chair of the story's title outlives its owner, and stands broken and abandoned in the attic long after the narrator's mother and father have died. It cannot be repaired, just as the past cannot be recovered: and when the narrator comes upon it just before he sells the empty house, its presence conjures up for him all that his parents lost in their move from country to city – 'the sweet tang of apples, and the crisp tang of autumn air, and the lovely musky smell of Limerick turf-smoke'.[46] The experience of moving from the farm to the city has made his parents into 'impostors' in their own home, displaced country folk who are caught between the ill-fitting comfort of their urban life and the lost traditions of their past.

The Bell demanded that its writers and readers accept the transitional state of contemporary Irish culture, and not be tempted to fixate their nostalgia on an idealized version of what it meant to be Irish. In contrast to de Valera's vision of rural Ireland, the reality of the 1940s was that urbanization was under way, fuelled by a growing dissatisfaction with the impoverished conditions of rural life.[47] O'Faoláin called for a realistic appraisal of rural life, and stated that 'if we listened to the breathing of our dead people and less to the bellowing of our live politicians, we would, I feel, think of Ireland and her problems more quietly, more constructively, and more happily'.[48] He went on to argue that the generations of the past would not want their descendants 'to live as they lived, in dirt and misery, talking Gaelic in hovels'.[49] O'Donnell described the common sentiment among small farmers in Donegal: 'It is not a question here of who is to inherit the holding but who is to be stuck with it, and with it the task of seeing to the old folk'.[50] Such feelings were echoed in short stories such as John

---

44 Ibid., p. 23. 45 Ibid., p. 25. 46 Ibid. 47 See Brown, *Ireland*, pp 199–206. 48 O'Faoláin, 'Shadow and Substance', *The Bell* 6:4 (July 1943), 273–9 (p. 278). 49 Ibid., p. 279. 50 O'Donnell, 'Emigration is a Way of Keeping a Grip', p. 115.

Dearden's 'Love One Another', in which Brigid Connolly, a spinster resentful of her role as her father's only caretaker, bars her four brothers from visiting him before he dies, and refuses to allow them into the house for his wake.[51]

The frustrations of rural life included a tradition of land inheritance that inhibited younger Irish men and women from marrying until their parents had died. O'Faoláin wrote about the abnormal Irish marriage pattern in a lengthy article for the American *Life* magazine which attracted vehement criticism from the *Irish Press,* and an equally vehement defence from Peadar O'Donnell in the pages of *The Bell.*[52] O'Faoláin's short story 'Childybawn' dramatizes the incidence of late marriage in its description of forty-one-year-old banker Benjy Spillane, whose doting mother connives to end his romance with a work colleague by getting him to read St Augustine. When his mother dies five years later, Benjy finally marries the woman, and 'a bachelor pal teased him at the wedding for marrying so young'.[53] Patrick Kavanagh's Tarry Flynn also lives the bachelor life with his mother, and fantasizes about many of the young women in his village. The first section of Kavanagh's long poem 'The Great Hunger', which expresses one farmer's feelings of sexual starvation, was published not in *The Bell* but in *Horizon,* whereupon the magazine's Dublin distribution was promptly censored, as editor Cyril Connolly noted with satirical self-satisfaction: '*Horizon* would like to take this opportunity to thank our English and American readers for their extreme forbearance in letting this poem pass with favourable comment'.[54]

Irish towns and cities, meanwhile, were failing to replace the communal social structures lost to internal migration and emigration. Nor did life in the city offer all of its inhabitants the comforts of economic security and a healthy standard of living. 'I Live in a Slum', a transcribed monologue printed in *The Bell*'s second issue, presented the experience of a thirty-six-year-old man who, with his wife and five children, shared a Dublin tenement house with fifty-six people, one water tap and one lavatory between them, with no means for cooking but an open fire.[55] Sheila May's article 'Two Dublin Slums' opens with a direct attack on de Valera's version of an ideal Ireland, contrasting his vision of self-sufficiency with detailed reports of the abject poverty experienced by slum dwellers. May charges the post-independence government with failing to bring about any improvements that go beyond cosmetic changes: 'Incidentally, only one change has occurred in these slums since we got our own government. [...] The names of the alley and the street have been changed from English into Irish'.[56] Peadar O'Donnell drew a direct link from poor living conditions in Irish

---

51 John Dearden, 'Love One Another', *The Bell* 18:5 (October 1952).   52 O'Faoláin, 'Love Among the Irish', *Life* (16 March 1953); Peadar O'Donnell, 'The *Irish Press* and O'Faoláin', *The Bell* 18:11 (Summer, 1953).   53 Sean O'Faoláin, 'Childybawn', *The Bell* 19:10 (November 1954), p. 20.   54 Editorial note, *Horizon* 5:29 (May 1942), p. 300.   55 'I Live in a Slum', *The Bell* 1:2 (November 1940).   56 Sheila May, 'Two Dublin Slums', *The Bell* 7:4 (January 1944), p. 356.

cities to the increasing rate of emigration, and he connected both to the failure of the native government's revolutionary ideals: 'The exiles are not in any mood to make excuses for it. They must be the bitterest lot ever forced from these shores by conditions. [...] The Ireland they freed has failed them and it hurts'.[57] O'Donnell ended one article on emigration with a call for city planners to provide 'housing suitable for men, women and children, for we want our cities transformed not patched and we want pictures of the transformed cities NOW'.[58]

Here again, *The Bell* extended its efforts beyond representation, towards the transformation of urban centres for contemporary Irish men and women. O'Faoláin captured the complexity of the relationship between country and city when he wrote about the need for careful town and city planning:

> Cities we will always have, and towns feeding them. Nobody could have any sentimental idea that there is anything inherently wrong with the life of a great city with all its clanging and stirring, its fine thinking and fine making. But when the cities begin to leech the countryside so that our villages are being killed one by one, then something evil is happening. For there must always be a nucleus – a community-centre – if any sort of civilised life is to flourish in the countryside. And that marks out the preservation of village-life in Ireland as a key-point in the effort to slow-down to a healthy tempo the otherwise normal adventure of our people into that more complex world where they must, sooner or later, play their full part as a modern nation.[59]

Rather than wait upon the government, *The Bell*'s editors decided to take the initiative. In December 1941, they invited architect Michael Scott, MRIAI, to write the lead article in a symposium on town and village planning, and followed up with commentary from experts in architecture and economics, including Erskine H. Childers, who was then a TD.

Scott's article, which was accompanied by two full-page drawings of plans to improve existing Irish villages, argued that the layout and appearance of most existing towns and villages 'might suggest despair', but that this need not always be the case.[60] Scott proposed that planning should focus on the social needs of the local residents: a community centre was essential, as were a crèche and nursery school. He suggested that every town have a clinic, hotel, shopping centre, and a block of small flats to accommodate workers currently living in 'digs'. The aim of these proposals, he stressed, was to stem the flow of internal migra-

---

57 Peadar O'Donnell, 'Call the Exiles Home', *The Bell* 9:5 (February 1945), p. 383. 58 Ibid., p. 384. 59 O'Faoláin, 'Beginnings and Blind Alleys', p. 5. 60 Michael Scott, 'The Village Planned', *The Bell* 3:3 (December 1941), p. 235.

tion from rural to urban areas: 'Remember that we are trying to preserve a decaying village-life and that if we do not make village-life as comfortable as city-life there may soon be no villages left'.[61] Erskine Childers struck a nationalist note in his response, noting that without planning, the design of Irish towns would be based on second-rate copies of British suburbs such as Surbiton, 'and God knows it is not Irish'.[62] One *Bell* article went so far as to propose a re-design of the traditional Irish cottage in a contemporary style, with a total building cost of £750.[63] In all of these articles, *The Bell* revealed its instructional impulses and its transformational agenda. Time and again, the magazine's writers and editors went beyond documentary representation and expressed their view of Ireland as a forward-looking nation which could maintain its intrinsic identity while meeting the challenges of modernization.

SOCIAL CONCERNS: FROM CLASS DIFFERENCES TO PRISON REFORM

The decline of rural communities was only one of the social concerns addressed by *The Bell*. Early in the life of the magazine, the editors made it clear that in its mission to represent an authentic version of Irish identity, *The Bell* would not gloss over the more problematic aspects of mid-twentieth-century Irish life. In his fifth editorial, O'Faoláin addressed what he saw as a weakness in the magazine's initial project of representation, and challenged contributors to address the social and political problems of the day:

> We are well satisfied with the first five numbers, and we have first-class general material on hand for several months to come: but we are weak in that particular section where our social problems and (having regard to war-conditions) our political problems should be bravely, and thoroughly delineated. Without these we should become a purely popular magazine, and, perhaps, in the end stand appalled by exactly that kind of a success which we do not in the least desire. We challenge our students to get down to it: and to note that apart from the exclusively literary *Dublin Magazine* this is the only independent, non-affiliated periodical in the entire country. This is the only native periodical open to *everybody*.[64]

It was not the editors' intention to publish a purely popular magazine, nor one that was exclusively literary. In addition to articles on rural migration and emi-

61 Ibid., pp 238–9.   62 Erskine H. Childers, 'The Village Planned', *The Bell* 3:5 (February 1942), p. 368.   63 Kenneth Bayes, 'A £750 Cottage', *The Bell* 4:3 (June 1942).   64 O'Faoláin, 'A Challenge', p. 6.

gration, *The Bell* published informative and argumentative articles on topics such as class differences, public health, education and prison reform. By presenting various aspects of Irish life that did not always find their images in the main-stream media, *The Bell* consciously tried to complicate its representation of contemporary Irish identity.

Class differences were a preoccupation from the very beginning. The first issue of *The Bell* juxtaposed an anonymous article called 'Orphans', transcribed from the oral history of Frank O'Connor's seventy-five-year-old mother,[65] who was raised in a convent orphanage, with an autobiographical essay titled 'The Big House', written by Elizabeth Bowen, which explained the economic and psychological difficulties of maintaining her life in Bowen's Court. Bowen's article stresses the importance of attacking the barriers that separate Irish people from one another, and notes that 'it must be seen that a barrier has two sides'.[66] Such a statement characterizes *The Bell*'s approach to the discussion of social differences across Irish society as a whole.

The Bell's primary agenda for the representation of class differences seems to have been to counteract the very idealism put forward by de Valera. In an editorial titled 'Shadow and Substance', printed four months after de Valera's 1943 St Patrick's Day radio address, O'Faoláin attacked the Taoiseach's 'romantic nationalism' and argued in favour of a 'realistic nationalism' based on the 'actuality' of Irish people's daily lives.[67] Towards the goal of realistic representation, *The Bell* published a four-part series of articles on 'Other People's Incomes' in 1943, each of which detailed the monthly budgets of families living at four different levels of income: £800 a year, £400 a year, £300 a year, and £100 a year. When the series concluded, after a discussion of the difficulties faced by families whose income was less than £325 a year, the authors closed with an editorial note that stated, 'We hope that these articles may have come to the eyes of our legislators, so that they may realise in what a struggling condition the majority of this class of people now live'.[68] Likewise, a series of three articles by Olivia Manning Robertson, who had been working for three years as a relief play-leader in Dublin Corporation playgrounds, paint a startlingly bleak portrait of the lives of children living in poverty in the slums of inner-city Dublin.[69]

But who was the intended audience for such representations of Irish life? The tone of one article in the 'Other People's Incomes' series suggests that it

65 O'Faoláin, undated letter to O'Connor, Gotlieb Archival Research Center. See also Ruth Sherry, 'Frank O'Connor's Autobiographical Writings' in Lennon (ed.), *Frank O'Connor: critical essays*, p. 184.   66 Elizabeth Bowen, 'The Big House', *The Bell* 1:1 (October 1940), p. 77.   67 O'Faoláin, 'Shadow and Substance', *The Bell* 6:4 (July 1943), pp 277–8.   68 'Other People's Incomes – 4 / Compiled', *The Bell* 7:2 (November 1943), p. 150.   69 Olivia Manning Robertson, 'Out Patients', *The Bell* 7:6 (March 1944); 'Deformed', *The Bell* 9:2 (November 1944); 'Court Circular', *The Bell* 10:5 (August 1945).

was not the lower classes themselves. Commenting on the monthly budget of Mrs K., a widow raising four daughters, under the subtitle 'How to Live on £100 a Year', the unnamed author writes: '"Live?" Well, maybe it would not be your idea of living, nor ours for that matter. But Mrs K. does not pity herself'.[70] Readers are encouraged not to pity her, either, but to witness Mrs K.'s 'moments of terrible discontent, moments of resentment against an order which makes her dependent on others for meals and clothing'.[71] Thus readers are asked to identify the separation between their own lives and that of Mrs. K., and also to consider the 'order' of Irish society which imposes a state of dependency upon her. It is a tacit assumption that *Bell* readers might be able to take action to change the prevailing social order, whether at the ballot box or within their own positions of influence.

Indeed, although *The Bell*'s purchase price was kept relatively low, suggesting that it was available to readers of all means, there is much evidence to suggest that many of its readers were drawn from the more affluent sections of Irish society. Advertisements for life insurance abound in the pages of the magazine, often with a tone of commendation, for example, the Irish Life Assurance ad that reads 'Congratulations Mr Breadwinner!' in 1944.[72] Barnardo's Furs was a frequent advertiser, appealing to *Bell* readers as people who would appreciate 'the work of the Artist-Furrier'.[73] Victor Waddington Galleries often ran ads for new exhibitions of paintings as well as for framing services available to those who possessed the means to own original art.[74] Maura Laverty, writing in 1943, described Dublin's 'mistress-and-maid problem' and efforts by both Louie Bennett, Secretary of the Irish Women Workers' Union, and the newly organized Domestic Employers' Association to resolve grievances between upper-class women and their domestic servants.[75] And D.J. Giltinan, who later wrote plays for the Abbey, contributed a short-lived series of articles titled 'Futures for Johnny and Jenny' which described employment in a solicitor's office, a library, and a veterinary surgery, presumably aimed at middle-class, urban parents who were in a position to guide their children's career choices.[76]

Yet there were also articles aimed at a broad cross-section of Irish society, particularly those which focused on problems of public health. The spectre of tuberculosis was raised in one of the earliest issues of *The Bell*, in an article by Dr Robert Collis, who later became known for his work with cerebral palsy patients, including the artist Christy Brown. Tuberculosis was widespread in Ire-

---

70 'Other People's Incomes – 3 / Compiled', *The Bell* 7:1 (October 1943), p. 58.   71 Ibid., p. 62.   72 Irish Life Assurance Company Limited, advertising in *The Bell* 9:1 (October 1944), inside page (unnumbered).   73 Barnardo's, advertising in *The Bell* 5:5 (February 1943), inside cover page (unnumbered).   74 See, for example, advertisement for Victor Waddington Galleries, *The Bell* 2:2 (May 1941), p. 82.   75 Maura Laverty, 'Maids *versus* Mistresses', *The Bell* 7:1 (October 1943).   76 D.J. Giltinan, 'Futures for Johnny and Jenny', *The Bell* 11:1 (October 1945), pp 609–16; *The Bell* 11:2 (November 1945), pp 697–702; *The Bell* 11:3 (December 1945).

land in the 1940s, causing approximately 4,000 deaths every year.[77] In 'The Delicacy', Collis characterizes popular attitudes towards the disease as a distinctively Irish problem: 'It is a lurking terror in the national mind; an evil thing; something to be feared and fled from; something best not spoken of, a shame which must be denied and hidden'.[78] As Collis points out, secrecy itself is counterproductive when attempting to treat tuberculosis, and in order to combat the lack of openness about the disease, *The Bell* juxtaposed his article with an optimistic first-person account of 'Two Years in a Sanatorium', a description of the clean and comfortable conditions in a tuberculosis treatment clinic, and the author's recovery from the disease under the care and guidance of the medical staff, who strap him to an iron frame to ensure absolute rest, and who teach him new routines to help him live more healthily as he recuperates. (Today's reader might be surprised to find that the tuberculosis patient's routines include enjoying 'the soothing influence of a cigarette' as he reads the morning newspaper.)[79]

The Bell's series of articles on tuberculosis provide yet another example of its dual project of representation and transformation. By combining the testimony of patients who have recovered from tuberculosis with the commentary of Dr Collis, *The Bell* employs both documentary and argument in the building of a case against the current Irish attitude towards the disease and against government inaction. One tuberculosis survivor, who describes thirteen months of treatment including an operation to collapse his tubercular lung, urges fellow sufferers to ignore social taboos and come forward to begin treatment: 'Do not be ashamed to admit that you have TB [...] Remember, too, it is *your life* that matters, and not the opinions of your *friends*. But that life may depend on how soon you get into a sanatorium'.[80] Meanwhile O'Faoláin, in his introduction to Collis' first article, contrasts the government's disproportionate spending on air-raid precautions with its inadequate regulation of dairy pasteurization, a fault of attention which often resulted in the spreading of tubercular bacilli through bottled milk.[81] The battle against tuberculosis is cast as a nationalist endeavour, as when Collis notes, in a later article, that 'while even Northern Ireland has succeeded in reducing its mortality rate under British guidance we, masters at last of our own destiny, have actually allowed the disease to gain on us'.[82] Short stories in later issues of *The Bell* reinforce the necessity of taking action. In 'The Weakness', forty-three-year-old Sara Carr listens with dread to the coughing of her oldest daughter Tess, recently

77 Greta Jones, *'Captain of all these men of death': the history of tuberculosis in nineteenth and twentieth-cenutry Ireland* (Amsterdam, 2001), pp 199, 206.   78 Robert Collis, 'The Delicacy', *The Bell* 1:5 (February 1941), p. 33.   79 Charles Woodlock, 'Two Years in a Sanatorium', *The Bell* 1:5 (February 1942), p. 42.   80 W.J. Heaney, 'I Fought T.B. – and Won', *The Bell* 8:4 (July 1944), pp 323–4.   81 Editorial note preceding Collis, 'The Delicacy', p. 33. The Milk Act of 1944 eventually enforced the pasteurisation of milk.   82 Robert Collis, 'A Description of Tuberculosis', *The Bell* 8:3 (June 1944), p. 211.

returned from seasonal work in Northern Ireland, and fears that she will die of 'the weakness' that has already killed several family members; and in 'Sanatorium Death', the narrator witnesses the death of a fellow patient who entered the sanatorium too late to be cured of his tuberculosis.[83]

For the editors of *The Bell*, social concerns were inextricably linked to questions of national identity. O'Faoláin connected the definition of 'Nationality' both to concrete objects such as súgán chairs and to the discussion of issues that would impact the lives of ordinary citizens:

> One may talk of 'Nationality' until one is green in the face and get no nearer the fact. But when somebody makes a chair that is patently an Irish chair, and not a Birmingham chair, that *is* Nationality. We want to know what to do with our surplus doctors; what to do with our illegitimate children; to see what is being done in our penal system; to see what we actually can produce in native dishes or native arts and crafts. We want to project the theory of the Nation in concrete form.[84]

Thus the autobiographical story of an Irish doctor, Fionan O'Shea, and his journey to a country practice in Glan yr Afon, Wales, where he attends 6,746 patients a year, is offered not only as a piece of documentary realism, but also as an example of a national trend. As O'Shea writes in his article's introduction, 'When I qualified in 1925 I never tried for a job in Ireland; in fact I never gave it a thought; I just packed my bag and left. It was a kind of tradition amongst us to quit as soon as degrees were conferred'.[85] While O'Shea writes in detail about the British panel system and its financial implications, another doctor, Peter O'Kane, compares his experience of the British system to his Irish practice, and evaluates the former's relative advantages.[86] A third doctor discusses the general surplus of Irish medical graduates and discusses ways to improve the training and living conditions of emigrating doctors; he also mentions the proposal for a National Health Service, 'at present hotly debated in Britain'.[87] Interestingly, none of these three writers express a desire to stem the flow of emigration among graduating medical students. Yet as each doctor tells of his own life in detail, he also suggests improvements to the Irish medical system, which would impact the wider society at large.

Likewise, a discussion of illegitimacy opens with the description of one individual young mother brought into court and charged with begging, then

---

83 Michael J. Murphy, 'The Weakness', *The Bell* 16:6 (March 1951); William J. Johnston, 'Sanatorium Death', *The Bell* 18:4 (September 1952).   84 O'Faoláin, 'Attitudes', *The Bell* 2:6 (September 1941), p. 11.   85 Fionan O'Shea, 'Doctors for Export', *The Bell* 2:2 (May 1941).   86 Anonymous, 'The Life of a Country Doctor', *The Bell* 3:1 (October 1941). 87 Earl McCarthy, 'Eire's Surplus Doctors', *The Bell* 9:2 (November 1944), p. 121.

expands its focus to describe the plight of other unmarried mothers, and suggests changes to government policy which might provide a better future for both mother and child. The author, who is named only with the initials 'M.P.R.H.', appeals to the Irish sense of national heritage in an attempt to soften readers' attitudes towards illegitimate children: 'Such great houses as the O'Neills, the Geraldines, the Burkes, always included bastards who were reared not on equal terms but certainly with equal humanity by their fathers'.[88] As a possible solution, the author points to Britain's National Council for the Unmarried Mother and her Child and its improvements in social services and public information surrounding illegitimacy, and then advocates for similar developments in Ireland. One *Bell* short story, 'The Rustle of Spring', portrays the fictional experience of a young unmarried mother who sought refuge with her farming cousins, only to be turned away for refusing to give up her baby.[89]

Edward Fahy, a barrister and professor of law at Dublin University, was commissioned to write two articles on prison reform, beginning in the second issue of *The Bell*. O'Faoláin introduced the articles with a statement that they provided information 'the importance of which it is not possible to overstress'.[90] Fahy's articles, like others in *The Bell*, weave together documentary representation and arguments in favour of social transformation. He describes the Irish prison system, comprising Ordinary and Convict Prisons, three divisions of prisoners in Ordinary Prisons, the organization of prison workshops, and the Progressive Stage System of rewards for industry (good behaviour). In his second article Fahy addresses the problem of juvenile crime and the Irish system of detaining juvenile offenders in adult prisons. He describes his visit to the Borstal Institute of Eire in Clonmel, County Tipperary, and compares the Irish Borstal institutions very unfavourably to their English counterparts, where the focus is on keeping young offenders from becoming habitual criminals: 'The object of Borstal detention is training, not punishment'.[91] In both his articles, Fahy calls for specific prison reforms, for example, longer hours at night for reading, education, or amusement instead of locking prisoners in their cells at 4:40 p.m. until the next morning.

The reality of prison life was further brought home to *Bell* readers in the well-known series of articles by an unnamed ex-convict who used the pseudonym 'D83222'.[92] *Bell* editors introduced the series with a statement that it 'should assist the public to form a more complete picture of jail-life in Ireland to-day,

88 M.P.R.H., 'Illegitimate', *The Bell* 2:3 (June 1941), p. 79.   **89** Eily O'Horan, 'The Rustle of Spring', *The Bell* 13:5 (February 1947).   **90** Editorial note preceding Edward Fahy, 'The Prisons', *The Bell* 1:2 (November 1940).   **91** Edward Fahy, 'The Boy Criminal', *The Bell* 1:3 (December 1940), p. 43.   **92** 'D83222' was presented to readers as the prisoner's serial number, but was actually Sean O'Faoláin's home telephone number (Furze, 'A Desirable Vision of Life', p. 84).

and interest all who are concerned with the problem of the discharged prisoner'.[93] In a series of six articles published in late 1944 and early 1945, D83222
described his sentencing for embezzlement, his one-month stay in Mountjoy
prison and his subsequent journey to Portlaoighise [*sic*] prison, where he experienced the full range of punitive and rehabilitative systems described in Fahy's
earlier articles. In a later series of three articles published in 1946, the former
prisoner went back in time and described the series of missteps he took as a
young bank clerk which led him into gambling, debt, and the act of fraud which
resulted in his prison sentence. Throughout the series, D83222's experiences are
presented both as individual and as representative of the Irish prison system —
and indeed, the Irish banking system — as a whole. The articles were later published as a collection by the Metropolitan Publishing Company, under the title
I did penal servitude, with a preface by O'Faoláin.[94]

   Comparisons to British policies and practice were common in *The Bell*'s discussion of Irish social problems, and they highlight the newly independent
nation's complicated relationship with its former colonial oppressor. As Fanon
noted, the inevitability of imitation poses recurring problems for the post-colonial intellectual:

> At the very moment when the native intellectual is anxiously trying to
> create a cultural work he fails to realize that he is utilizing techniques
> and language which are borrowed from the stranger in his country. He
> contents himself with stamping these instruments with a hall-mark
> which he wishes to be national, but which is strangely reminiscent of
> exoticism.[95]

So, for example, when Fahy writes about Irish prisons, he makes frequent comparisons to conditions in English prisons and to English critics of the prison
system, without apology or any evidence of self-consciousness. A 1942 article on
'The Postage Stamps of Ireland' is accompanied by an illustration of all nineteen
Irish stamps printed to date, including two British stamps on which the head of
King George V is over-printed with the words 'Saorstat Eireann' in Gaelic script;
the author explains that the last British stamps were replaced as late as 1937.[96] And
in the March 1943 issue of *The Bell* there appears an advertisement for a product
that could be said to epitomize Irish anxieties about post-colonial identity in the
mid-twentieth century. A full-page ad for 'T.D. Sauce' depicts a bottle identical

93 Editorial note preceding D 83222, 'I Did Penal Servitude: Journey to Fear (Part I)', *The Bell* 9:1 (October 1944),
p. 41.   94 Another well-known prison narrative, Brendan Behan's *Borstal Boy*, also saw its first excerpt published in
The Bell, under the title 'I Become a Borstal Boy', *The Bell* 4:3 (June 1942).   95 Fanon, p. 180.   96 W.D. Robertson,
'The Postage Stamps of Ireland', *The Bell* 4:3 (June 1942).

in shape to the well-known square bottle of H.P. Sauce, but with one important difference: the label carries a picture of Leinster House in place of the Houses of Parliament, and bears the inscription 'has the right constituents!' (see Figure 1).[97] The perceived need for an independent bottle of brown sauce parallels the uncertainty faced by Irish writers and other intellectuals in the early decades of independence: How far to banish British influence? How to establish indigenous modes of thought, and of day-to-day life, without being obscured in the long shadow cast by the British Empire? O'Faoláin addressed questions such as these in an editorial titled 'New Wine in Old Bottles', in which wrote of the growing difference between Irish and British social realities, and the impossibility of continuing with Irish life in the colonial mode:

> Indeed, it is only now, twenty years after [independence], that we are feeling the full force of the cold blast of social change. At first the old British-made bottles seemed able to carry the new Irish wine fairly well. But the Irish wine has begun to ferment, and pop go the corks, and the stuff is beginning to run all over the place.[98]

O'Faoláin lists a series of necessary changes that were not adequately planned for in the days of the Irish revolution: the redistribution of land after the collapse of the Irish Ascendancy, the reconfiguration of towns that had depended on English garrisons, the replacement of income from British pensions and emigrants' remittances, and the redirection of agricultural work in favour of tillage rather than livestock production.

O'Faoláin here again insists, somewhat disingenuously, that the writer's only work is the project of representation. He argues that the work of decolonization is a job for politicians, not writers:

> Our statesmen do not seem capable of realising this — that we are in a period of psychological chaos, that if the country is to be given hope and set to work it must first be inspired by the feeling that it is working inside a great, coherent social idea towards some new order which they can visualise in terms of a desirable image of life.[99]

Yet by pointing out the dissonance between de Valera's ideal Ireland and the realities of the social issues that confronted the new nation, *The Bell* did more than simply 'record the growing demoralisation of the gamblers and wirepullers', to use O'Faoláin's phrase.[1] By consistently representing many of the most prob-

97 T.D. Sauce, advertising in *The Bell* 5:6 (March 1943), p. 512.   98 O'Faoláin, 'New Wine in Old Bottles', *The Bell* 4:6 (September 1942), p. 382.   99 Ibid., p. 387.   1 Ibid.

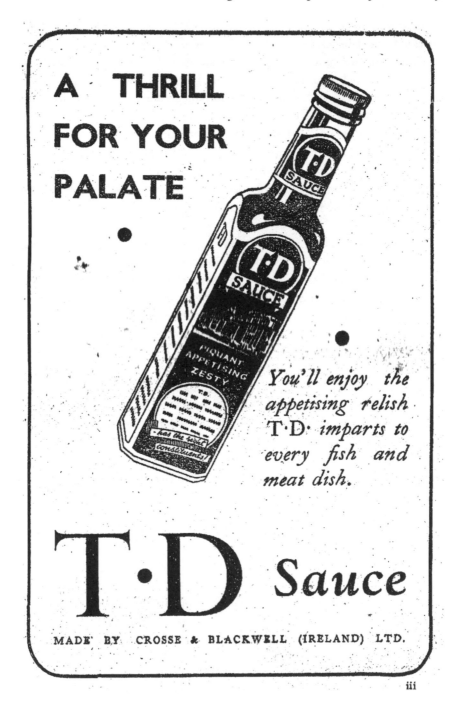

Figure 1: Advertisement in *The Bell* for T.D. Sauce

lematic aspects of contemporary Irish life, *The Bell* attempted to transform the
debate over the present social conditions of Irish men and women, as well as
the future of Irish society.

THE GAELIC QUESTION: LANGUAGE, LITERATURE AND THE GAELIC LEAGUE

F.S.L. Lyons notes that in the early twentieth century, it was Patrick Pearse who
'consecrated, as it were, the union of language and nationality', beginning with
his own bilingual school, St Enda's, which he founded in 1908 to educate children in an Irish context, as opposed to the colonial, English-oriented education
system.[2] When Pearse's political revolution came to fruition, the newly independent Irish government took up the language question as one of its first priorities, and schools were part of the response from the beginning. Proficiency
in Irish had been an entrance requirement for the National University since 1913,
and in 1922, the Provisional Government legislated that 'Irish should be taught
or used as a medium of instruction in all primary schools for not less than one
hour a day during the ordinary school hours where there was a teacher competent to do so'.[3] The fact that the majority of teachers were not competent in
Irish meant that the new government had to redouble its efforts to improve
teacher training in the language. However, if the Gaelic League had had its way,
Irish would have been regarded as the principal language of schools throughout the country, and been taught in its spoken form for an hour a day where
teachers were available. The Gaelic League itself had become politicized when
a majority of its members voted to support Irish independence in 1915, a controversial action which resulted in the resignation of the League's founder, Douglas Hyde;and by the early 1930s, as Ferriter explains, 'The most notable activities of the Gaelic League were campaigns against the appointment of
non-Irish-speakers to educational or cultural posts, as they aligned themselves
with the zealots of the *Catholic Bulletin*'.[4]

The editors of *The Bell* made their position on the Gaelic question clear in
the very first issue of the magazine. Although the magazine only rarely used
quotations as page fillers, on the bottom half of one page was printed a quotation from Æ, writing in the *Irish Statesman* on 'The Two Traditions':

> There are still those who regard the Anglo-Irish as aliens. But anything
> is national that vitalises the nation. However hateful and unjust the inva-

2 F.S.L. Lyons, *Ireland since the Famine* (London, 1971), p. 635 and pp 331–2. 3 Ibid., pp 635–8. 4 Ferriter, *Transfor-mation*, p. 351.

sion of Ireland, the blending of races and cultures finally brought about a more vital and complicated mentality. Gaelic literature is pre-eminent in imagination, in beauty, but it is lacking in intellect. But the fusion of Saxon and Norman with the original stock created the Anglo-Irish with their amazing intellectual vitality. The Gael has as much to learn from science, from the new and the aged thought of the world, as the Anglo-Irish have from the Gaelic tradition. No country can rid itself of its history, and I believe that if this country is to come to anything it will only be by the continuance of the two traditions, each vitalising the other.[5]

The Bell's editors were resolutely opposed to any promotion of the Irish language and its literature that came at the expense of the Anglo-Irish tradition, a position which was championed by O'Faoláin and which has led some critics to consider him an early proponent of revisionism.[6] Gibbons, for example, cites O'Faoláin's *Bell* editorials on the Gaelic question as being among 'the first direct challenges to the orthodoxies of the national revival'.[7] A closer examination, however, of O'Faoláin's statements about Gaelic culture, language, literature and the Gaelic League, as well as a consideration of *The Bell's* substantial body of critical work on literature in Irish, yields a more complicated assessment of O'Faoláin's position, and of *The Bell's* approach to the Irish language.

By the time he became editor of *The Bell*, O'Faoláin was well positioned to appreciate the importance of Gaelic heritage to Irish culture. In his youth, O'Faoláin had embraced the Irish language as part of the nationalist movement, and had made frequent visits to the Gaeltacht in order to develop his language skills. Images inspired by these visits appear frequently in his short stories for *The Bell*, for example, 'The Man Who Invented Sin' and 'The Silence of the Valley'.[8] He changed his name from Jacky Whelan to the Gaelicized Sean O'Faoláin at the age of eighteen, and later became secretary of a Cork branch of the Gaelic League, as well as the editor of an Irish-language literary magazine, *An Grianán*. His first attempts at publication, moreover, were of short stories written in Irish, printed in the pages of *An Grianán* itself.[9] There is no reason, therefore, to doubt O'Faoláin's sincerity when he writes, in an editorial on 'The Gaelic League', that 'In a word, Gaelic is essential if we wish to inform ourselves about ourselves'.[10] In his view, the Irish language was an invaluable tool in the work of understanding Irish identity:

5 Æ, 'The Two Traditions', quoted in *The Bell* 1:1 (October 1940), p. 53.   6 Shovlin, *The Irish literary periodical*, p. 107.
7 Gibbons, 'Challenging the Canon: Revisionism and Cultural Criticism', *The Field Day anthology of Irish writing*, ed. by Seamus Deane (Derry, 1991), p. 562.   8 O'Faoláin, 'The Man Who Invented Sin', *The Bell* 9:3 (December 1944); 'The Silence of the Valley', *The Bell* 12:6 (September 1946).   9 Harmon, *Sean O'Faoláin: a life*, pp 43–5, 63.   10 O'Faoláin, 'The Gaelic League', p. 81.

That entire and so slowly formed psychosis which, in Arnold's word,
we sometimes call the 'genius' of our race opens itself fully only to
those who can touch, through Gaelic, the folk-world of our people's
imagination, their ancient ways, the charm of their literature, their
wilful modes of life, even their tabus and fetishes and pious simplici-
ties, all preserved uninterrupted for too many centuries to be worn out
of us by even two centuries of Europeanisation.[11]

O'Faoláin's equation of the 'genius' of the Irish race with a 'psychosis' hints
strongly at his distaste for notions of Irish racial purity. Yet his statements about
the importance of the Irish language mirror his editorial vision for *The Bell* and
his emphasis on the value of documenting everyday Irish experiences. Those
who do not speak the language, he argues, cannot fully understand how 'even
the most plebeian memories, the most vulgar tales, the most humble customs'
become 'sanctified' by their intrinsic connection to Irish heritage and Irish life.[12]

It was the politicization of Irish, however, to which O'Faoláin objected, and
which fuelled the fire of his most strident editorials against the Gaelic League
and against the heavy-handed promotion of the Irish language by de Valera's
government. Between November 1941 and December 1944, O'Faoláin wrote several *Bell* editorials attacking what he called 'The Gaelic Cult', often in response
to articles in other Irish periodicals or in pamphlets published by the Gaelic
League. One attack, published in an English periodical, earned him a direct
response in the pages of *Comhar*, the Irish-language journal established in 1942.
Under the heading 'Johnny, I hardly knew you!' one *Comhar* editor mocked
O'Faoláin for criticizing others who took Gaelicized names, and wrote: 'Ach,
duine a bhí tamall na eagarthóir ar The Bell, ba cheart go seachnódh sé geáitsí
an stage-Irishman' ['When one is editor of *The Bell*, one should avoid stage-Irishman gestures'].[13] O'Faoláin never wavered from his determination to reconcile
and celebrate both the English and Irish languages. Although he recognized 'a
natural, and indeed a commendable eagerness to discover some thread of continuity that would lead us from the present to the past', he urged proponents
of the Irish language revival to acknowledge 'that we are now an English-speaking people, that we have only the broken shards of a folklore, and no Gaelic literature at all, because we broke, or were broken from all these things two hundred years ago'.[14]

Perhaps most provocative were O'Faoláin's comparisons of 'neo-Gaels' to
propagandists for racial purity in Nazi Germany.[15] In response to an early letter

11 Ibid. 12 Ibid. 13 'Cúrsaí Reatha', *Comhar* 6:2 (February 1947), p. 5. 14 O'Faoláin, 'The Gaelic and the Good',
p. 98. 15 For an example of O'Faoláin's use of the term 'neo-Gael', see 'The Gaelic and the Good', p. 102.

to the editor, in which the writer, Gearóid Ó Cuinneagáin, a pro-Gaelic (and pro-Fascist) activist, argues for his family's status as Gaels (in reference to a line from a previous issue of *The Bell*), O'Faoláin writes:

> His present anxiety to prove himself a 'Gael' is like somebody sweating to prove himself of pure Aryan blood [...] Let us be content to be 'Irish' and have done with this childish *raiméis* about 'Gaels'.[16]

O'Faoláin had previously attacked Ó Cuinnegáin and his organization Ailtirí na hAiséirghe, in Irish, in an opinion piece published in *Comhar* in 1942.[17] In his response to Ó Cuinnegáin's letter to *The Bell*, O'Faoláin's tone may be read as dismissive, and one may interpret his self-conscious inclusion of the Irish word *raiméis* [nonsense] as an assertion of his right to move in and out of the Irish language. But in a later editorial, O'Faoláin explicitly describes the 'master-type' of 'The Gael' in terms of its similarity to Nazi propaganda:

> It is a mystique, and like all mystiques it has a basis in fact, or rather an impossible bundling together of disparate facts. In sum the mystique has tried to discover in the old Gaelic world a model, or master-type – rather like the National Socialist mythology of the Pure Aryan – to which we must all conform.[18]

Here the implications of the Gaelic revival are cast as ominous and destructive. In fact it was the Gaelic League's insistence on compulsory Irish in various areas of Irish life, and its denial of the multiple roots of contemporary Irish culture, including its Anglo-Irish influences, which caused much of O'Faoláin's concern.

O'Faoláin identified the importance of restoring the voluntary aspect of participation in Irish-language activities as a key element in keeping the language alive in modern Ireland. In an editorial entitled 'Gaelic – The Truth', he demanded that the Gaelic League should formally disband as a political institution, and that the 'inspirational quality of Gaelic' should be emphasized in public efforts to revive the language.[19] Second, he argued, it was necessary 'that we be honest and realistic, and admit that our object is not unilingualism, but

16 O'Faoláin, response to letter in 'Public Opinion', *The Bell* 5:4 (January 1943), pp 316–17. 17 O'Faoláin, 'What's This about the Gaelic League', *Comhar* 1:2 (June 1942), p. 10. O'Faoláin wrote this piece (in Irish) in response to Daniel Corkery's pamphlet of the same title, published (in English, and with Corkery credited as Dónall Ó Corcora) by the Gaelic League in 1942. For more on their exchange, see Philip O'Leary, *Writing beyond the Revival: facing the future in Gaelic prose, 1940–1951* (Dublin, 2011), pp 266–71. For more on Ó Cuinneagáin, see R.M. Douglas, *Architects of the resurrection* (Manchester, 2009). 18 O'Faoláin, 'The Gaelic Cult', p. 187. 19 O'Faoláin, 'Gaelic – The Truth', *The Bell* 5:5 (February 1943), p. 339.

that we should speak, according to our moods and needs, both Gaelic and English'.[20] In particular, O'Faoláin stressed the need for giving schools the right to determine in which language they would instruct their pupils, and he quoted a lengthy passage from Patrick Pearse's anti-colonial manifesto on education in Ireland, *The murder machine*, to support his argument in favour of school autonomy when it came to the teaching of Irish.[21]

It would remain the work of *The Bell*'s documentary articles to describe the experiences of teachers and students labouring under the requirements of compulsory Irish in the schools. The first such article, 'Gaelic – With the Lid Off', was contributed by an anonymous secondary school teacher who, *Bell* readers were told, had sixteen years of experience, was rated 'Highly Efficient', and had taught students who had received awards in Gaelic at the Feis Ath' Cliath and elsewhere. Yet this teacher complained that having to teach 'Irish Reading, Irish Grammar, Irish Spelling, Irish Dictation, Irish Composition, Irish Poetry and Irish Conversation' as well as their counterparts in English, without any increase in the length of the school day, was a virtual impossibility.[22] Noting that 'after twenty years of native government', most Irish children still couldn't speak the language, the author concludes: 'Maybe I'm wrong, but it is my opinion that languages come up from below not down from above'.[23] A second anonymous author, whose name was given as 'Naosc a' Ghleanna' ['Snipe of the Glen'], suggested the abolition of Irish-medium education and, among other policies, the promotion of high-interest reading materials in Irish, rather than translations of books already available in English.[24] An article by the noted Irish translator Arland Ussher criticized government policies to mandate Irish in schools, and finally, in 1947, one *Bell* contributor declared that 'National policy since 1922 set the Primary Schools the task of restoring the national language and to this end the giving of education was frankly subordinated'.[25]

While O'Faoláin and his fellow editors campaigned against the imposition of compulsory Irish on primary school children, they nonetheless consistently made space for reviews of literature written in Irish, and vigorously promoted discussion among writers working in the language. In one of his editorials on the Gaelic League, for example, which may contain one of the earliest uses of the current phrase 'Irish literature in English', O'Faoláin decried the rejection of Anglo-Irish literature in favour of work written in Irish: 'This hatred of the Gaelic League for Irish literature in English is not nice to contemplate, and by putting two good things against one another it is simply creating an utterly

20 Ibid.   21 Ibid., p. 340.   22 'A National Teacher', 'Gaelic – With the Lid Off', *The Bell* 3:3 (December 1941), p. 222.   23 Ibid., p. 227.   24 'Naosc a' Ghleanna', 'Twenty Years A-Withering', *The Bell* 3:5 (February 1942).   25 Arland Ussher, 'Can Irish Live?', *The Bell* 9:5 (February 1945); Patrick O'Callaghan, 'Irish in Schools', *The Bell* 14:1 (April 1947), p. 62.

pointless dissension'.[26] Through its own publishing practice, *The Bell* strove to demonstrate that it was possible to embrace both languages and both literatures. In the absence of an apolitical Irish-language magazine, a lack that O'Faoláin lamented in his early editorials on the Gaelic League[27] (he apparently excluded the fledgling *Combar* from this category), *The Bell* provided a forum of literary debate for both critics and writers of Irish-language literature.

English-language reviews of Irish-language books appeared in nearly every issue of *The Bell*, as did advertisements for books from the state Irish-language publisher, An Gúm. Several of the earliest book reviews were contributed by Roibeárd Ó Faracháin, also known as Robert Farren, who later wrote the epic poem *The First Exile* about St Colmcille, and who was one of the first officers of Radio Eireann. In his reviews, Ó Faracháin consistently comments on the style of contemporary writing in Irish, as for example, when he praises Seosamh Mac Grianna's book *Eoghan Ruadh*: 'Mac Grianna has here achieved a style in Ulster Irish which preserves its vigour and at the same time smooths, refines, and subtilizes it'.[28] Rather than ask for Irish-language writers to copy the style of their ancestors, Ó Faracháin values Mac Grianna's efforts to refine the style of the written language, and to draw upon sources other than those that were historically Irish; for example, Ó Faracháin writes that 'in mood and texture, it [Mac Grianna's unfinished novel *Dá mbiodh ruball ar éan* [*If the bird had a tail*]] reminded me constantly of French novelists, now of Mauriac's *Noeud de Vipères*, again of Duchamel'.[29]

Moreover, in many *Bell* reviews, Ó Faracháin and other reviewers make reference to the larger body of contemporary Irish-language literature, critiquing general trends in style and technique, whether positive or negative. In a review of *An Doras do Plabadh*, a 'workmanlike thriller' by Seoirse Mac Liam, Ó Faracháin comments that 'The general level of competency in modern Gaelic writing is rising', and he again praises the writer for bringing the ancestral language up to date with contemporary realities: 'As I know from experience the difficulty of adapting the ruralities of Irish to the life of Dublin I appreciate the success of Seoirse Mac Liam'.[30] Another reviewer, identified in *The Bell* only as 'G.M.', comments on the difficulty of adapting spoken Irish to the written page, when he writes that 'cold print is not always suited to interjections which may sound quite natural in the warm flow of conversation'.[31] Indeed, one of the main concerns of *Bell* reviewers was that Irish-language writing should become more than an academic or nationalist exercise. It was hoped that writing in Irish would

---

26 O'Faoláin, 'The Gaelic League', p. 83. 27 See, for example, 'The Gaelic League', p. 86. 28 Roibeárd Ó Faracháin, 'Seosamh Mac Grianna', *The Bell* 1:2 (November 1940), p. 67. 29 Ó Faracháin, 'Seosamh Mac Grianna', p.67. 30 Roibeárd Ó Faracháin, review of *An Doras do Plabadh* by Seoirse Mac Liam, *The Bell* 1:6 (March 1941), p. 96. 31 G.M., review of *Fir Mhóra an t-Sean-Phobail* by Eibhlín Bean Uí Churraoin, *The Bell* 5:1 (October 1942), p. 70.

evolve into a living form of contemporary literature, no less vibrant than Irish literature in English. As P.S. O'Hegarty wrote in 1944, in a review that compared the work of Pádraic Ó Conaire to other, less skillful writers in Irish:

> A great deal of writing in Irish is difficult to read. Many of the writers have no natural talent for writing, and their writing is in the nature of a grammatical exercise. [...] That sort of writing in Irish perhaps constitutes an inevitable phase, and there are hopes that it is passing.[32]

Through their continued commitment to providing a nuanced critique of Irish-language literature, the editors of *The Bell* intended to play a part in the nurturing of the written language, helping it through its contemporary growing pains and towards its resuscitation as a vehicle for literary creativity.

The efforts of Irish-language writers themselves, however, were not always rewarded by the rest of the Irish reading public, nor indeed by the state institutions established to promote their work. Writing in May 1946, Séamus Ó Néill, editor of the new Gaelic literary monthly 'An Iris', commented on the twenty-year history of An Gúm, the publishing house founded by the Department of Education to produce translations and original books in the Irish language. Ó Néill noted that more than 800 works had been published to date, 'but if the true result is to be seen in the use the public makes of the published works, time and money have been largely wasted'.[33] He referred to the almost moribund rate at which Irish-language books were borrowed from public libraries, and described his own experience as an Irish-language writer, having been awarded a Gúm contract, but then having waited seven years for the publication of only 500 copies, with no plans for a timely reprint. Furthermore, he noted, since the Gúm was directly funded by the Minister for Education, it was subject to a stringent censorship, which was 'bound to put shackles on writers of originality'.[34] As Proinsias Ó Drisceoil recently noted, in reviewing a biography of Seosamh Mac Grianna, whose first novel *An Druma Mór* [*The big drum*] was suppressed by An Gúm for thirty-seven years, from its submission in 1932 until its eventual publication in 1969, 'while writers in English found themselves the object of an increasingly repressive censorship, writers in Irish were being published by the censors themselves'.[35]

The most popular Irish-language writer of the 1940s was Séamus Ó Grianna, the brother of Seosamh Mac Grianna, who wrote under the pseudonym 'Máire' and whose autobiography, *Nuair a bhí mé óg* (*When I was young*), sold two

---

32 P.S. O'Hegarty, 'Pádraic O Conaire', *The Bell* 8:3 (June 1944), p. 237. 33 Séamus Ó Néill, 'The Gúm', *The Bell* 12:2 (May 1946), p. 136. 34 Ibid., p. 139. 35 Proinsias Ó Drisceoil, 'Tragic Fragments Revealed', *Irish Times* Weekend Review (10 November 2007), p. 11.

thousand copies in its first year of publication by the Talbot Press.[36] Yet despite
his success, it was 'Máire' who contributed a bitter commentary on the thank-
less life of the Irish-language writer, which appeared in English translation in
The Bell in February 1947. Addressing young writers who hoped to publish in
Gaelic, 'Máire' wrote, 'Ireland is lying in the mud. If you attempt to raise her
with your pen, you will suffer for it [...] You will get blows and stripes and kicks
a hundred-fold'. In the interests of personal advancement, he advised, 'steer clear
of the truth'.[37] These sentiments may be seen to echo comments made by
Roibeárd Ó Faracháin on the double isolation of writers in Irish: 'the double
isolation, indeed, of the man born to the language of the minority, and born
as well to artistic endeavour in that language'.[38] But while Ó Faracháin speculated that the Irish-language writer might draw strength as well as creativity from
his dual sense of isolation, 'Máire' took no such comfort: 'If he becomes a great
Gaelic writer, let him not expect any reward other than to be crucified'.[39] 'Máire'
pointed, as an example, to his brother Seosamh Mac Grianna, who, disillusioned,
had given up writing in 1935, and who, though 'Máire' does not mention the fact,
spent much of his later years in psychiatric treatment for depression.

Until the very end of its publishing run, *The Bell* hosted debate over issues
of Irish-language literature and published reviews of writers working in the
language. Its importance as a forum for discussion of language-related issues
may be seen in that even a passing reference, in a half-page book review, to
Séamus Ó Néill as a writer of 'revival-Irish', as opposed to the Irish of native
speakers, provokes a page-long letter to the editor from 'Máire', arguing against
labelling non-native speakers with a term that implies 'an atrocious jargon that
can only be understood (in as far as it is understandable at all) by translating
it into English'.[40] The need for a standardized form of Irish to mitigate the
sometimes conflicting forms of local dialects is taken up in a review of Niall
Ó Domhnaill's *Forbairt na Gaeilge*, and is swiftly answered by a two-page letter
from the Irish-language writer Máirtín Ó Cadhain. (An Caighdeán Oifigiúil,
or Standard Irish, was not formulated by the Dáil's translation office, Rannóg
an Aistriúcháin, until the 1950s.) When Seán Ó Riordáin's collection *Eireaball
Spideóige* appeared in 1952, marking the first published book by an author 'hailed
as the greatest Gaelic poet for three centuries', *The Bell*'s review was reverent
and congratulatory: 'Whatever happens, his book will remain as a milestone
on the still-narrow road of Gaelic literature'.[41] It was part of *The Bell*'s project

36 Ó Néill, p. 138.   37 'Máire', 'From the Gaelic of "Máire"', *The Bell* 13:5 (February 1947), p. 17.   38 Ó Faracháin,
'Seosamh Mac Grianna', p. 66.   39 'Máire', 'From the Gaelic of "Máire"', p. 18.   40 'Máire', 'Seamus O Neill and
his Book', *The Bell* 11:2 (November 1945), p. 725; G.M., reviews of *An Sean-Saighdiuir agus Scéalta Eile* by Séamus Ó
Néill and *An Aibidil a Rinne Cadmus* by 'Máire', *The Bell* 10:6 (August 1945), p. 456.   41 Richard Power, review of
Eireaball Spideóige by Seán Ó Riordáin, *The Bell* 18:12 (Autumn, 1953), pp 129, 130.

of representation and transformation to contribute towards the widening of that road.

NORTHERN IRELAND: BRIDGING THE GAP

The Bell's stance towards Northern Ireland formed another key element in its representation of Irish identity, one that evolved throughout the life of the magazine. To read the body of the magazine's articles on the North is to witness the reification of the border as the two parts of the island grew more distant from one another, both because of ideology and because of their differing experiences of the war years. In his introductory editorial to the first Ulster Number, in 1941, O'Faoláin described the contrast between North and South in terms of the North's connections to the vastness of the British Empire versus the South's intentional drive towards self-sufficiency. O'Faoláin predicted that in time the differences between the two would drive them further apart:

> [T]hat outward-looking eye, and this introversion and exclusiveness not only help to distinguish, and therefore to divide the two parts of the island, but, as time goes on, they must increase the gap beyond bridging by creating two completely dissonant modes of life.[42]

It was *The Bell's* original goal that the gap not grow beyond bridging. In publishing its Ulster issues, as well as its frequent contributions from Northern writers, the magazine attempted to maintain dialogue between the two parts of the island. In the later years of *The Bell's* publication, as the border gained a stronger sense of permanency, that dialogue became more and more fraught. Yet the editors' commitment to the authentic representation of Northern life would lead Hubert Butler to write, two decades after the magazine's demise: 'I believe that for the truth about Ulster you must still look to *The Bell* and not to the sensationalism of the contemporary press'.[43]

In July 1941, timed to coincide with annual commemorations of the Battle of the Boyne, *The Bell* published its first Ulster Number, a collection of short stories, poems, and documentary articles by Northern writers. An examination of the contents reveals an openness towards Northern voices as well as a frank expression of hopes for 'Irish unity',[44] a phrase which, though initially undefined, would gradually take on political overtones in *Bell* articles on the North. The first Ulster Number mirrors the original intentions of *The Bell*: its stories,

42 O'Faoláin, 'Ulster', p. 4.   43 Butler, p. 68.   44 O'Faoláin, 'Ulster', p. 8.

poems and articles are largely representative, not argumentative, and aim to explore various aspects of daily life in Northern Ireland. Short stories by Michael MacLaverty and Lynn Doyle describe, respectively, a schoolteacher who contrives to make poitín in the guise of a science experiment, and an old woman who plans her own memorable burial.[45] One documentary article preserves the writer's memories of 'street-hawkers, beggars and ballad singers' in late nineteenth-century Belfast, another explains the provenance of various expressions of Belfast slang, and a third recalls the writer's childhood in an Ulster workhouse.[46] Only one article, 'The Battle of Scarva', touches on the potentially divisive topic of the Twelfth of July celebrations; but the writer, H.L. Morrow, filters the experience through the bewildered observations of an English colleague from the BBC, and casts much of the event in a humorous light, noting, for example, that at Scarva the battles of Derry, Aughrim, Enniskillen, and the Boyne are all compressed into one re-enactment lasting 'just under fourteen minutes'.[47] Poems by John Hewitt and W.R. Rodgers focus on politically neutral, pastoral themes; only Rodgers', with its choice of title, 'Ireland', for a description of the Mourne Mountains, could be read as even faintly sympathetic to nationalist aspirations.[48]

The Bell's publication of its Ulster Numbers was primarily based on its recognition of two facts: first, that a disproportionately high number of its contributors wrote from north of the border, and second, that the topics and themes chosen by Northern writers varied significantly from those taken up by their Southern counterparts. In February 1942, Geoffrey Taylor noted that about half of the poems submitted to The Bell each month came from 'our industrial north-east corner',[49] a region, as O'Faoláin noted, 'less than one-fifth of the size of the whole country'.[50] For the second Ulster Number, in July 1942, The Bell received so much material that the editors chose to fill the next month's issue with the overflow. There is also evidence that in the absence of a Northern literary magazine (Lagan was not founded until 1943; Rann not until 1948), The Bell was at least as widely read in Northern Ireland as it was in Eire. The first advertisement for a Belfast firm, George Morrow & Son Interior Decorators, appeared in January 1942;[51] others followed, including two large advertisements for Belfast booksellers D.A. McLean and Derrick Mac Cord in the Christmas

45 Michael MacLaverty, 'Moonshine', *The Bell* 2:4 (July 1941); Lynn Doyle, 'The Burying of Maryanne Corbally', *The Bell* 2:4 (July 1941). 46 Hugh Quinn, 'Old Belfast Street Characters', *The Bell* 2:4 (July 1941); Joseph Tomelty, 'A Note on Belfast Slang', *The Bell* 2:4 (July 1941); Patrick Roe Ward, 'In an Ulster Workhouse', *The Bell* 2:4 (July 1941). 47 H.L. Morrow, 'The Battle of Scarva', *The Bell* 2:4 (July 1941), p. 20. 48 W.R. Rodgers, 'Ireland', and John Hewitt, 'Hay', both in *The Bell* 2:4 (July 1941). 49 Geoffrey Taylor, review of *Poems from Ulster*, ed. Robert Greacen, *The Bell* 3:5 (February 1942), p. 403. 50 O'Faoláin, 'Fifty Years of Irish Literature', *The Bell* 3:5 (February 1942), p. 330. 51 George Morrow & Son Ltd, Interior Decorators, advertising in *The Bell* 3:4 (January 1942), inside page (unnumbered).

issue of 1943, suggesting a sizeable Northern readership.[52] In January 1944, 'Gulliver' wrote that for one monthly competition that 'Far more letters came from the North of Ireland than from all the twenty-six counties'.[53]

In the 1940s, Northern Ireland was experiencing something of a literary renaissance. Poetry was flourishing in Belfast, in contrast to Dublin, where, O'Faoláin noted with regret, 'The decline of poetry is almost complete'.[54] But Belfast poets, O'Faoláin wrote, were generally 'not preoccupied with depicting a traditional mode of life'.[55] Their poetry, instead, was often set against the backdrop of their industrialized capital city, which, O'Faoláin quoted one observer as stating, 'does not amount to saying that they are not Irish but merely that they are twentieth century industrialised Irish'.[56] Although *The Bell*'s editors chose pastoral poems by Hewitt and Rodgers for both the 1941 and 1942 Ulster Numbers, they nonetheless took up, in prose, the discussion of life in industrialized Belfast, and published articles which staked a claim to Belfast as an Irish city.[57] In the Ulster Number of 1942, the magazine's editors also included several articles discussing contemporary literature in Northern Ireland and suggesting books for Southern readers who wished to learn more about life in the North.[58] Commenting on the second Ulster Number, Peadar O'Donnell urged Belfast writers to 'speak for the whole of Ireland', and expressed the hope that Northern Irish literature would explore the complexity of the various characters in Northern society: 'The darkest Orangeman of them all needs to be revealed with sensitiveness and a sense of history'.[59]

The tone of *The Bell*'s Ulster Numbers of 1941 and 1942 is often conciliatory, even deferential, to Northern writers, especially to Northern Protestants. At the initial stages of *The Bell*'s discussion about Northern Ireland, writers in the magazine were careful not to question the legitimate identity of their counterparts across the border. O'Faoláin sounded a note of caution to his Southern compatriots:

> [O]ur fellow-Irishman in the North may not have precisely the same picture that we may have in the South about what constitutes 'a native culture.' And I sincerely trust that nobody will suggest that because a man is an Ulster Presbyterian, let us say, or even a Belfast Orangeman, he is not therefore a 'fellow-Irishman' with as much right as any Southern Catholic to speak on such matters.[60]

52 D.A. McLean, Bookseller, Belfast, and Derrick Mac Cord, Belfast, advertisements in *The Bell* 7:3 (December 1943), p. 276.   53 Michael Farrell, 'The Open Window, A Monthly Perambulation Conducted by Gulliver', *The Bell* 7:4 (January 1944), p. 371.   54 O'Faoláin, 'Ulster', p. 7.   55 Ibid.   56 Ibid., p. 8.   57 Thomas Carnduff, 'Belfast', *The Bell* 4:4 (July 1942); John Dowling, 'In Defence of Belfast', *The Bell* 4:5 (August 1942).   58 'The Best Books on Ulster', *The Bell* 4:4 (July 1942); P.S. O'Hegarty, 'About Ulster Novelists', *The Bell* 4:4 (July 1942); Denis Ireland, 'Books and Writers in North-East Ulster', *The Bell* 4:5 (August 1942).   59 Peadar O'Donnell, 'Belfast – Village or Capital?', *The Bell* 4:6 (September 1942), pp 391, 392.   60 O'Faoláin, 'Ulster', p. 11.

Northern Protestant contributors, however, made it clear that they considered themselves distinct and different from their Southern neighbours. One example of *The Bell's* attempt to engage Northern Protestants in discussion of their status and identity is the long article 'Conversation Piece' with an unnamed 'Ulster Protestant', who has since been identified as W.R. Rodgers.[61] In a lengthy dialogue with an unnamed questioner from the South, the Ulster Protestant explores the roots and manifestations of difference between Northern Protestants and Catholics, and explains the significance of religion in Northern society, a society which, he argues, still finds its basis in rural life, despite the increasing industrialization of Belfast. The editorial note preceding the 'Conversation' claims that 'It is one of the first attempts that has been made to put the case for Ulster from the intelligent, humanist point of view'.[62]

In *The Bell's* early articles by Ulster Protestants, the authors, though often unnamed, offer candid explanations for their opposition to a thirty-two-county government. Rodgers, as the unnamed Ulster Protestant of 'Conversation Piece', quite frankly expresses the attitude of fear on which opposition to a united Ireland is based:

> It is impossible to convince an Ulster Protestant farmer that, in the event of an all-Ireland government being formed independent of Westminster, his farm will not be taken away from him, and given to his Catholic neighbour. And, mark you, it is equally impossible to convince the Catholic neighbour that *he* will not be given the Protestant's farm.[63]

Similarly, in an article titled 'Speaking as an Orangeman', an author named only as 'One of Them' explains that the 'modern Orangeman' fears that in an all-Ireland government, the role of the Catholic Church would be greatly expanded, and offers the Censorship Board's power to ban books and films as an example of the kind of interference he would shun. Yet the author asserts that it is only through honest and open conversation that the two parts of the island of Ireland will come to mutual understanding: 'I say all this without rancour, but merely as a statement of facts which must be taken into consideration. And nothing except frank discussion can ever hope to resolve such differences'.[64]

The publication of the pamphlet *Orange Terror* as part of the 1943 *Capuchin Annual* marked a turning point in *The Bell's* approach to the question of partition. *Orange Terror*, which may have been published in response to the 1943 appointment of the staunchly Unionist Basil Brooke as Northern Ireland Prime

61 See Brown, *Northern voices: poets from Ulster* (New Jersey, 1975), p. 232.   62 Editorial note preceding 'Conversation Piece: An Ulster Protestant', *The Bell* 4:5 (August 1942).   63 'Conversation Piece', pp 313–14.   64 'Speaking as an Orangeman, by One of Them', *The Bell* 6:1 (April 1943), p. 26.

Minister, opens with the same type of documentary realism that characterized many articles in *The Bell*. Under the heading 'I Live There', the anonymous author, 'Ultach' ['Ulsterman'] describes his family's persecution during the 1920s, when his father, a moderately successful Catholic business owner with no involvement in politics, was first intimidated and then victimized by extortion to the point of near poverty. As 'Ultach' recalls, 'We cleared out with just enough to take us abroad – but not before one member of the family was shot, and died, and my father, his nerves shattered, began the slow death which lasted seven years before he was released from suffering'.[65] *Orange Terror* then widens its focus to include statistical evidence of anti-Catholic gerrymandering and Stormont-sanctioned injustices in the court system as well as in employment and education. Statistics on the 514 Catholic families evicted – most by violent mobs – during the 1935 'Belfast pogrom' demonstrate that violence against Catholics was widespread.[66] The aim of *Orange Terror*, its author stated, was to raise awareness, especially in England, of the 'totalitarian state' that had evolved in Northern Ireland, and to appeal for the intervention of the British government.[67] 'Ultach''s essay was followed by twenty pieces of commentary written by authors as diverse as Lady Yarrow, Maud Gonne MacBride, and the Catholic bishop of Down and Connor, all of whom supported 'Ultach''s argument to varying degrees and all of whom called for the ending of Partition.

In his 1945 book *Counties of contention*, Benedict Kiely devotes a substantial number of pages to discussion of *Orange Terror* and the subsequent Stormont debates over its claims of Catholic persecution.[68] The Northern Ireland Parliament voted to ban the pamphlet's distribution in Northern Ireland in early 1944.[69] An article in *The Bell* contributed by the anonymous 'Ultach Eile' ['Another Ulsterman'] sought to recast Protestant-Catholic conflicts in the North as a problem resulting from the competition for employment: 'The persecution of the Catholics in the Six Counties arises from the scarcity of jobs and the system of Orange foremen under a Government which derives its support from the conflict thus engendered'.[70] A second *Bell* article, by Associate Editor Harry Craig, reported on interviews with Northern Protestants which lent support to 'Ultach Eile''s position. But Craig also warned fellow Protestants in the South to be concerned about sectarian violence: 'this is done in the name of *Our* Religion'.[71]

65 'Ultach', *Orange terror: the partition of Ireland* (Dublin, 1943), p. 4. 66 Ibid., pp 22–3. 67 Ibid., p. 8. 68 Benedict Kiely, *Counties of contention* (Cork, 1945, 2004), pp 156–60 and 171–83. 69 *Orange terror* remains a provocative text; the University of Ulster's copy, for example, has been defaced so that the title reads 'Orangeism Forever', and Father John Senan, editor of the *Capuchin Annual*, is labelled a 'Taig Bastard'. 70 'Ultach Eile', '"Orange Terror": A Demurrer', *The Bell* 7:2 (November 1943), pp 139–40. 71 Harry Craig, 'A Protestant Visits Belfast', *The Bell* 7:3 (December 1943), p. 244.

With religion thus returned to the centre of the debate, the Protestant dean of Belfast, William Shaw Kerr, submitted his own 'Rebuttal' of *Orange Terror* to *The Bell*, and countered the original pamphlet's claims of Catholic persecution with accusations of his own. He ascribed the roots of sectarian violence to the actions of the clandestine IRA, and focused attention on the Belfast riots of 1920–2 as well as the riots of 1935, which began, the Dean claimed, with attacks on an Orange Order march on the Twelfth of July.[72] The Dean in turn was answered by the Committee of the Ulster Union Club, a misleadingly named group of Protestant Nationalists, whose President was the writer Denis Ireland. In their letter to *The Bell*, they stated that the degeneration of the original argument into a tit-for-tat listing of grievances on each side was 'just what we feared when the pamphlet *Orange Terror* was originally published'.[73]

Yet the naming of injustices suffered by Protestants, on both sides of the border, was an important factor in discussions about Unionists' fear of a united Ireland. In one letter to *The Bell*, the Protestant rector of Manorhamilton, Co. Leitrim, listed inequalities he had noticed in the South before pointing out that 'in a United Ireland more than one quarter of the population would be Protestants, a larger minority than many countries whose minorities give far more trouble'.[74] Professor W.B. Stanford's article 'Protestantism Since the Treaty', excerpted from his pamphlet *A Recognised Church*, alluded to the 'alarm, bewilderment and apathy' felt by many Southern Protestants since Irish independence and Partition, and 'the loss of influence' of the Church of Ireland in the political and public arena.[75] In response, O'Faoláin took Stanford to task for privileging his Protestant identity over his Irish identity: 'I strongly resent being compelled to think of myself as a Catholic, or of seeing other people compelled to think of themselves as Protestants, when we should all feel quite content to think of ourselves as Irishmen'.[76] O'Faoláin's impatience with the frustrations of Southern Protestants offers a marked contrast to his earlier welcoming of Stanford's contribution on 'The English Strain' for the Five Strains symposium.

Following *Orange Terror*'s exposition of Catholic persecution in the North, and the retaliatory accusations made by Protestant leaders on both sides of the border, the frank discussions of Northern Ireland sponsored by *The Bell* were gradually clouded by elements of the rancour that the editors had initially sought to avoid. In a 1945 editorial, O'Faoláin, who had so scrupulously avoided criticizing the political viewpoints of Northern Protestant contributors, now vehemently attacked de Valera's continued acceptance of Partition, describing

---

72 Dean of Belfast [William Shaw Kerr], '"Orange Terror": A Rebuttal', *The Bell* 7:5 (February 1944).   73 'Ulster: A Reply', *The Bell* 7:6 (March 1944), p. 475.   74 (Revd) D.C. O'Connell, letter in 'Public Opinion', *The Bell* 8:1 (April 1944), p. 76.   75 W. B. Stanford, 'Protestantism Since the Treaty', *The Bell* 8:3 (June 1944), p. 219.   76 O'Faoláin, 'Toryism in Trinity', *The Bell* 8:3 (June 1944), p. 186.

Irish political unity as 'purely and simply a natural human necessity'.[77] Whereas both parts of the island of Ireland had earlier been viewed in *The Bell* as legitimate cultural entities, O'Faoláin now wrote: 'Our Irishism is only half-Irish without the Northern strain, just as the North is only an artificial half-alive thing without the blood of Ireland running through its veins'.[78] A 1946 theatre review in *The Bell* makes reference to a fictional Ulster town as being located in 'Occupied Ireland', a heavily loaded remark in a journal that had previously treated Northern Protestants so delicately.[79] And in one of his first commentaries as editor, O'Donnell refers to current debates over the future of Northern Ireland, attacking, as did O'Faoláin, de Valera's failure to take decisive action against the Westminster government: 'The fact is that Britain is guilty, before history, of the partition of Ireland'.[80] Such unequivocal statements of blame stand in stark contrast to the earlier, conciliatory tone of *Bell* editorials on the North.

Ulster Protestants responded in kind. In answer to O'Donnell's editorial, William Douglas, Secretary of the Ulster Unionist Council, submitted an article titled 'Impossibility of Irish Union', in which he assigned the blame for Partition to the Free State government of 1920: 'The real partitioners were the agitators in Southern Ireland, who demanded complete separation from the United Kingdom and the establishment of a State owing no allegiance to His Majesty the King'.[81] Secretary Douglas took particular offence at Eire's assertion of neutrality in the Second World War, during 'the crisis of the Empire's fate', and wrote that public opinion in the North had hardened against the South because of it. Rather than offer an opening for frank discussion, he firmly closed the door on considerations of future political unity: 'I merely want the fact to stick out a mile that Ulster so far from wanting to join Eire will resist any such proposal to the death'.[82]

O'Donnell's editorial for December 1950, demonstrates the difference in tone between early and later *Bell* approaches to Northern Ireland. In contrast to the inclusive language used by O'Faoláin in his first editorial on Ulster, O'Donnell's choice of phrasing sets Northern Protestants at a distance, even as he expresses interest in understanding their point of view:

> The section of our people who intrigue the imagination most to-day are those who have shut themselves into a rebel statelet in North-east Ulster. They offer as sharp a challenge as the western seaboard in the days of Synge. What measure of reality is in the fears they parade? How

---

77 O'Faoláin, 'Eamon De Valera', *The Bell* 10:1 (April 1945), p. 7. 78 Ibid. 79 Roger McHugh, 'Dublin Theatre', *The Bell* 12:2 (May 1946), p. 162. 80 Peadar O'Donnell, 'Whose Bridgehead?', *The Bell* 13:5 (February 1947), p. 1. 81 W. Douglas, 'Impossibility of Irish Union', *The Bell* 14:1 (April 1947), p. 33. 82 Ibid., pp 39–40.

far are they one of those manifestations which arise when people do things of which they are vaguely ashamed?[83]

O'Donnell's editorial, titled 'A Welcome to a Contributor', welcomes the commentary of the Revd Frederick S. Leahy, a member of the Executive Committee of the National Union of Protestants, who had recently failed to obtain a meeting with Seán MacBride, the Minister for External Affairs. As such, *The Bell's* editorial decision to print Leahy's article on the 'Fears and Convictions of Ulster Protestants' may be read as an effort to maintain North-South dialogue and to protest against the mishandling of moderate Unionists by the Irish government.[84] Yet it is worth noting that O'Donnell introduces Leahy as an outsider in need of a formal welcome, not as a 'fellow-Irishman', as in O'Faoláin's earlier turn of phrase. Northern Protestants, in the excerpt quoted above, are named as 'they', not as a part of 'us', and it is 'they' who have shut themselves out of Ireland, a formulation that suggests their active participation in Partition, rather than their role, implied in earlier *Bell* articles and editorials, as victims of British imperialism and Irish inaction.

Southern Protestants, too, came under increasing criticism from *The Bell* in the later years of its publication. Though writers such as George Gilmore and the Revd C.M. Stack were permitted to use the magazine's pages to point out examples of discriminatory policies and practices against Protestants in the newly declared Irish Republic, Peadar O'Donnell countered by headlining his editorial pages with titles such as 'When a Minority Sulks' – a call for Protestant clergymen in the Republic to 'go before their co-religionists in North-East Ulster and say to them that whatever privileges they would put in jeopardy by coming into United Ireland the right of free exercise of their religion would not suffer'.[85] Though open discussion of Northern Protestant misgivings about Irish unity had marked *The Bell's* early articles on the subject of Partition, by the 1950s, a sense of frustration with perceived Protestant intransigence dominated the magazine's editorial stance on the issue.

Nonetheless, *The Bell* continued, throughout its final years, to examine the lives of Northern Protestants and to discuss the literary contributions of Northern Irish writers. One strand of continuing interest was the attempt to demystify the Orange Order, which was the subject of a number of articles in

83 Peadar O'Donnell, 'A Welcome to a Contributor', *The Bell* 16:3 (December 1950), p. 7. 84 Revd Frederick S. Leahy, 'Fears and Convictions of Ulster Protestants', *The Bell* 16:3 (December 1950). 85 Peadar O'Donnell, 'When a Minority Sulks', *The Bell* 16:4 (January 1951), p. 5; George Gilmore, 'The Republic and the Protestants', *The Bell* 16:5 (February 1951); Revd C.M. Stack, 'Unity, the Republic and the Church of Ireland', *The Bell* 16:4 (January 1951). Gilmore and Stack focus largely on the privileged position of the Roman Catholic Church and the lack of ceremonial courtesy paid to Protestant churches and clergy by the Irish government.

The Bell. In May 1943, Campbell Barton, an aging Orangeman, had contributed a documentary article on his experiences in the Orange Order, downplaying the significance of the Twelfth and stressing that 'in all my associations with the Orange Order, I never once heard the Pope mentioned. If ever you hear a rowdy shouting "To Hell with the Pope," you will be safe in laying a shade of odds that he is not an Orangeman'.[86] Similarly, an article on 'The Orange Society' by the socialist writer Thomas Carnduff, a former Worshipful Master of an Orange Lodge and a friend of Peadar O'Donnell, endeavoured to distance the Order from its stereotypical image as an organization of the Protestant upper and middle classes. Carnduff pointed out that the Orange Order 'began with the people', and that it had been manipulated by the land-owning classes to ensure continuing divisions between Protestant and Catholic workers, as in the Belfast dockers' strike of 1907.[87] Likewise, in an article based on a review of fifty years' worth of minutes from one Orange Lodge, Peadar O'Donnell concludes of Lodges in general that 'the men who enter them are pretty normal Irishmen' and that 'I know of no better way of making clear how unreal are the fears that divide us than thumbing thro' these pages of heavy-fisted writing where each chapter opens with "a prayer and a reading from Scripture"'.[88]

Northern writers, meanwhile, continued to make use of *The Bell* as a forum for the publication and discussion of their work, tacitly accepting, at least in cultural terms, the persistence of the border and its implications for the development of a Northern Irish literary community. In August 1944, one *Bell* reviewer had remarked that 'those [writers] in the North are faced with the difficult task of creating a tradition where none existed before',[89] suggesting that the political imposition of the border necessitated the creation of a new literary identity for Northern writers, distinct from their own literary history and from that of the rest of the island. This view went unchallenged in the pages of *The Bell* despite its apparent contradiction of the magazine's political opposition to Partition. In July 1952, after several years that marked an increase in artistic and literary production in the North, John Hewitt asked: 'Can it be [...] that Northern Ireland, as a community, is coming of age?'[90] Hewitt urged his fellow writers to avoid the perils of exile and of rarefication, which he defined as 'withdrawal from the community, from the day-to-day, from the topic of the time, into memories of childhood, nostalgia, the pastoral, the slightly fantastic, the rather obscure'.[91] When the International P.E.N. Congress took place in Dublin, *The Bell* commissioned Hewitt and Roy McFadden to write an eight-

---

86 Campbell Barton, 'An Arch Purple Past', *The Bell* 6:2 (May 1943), p. 131.   87 Thomas Carnduff, 'The Orange Society', *The Bell* 17:4 (July 1951), p. 26.   88 Peadar O'Donnell, 'The Orangeman', *The Bell* 19:1 (December 1953), p. 183.   89 Harrison, review of *Irish poems of to-day*, p. 452.   90 John Hewitt, 'Some Notes on Writing in Ulster', *The Bell* 18:4 (July 1952), p. 197.   91 Ibid., p. 201.

page summary of the event, which included a day trip to Belfast for Congress participants, experienced by the two Belfast poets with a mixture of pride and nervousness. Roy McFadden recalled: 'There we were, travelling in selfconscious solemnity to our own backdoors [...] wondering – with bristling northern inferiority – what they would make of the Black City'.[92] The excursion represented an acknowledgment of Belfast's arrival onto the international literary scene; it also marked the distance between Northern and Southern literary circles.

In many ways, *The Bell*'s handling of Northern Ireland can be read as a chronicle of the growing distance between the two parts of the island as the Civil War faded into memory and as the Second World War further divided Northern and Southern political realities. *The Bell*'s last mention of Northern Ireland came in early 1954, in an editorial by Peadar O'Donnell on the arrest of Tyrone republican Liam Kelly, who had made a highly incendiary speech against Partition, the Queen, and the British government, and who was elected a Member of Parliament while in prison.[93] In November 1955, Kelly's republican splinter group, Saor Uladh [Free Ulster] would attack the RUC barracks in Roslea, Co. Fermanagh, an event that foreshadowed the IRA's anti-Partition border campaign of 1956–62, itself a precursor to the Troubles that erupted in the late 1960s, which significantly altered any future considerations of the border and its impact on Irish identity. *The Bell*'s discussion of Northern Irish identity and literature took place in a period of relative peace in the region, and the openness with which Northern writers, Protestant and Catholic, addressed the issue of Partition stands both as a marker of the magazine's commitment to representation and as something of a historical anomaly. By the time that the widespread use of violence returned to the Northern conflict, *The Bell* had ceased publication. Nonetheless, its perseverance in representing the changing attitudes on both sides of the border offers a powerful example of its response to the transformation of modern Irish society, a theme which will be further explored in the next chapter.

92 John Hewitt and Roy McFadden, 'International PEN in Dublin: Impressions', *The Bell* 18:12 (Autumn 1953), p. 77.   93 Peadar O'Donnell, 'Up Stormont Way', *The Bell* 19:2 (January 1954).

CHAPTER FIVE

The Bell and transformations in Irish identity

A s Irish society emerged from its wartime isolation and joined the global post-war process of modernization, *The Bell* actively worked against what O'Faoláin had called the 'sense of contraction' in Irish life during the war years.[1] As we have seen, the magazine's project of expanding and redefining Irish identity had started well before the end of the Emergency era. As the war drew to a close, *The Bell's* editors continued to push the boundaries of Irish cultural and political thought, and to re-orient Irish identity in the light of newly defined external relations with Europe and America as well as new influences from within, such as the development of Irish radio broadcasting, a growing popular interest in the cinema, and the increasing urbanization of Irish society. Though *The Bell's* role as an agent of transformation diminished somewhat in the post-war period, the magazine remained true, in its later years, to its original mission of representation. Its editorials and essays often commented on changes in technology and media as well as on Ireland's increasingly active role in international affairs.

The Bell's response to the transformation of post-war Irish society takes in many elements of modernization, most notably globalization, technological advances and urbanization. This chapter begins with an exploration of the effects of wartime censorship on the magazine's attempts to discuss Ireland's position in the world during the Second World War. The declaration of neutrality itself played a significant role in the development of post-war Irish identity, as evidenced by *Bell* short stories and by excerpts from Denis Johnston's war diaries, both as they were published in *The Bell* and as they were later amended for inclusion in his fictionalized memoir *Nine rivers from Jordan*. During wartime and immediately afterward, *The Bell* published commentary on Ireland's position in the international arena, especially in relation to the newly formed British Commonwealth and to the United States' offer of aid under the Marshall Plan. Later, the magazine's contributors discussed the influence of technological advances, especially in the media, on Irish culture. Taken together, *The Bell's* representations of life in Ireland during the late 1940s and early 1950s address the continuing development of Irish identity as it came face to face with the modern era.

1 O'Faoláin, 'Silent Ireland', *The Bell* 6:6 (September 1943), p. 457.

WARTIME CENSORSHIP AND NEUTRALITY

Irish neutrality during the Second World War has frequently been interpreted as a sullen refusal to take part in the greatest human drama affecting Europe in the twentieth century. Clair Wills has summarized this perspective as presenting a negative view of the Irish experience of the war: 'One version of Ireland's wartime story is that it is all about absence – the absence of conflict, of supplies, of social dynamism, of contact with "the outside world"'.[2] Wills and others have since worked to reveal the more complicated cultural and social developments of the Emergency era, but to many observers at the time, the contrast between Irish and British political and cultural commentary during the war years was so stark as to suggest a wilful denial of reality on the part of the Irish press. In his 1944 review of British and Irish literary magazines, for example, Denys Val Baker praised *The Bell* and its editors, but remarked of the magazine that 'To our eyes, it seems somewhat unreal with its studious avoidance of war influences'.[3] Cyril Connolly, the editor of *Horizon*, published several editorials on the reactions of British writers and artists to the ongoing war;[4] O'Faoláin, on the other hand, rarely mentioned the conflict in the pages of *The Bell*.

It would not be until after German defeat that the reading public would learn the full extent of the censorship which had forced the Irish media into silence. Wills has documented the extremes of Irish film censorship, which went so far in the interests of preserving Irish neutrality as to cut the word 'war' itself from any film imported for Irish viewers. Newsreels produced in England and America were severely edited in order to avoid any implication of propaganda, which meant that references to 'our troops' or 'the enemy' were cut, and voiceovers such as 'Well done the RAF' were excised as well.[5] The cumulative effect of the edits was to amplify the dissonance between the Irish view of the war and that experienced by much of the rest of Europe:

> While cinema audiences in the rest of Europe watched coverage of battles, shattered towns and cities, refugees, prisoners, the shell-shocked and wounded (albeit from very different perspectives), the war was glossed over for Irish filmgoers, who were informed instead about horse racing, annual festivals, the work of the Irish army and the LDF [Local Defence Force], and the activities of the Pope.[6]

Newspapers and magazines were similarly censored. The Emergency Powers Order required print coverage to maintain a balance between Allied and Axis

2 Wills, *That neutral island*, p. 10.   3 Denys Val Baker, *Little reviews, 1914–43* (London, 1943), p. 44.   4 See, for example, 'Comment' by Cyril Connolly, *Horizon* 5:29 (May 1942).   5 Wills, *That neutral island*, pp 271–2.   6 Ibid., p. 273.

perspectives, and to avoid any statement of opinion or comment beyond the detached reporting of military advances and defeats.[7]

Along with other Irish publications, *The Bell* was under considerable restrictions to refrain from comment on the war. Donal Ó Drisceoil notes that after October 1940, all newspapers and periodicals were required to submit to the Controller of Censorship any material they proposed to publish that related directly or indirectly to the war.[8] The extreme censorship exercised under the Emergency Powers Order forbade any press coverage which was deemed 'prejudicial to international relations',[9] a ruling which, O'Faoláin later noted, differentiated Ireland from the other neutrals, who, with longer histories of political independence, were 'more accustomed to the uncomfortable position of small nations'.[10]

The results of Irish wartime censorship played out in ways that may be surprising to a reader of today. For example, although the November 1944 issue of *The Bell* promised that Dr A.J. Leventhal's article 'What It Means to Be a Jew' would appear as the fifth in the 'Credo' series,[11] it was silently replaced by the article 'What It Means to Be a Quaker', with no explanation given until June 1945, when the lifting of wartime censorship prompted the publication of Leventhal's article, along with the following editorial note: 'Readers will understand that the Censorship did not allow us to mention that it [the article] even existed'.[12] Under the censorship, the pre-publication text of 'What It Means to Be a Jew' had been cut from its original length of 3,300 words to just under 1,200 words – almost two-thirds of the article was deemed a threat to neutrality. Text that commented on 'a rising national movement which aimed to found a home for Jews in Palestine' was not censored, nor were mentions of German Jews. But all references to anti-Semitism, whether state-sponsored or personal, whether occurring in Dublin or Limerick or France, were cut, as were Leventhal's childhood recollections of reading the *Jewish Chronicle*, a London weekly publication which brought news of anti-Jewish pogroms in Russia and of the impassioned speeches of Theodor Herzl, the Austrian Zionist.

Far from being a political diatribe, Leventhal's article is highly personal, and it is not clear why the censor felt the need to cut large sections such as the description of street taunts sung by rival groups of Jewish and Christian boys in early twentieth-century Dublin. Perhaps it was feared that any accusation of anti-Semitism, at whatever level, would raise questions of anti-German bias. Indeed, in the midst of a section which is largely uncut, one phrase describing the Rabbi Aimé Pallière, 'whose death in a German concentration camp has just

7 Ibid., p. 274. 8 Donal Ó Drisceoil, *Censorship in Ireland, 1939–1945: neutrality, politics and society* (Cork, 1996), p. 118. 9 Rex Mac Gall, 'How Your Films Are Censored', *The Bell* 10:6 (September 1945), p. 499. 10 O'Faoláin, 'The Price of Peace', *The Bell* 10:4 (July 1945), p. 288. 11 Editorial note, *The Bell* 9:2 (November 1944), p. 162. 12 Editorial note, *The Bell* 10:3 (June 1945), p. 207.

been reported', is singularly excised. In 1944 it was still not allowable to name the existence of Nazi death camps in print. Andrée Sheehy Skeffington, the widow of Owen Sheehy Skeffington, who had preserved the censored version among his personal papers, noted that Emergency-era editors were 'not allowed to hint that censorship had been at work, either in a brief statement or by leaving blanks in the text'.[13] Faced with the censor's drastic reduction of Leventhal's original text, *The Bell*'s editors decided not to print the article at all until after the war.

The only other specific reference made by *The Bell* to wartime censorship was a comment made by Michael Farrell, writing as 'Gulliver', on a line from a letter he had received during the war, written by a soldier stationed in 'a desert in the Middle East' who 'says he has been reading Gulliver in "the shade provided by a tank"'.[14] In August 1945, after the war's end, Farrell explained to his readers that he had been forbidden even to mention the letter before the German surrender, and he took the opportunity to criticize the overly cautious stance taken by the Emergency-era censors:

> Our Censors must have decided that those sentences could constitute a danger to this State or an offence to warring States. But Gulliver's decision was, and is, that such an exercise of censorship was truly a danger, perhaps not to this State, but to this Nation, and an offence against the courtesies of intercourse in war or peace.[15]

Farrell believed that the excision of the war from Irish discourse was, in itself, harmful to national life. O'Faoláin echoed this opinion with the statement that Irish moral judgment and intellectual engagement had been 'starved' by the censorship of war coverage.[16] One can only assume, then, that the absence of further commentary during the war was not, as Baker had initially suggested, a display of studious avoidance, but the outcome of the editors' experience with the Irish government's extremely restrictive censorship under the Emergency Powers Order.

The editors of *The Bell* were painfully aware of accusations that the Irish were ignoring the war. In January 1944, O'Faoláin wrote in the first of his 'One World' editorials that 'If there are any charges which we resent more sharply than others to-day they are the charges of being ignorant or indifferent about the war: especially the latter'.[17] O'Faoláin quoted British and American journalists for *War Illustrated*, the *Daily Telegraph* and the *New York Times*, all of whom

13 Andrée D. Sheehy Skeffington, 'What the Censor did in 1944', in 'The Emergency', a supplement to the *Irish Times*, 8 May 1985, p. 4. 14 Michael Farrell, 'The Open Window: A Monthly Perambulation Conducted by Gulliver', *The Bell* 10:5 (August 1945), p. 461. 15 Ibid. 16 O'Faoláin, 'The Price of Peace', p. 288. 17 O'Faoláin, 'One World', *The Bell* 7:4 (January 1944), p. 281.

expressed shock and dismay at the Irish lack of involvement with the war, and he asked why the neutrality of Switzerland, Sweden and Spain was not challenged on similar grounds.[18] He pointed out that many Irish people received information from British and American radio, newspapers, and magazines, and that ignorance of the war was therefore out of the question. As for the lack of public comment, O'Faoláin wrote, succinctly, that in the interests of maintaining neutrality 'this country has had to sacrifice speech to peace'.[19]

Nonetheless, O'Faoláin recognized the need for some form of public discussion of international issues, despite the restrictions of wartime censorship, and to this end he initiated a series of outward-looking editorials under the title 'One World'. Though he did not explicitly express disagreement with the strictness of the censorship during the war, he did state, somewhat ominously: 'Our only internal problem is to be sure that this silence does not endanger thought'.[20] The 'One World' editorials stand as one example of *The Bell*'s attempts to counter the inward-looking impulse engendered by Irish neutrality and its accompanying censorship. As O'Faoláin asserted in his second 'One World' editorial:

> It is, indeed, One World. We are no different to any other peoples. Our problems are not unique. Our future is locked with the future of Europe. Or, to put it in another way – as we put it here some months ago – every problem of nationality is, in the end, a problem of civilisation.[21]

The series of ten 'One World' editorials, which began in January 1944, and ran intermittently until the end of O'Faoláin's editorship, in 1946, constitute an effort to re-direct and re-shape Irish conceptions of national identity in light of the new world order that was emerging towards the end of the war. Later 'One World' editorials carried two epigraphs which suggested O'Faoláin's view of *The Bell*'s activist role in the formation of Irish identity: 'God has placed us upon this great city like a hornet upon a noble horse to sting it and keep it awake', attributed to Socrates; and 'Du ciel de sa Providence infinie, Dieu a donné à chaque peuple une différente génie' ['From heaven, in his infinite Providence, God has given to each people a unique genius'], attributed to Corneille.[22]

The declaration of neutrality had represented, for Ireland, an assertion of its right to make decisions as an independent nation, regardless of British interests. Yet national sovereignty, which was integral to definitions of Irish identity in the decades after independence, represented a challenge to the importance

18 O'Faoláin, 'One World', *The Bell* 7:4 (January 1944), pp 281–2. 19 Ibid., p. 282. 20 O'Faoláin, 'One World', *The Bell* 7:4, p. 282. 21 O'Faoláin, 'One World', *The Bell* 7:5 (February 1944), p. 380. 22 Epigraphs to 'One World', *The Bell* 8:2 (May 1944), p. 93.

of international co-operation after the war, in the wake of the rise and fall of über-nationalist Germany. In one of his 'One World' editorials, O'Faoláin cited Lionel Curtis, an architect of the Commonwealth of Nations, as the author of the idea that 'there will be another world-war in our time if we do not make a beginning of the end of national sovereignty'.[23] Several of the 'One World' editorials discuss post-war plans for a British Commonwealth, a new League of Nations, and other proposals for international relations. O'Faoláin did not want independence to become synonymous with isolationism; as he had written earlier in the war, 'The test of a true national spirit is whether it is inclusive'.[24] Thus while he took the view that the declaration of neutrality had been integral to the young nation's assertion of its right to sovereignty, this need not imply that Ireland would continue to cut herself off from the world once the war was over.

Irish emphasis on national sovereignty inevitably highlighted tensions over Partition and the continued existence of the six-county 'statelet' of Northern Ireland.[25] Some seemed to hope that a new era of post-war co-operation between Ireland, Britain, and the nations of the world might put pressure on the British government to relinquish its claims to the North.[26] In his 'One World' editorials, O'Faoláin extended the practice of opening windows on the experiences of people in countries around the world which had started with the International Numbers of *The Bell*, beginning in 1943. But the editor's long discursions on the politics of foreign countries were not merely informational. After discussing such topics as the formation of Serbo-Croat Yugoslavia or the federation of French- and English-speaking Canada, O'Faoláin consistently returned to their implications for the island of Ireland. In each case, he urged his readers to look beyond Irish borders for reflections of problems similar to their own, and for potential solutions to the questions of Union and Partition:

> They are questions that, to live, must be given the broad view which does not try to pretend that they are purely local, domestic, or national questions, which realises and which admits that they are linked up inextricably, like the tangled problem of Canada, with the whole international question of the economic and political future of Europe and the World.[27]

In his 'One World' editorials, which he later described as a 'modest contribution against Isolationism and Little Irelandism', O'Faoláin attempted to re-

23 O'Faoláin, 'One World', *The Bell* 7:6, p. 467. 24 O'Faoláin, 'Ireland and the Modern World', *The Bell* 5:6 (March 1943), p. 427. 25 O'Donnell, 'A Welcome to a Contributor', p. 7. 26 See, for example, O'Faoláin, 'One World', *The Bell* 8:4 (July 1944). 27 O'Faoláin, 'One World', *The Bell* 8:4 (July 1944), p. 286.

orient Irish thought, and to promote a version of Irish identity which did not depend solely on political definitions of national sovereignty.[28]

With the end of the war came the end of the Emergency Powers Order and its restrictions on public comment, and *The Bell* was free to print accounts of wartime events as well as reflections on how the war had affected conceptions of Irish identity.[29] O'Faoláin conceded that many of his 'One World' editorials had been limited by the censorship's 'circumscription on all comment', admitting that 'nobody realised better how inadequate, indeterminate, over-generalised and merely allusive these articles have, perforce, had to be'.[30] From the end of the war until his resignation as Editor, O'Faoláin ceded his editorial space to other writers who commented on international developments. *The Bell* also referred to the war and its effects in numerous short stories, poems, and personal accounts, the most famous being Denis Johnston's war diaries, excerpts from which were serialized in the magazine in 1950–1.

The Bell's account of the Second World War reflects the same diversity of experience that had marked its exploration of Irish life from its inception. For many Irish men and women, the war years were marked by deprivation, both material and cultural. Shortages were faced by all sectors of the Irish population, as evidenced by recurrent advertisements from the Department of Agriculture exhorting *Bell* readers to grow their own vegetables in order to replace the loss of imports and ensure a varied diet.[31] At the lower end of the socioeconomic scale were the experiences depicted in *Bell* short stories published after the war: Seamus de Faoite's 'Pictures in a Pawnshop', for example, in which two friends, Jack and Joe Jack, decide to walk the twenty-one miles from their hometown to a football match in Tralee because of wartime restrictions on trains, petrol, and car journeys.[32] At the upper end of the class spectrum were the losses felt by readers of Michael Farrell's 'Gulliver' columns, who responded to his post-war call for memories of Europe, 'joyful things of the past which we hope to find still there, unscarred by war', with lists of cathedrals, art museums, and hotels they had visited and hoped to see again.[33] More poignant was the excerpt from Maura Laverty's novel *Lift up your gates,* in which Dublin children burrow in a dump for salvageable coal cinders to sell during wartime, in spite of their memories of one boy who was killed when the cinder pile collapsed.[34]

The difference between Northern and Southern experiences of the war comes to light most vividly in *The Bell's* short stories, though it is occasionally

28 O'Faoláin, 'All Things Considered – 1', *The Bell* 11:2 (November 1945), p. 649. 29 O'Drisceoil (p. 284) reports that wartime censorship was officially lifted on 11 May 1945. 30 O'Faoláin, 'All Things Considered – 1', p. 649. 31 See, for example, Department of Agriculture, advertisement in *The Bell* 7:6 (March 1944), p. 552. 32 Seamus de Faoite, 'Pictures in a Pawnshop', *The Bell* 19:2 (January 1954). 33 Michael Farrell, 'The Open Window, A Monthly Perambulation Conducted by Gulliver', *The Bell* 10:3 (June 1945), p. 273. 34 Maura Laverty, 'Work in Progress, No. 2, Lift Up Your Gates (Extract)', *The Bell* 11:4 (January 1946).

mentioned in documentary articles such as 'The Life of a Country Doctor', in which the doctor halts his conversation because of the drone of a bomber overhead, flying Northward, and offers the sound as a tacit explanation of his wish to stay in the rural South, away from the threat of attack.[35] In one of *The Bell*'s Ulster Numbers, there appears a short story about Holy Joe, a Belfast street preacher who is normally ridiculed by the local children but who hushes them by performing an impromptu prayer service in an air-raid shelter during the night of the Belfast blitz.[36] The setting contrasts sharply with Elizabeth Bowen's short story 'Sunday Afternoon', which appeared in *The Bell* two months later, and which depicts Henry Russel, a forty-three-year-old man, as he returns from bomb-scarred London to attend a tea party at his friend Mrs Vesey's Dublin villa. Having lost his flat and all its contents in a recent bombing, Henry's world view contrasts sharply with that of the other party guests, who still chat languorously as they lunch on cucumber sandwiches. Though he finds it hard to make them understand the reality of wartime London, he cautions Mrs Vesey's niece, who wants to live in London, that leaving Dublin society behind will occasion a loss of selfhood: 'You will have an identity number, but no identity'.[37] Henry's wistfulness for neutral Dublin, cosseted though it is, reflects an acknowledgment of the war as a watershed, both for its participants and for its observers.

One of the most remarkable pieces based on the Northern experience of the war is Mary Beckett's first *Bell* short story 'Theresa', the story of a young Irish woman who becomes pregnant with the child of a black American soldier.[38] The deployment of American troops to Northern Ireland in 1942 generated anxiety in the South, as many observers worried that the American presence would drag Eire into the war.[39] But for residents of Northern Ireland, interaction with American soldiers sometimes carried complicated personal consequences. In Beckett's 1951 story it is the parish curate who, speaking from the pulpit, encourages local girls to bring home any babies they might have left in the orphanage during the war, promising to publicly disgrace any parishioner who criticizes the unmarried mothers. Bolstered by the curate's words, Theresa collects her baby girl, Deirdre, and persuades Harry Mulholland, her one-time suitor, to marry her, hoping that having a husband will shield her and her daughter from her parents' scorn. Throughout Deirdre's childhood, however, Theresa frets over the difference between her dark skin and the pale complexions of the neighbouring children. Deirdre goes to school and makes her first Holy Communion with the rest of the children, despite Theresa's fears that the

35 Anonymous, 'The Life of a Country Doctor', p. 27.   36 Arnold Hill, 'The Fisher of Men', *The Bell* 4:5 (August 1942).   37 Elizabeth Bowen, 'Sunday Afternoon', *The Bell* 5:1 (October 1942), p. 27.   38 Mary Beckett, 'Theresa', *The Bell* 17:2 (May 1951).   39 See Wills, *That neutral island*, pp 230–5.

event will be an 'ordeal': 'She would be dressed in a white frock and veil that would make her blacker than ever and she would have to walk down the aisle facing a packed church'.[40] The parish's acceptance of Deirdre, in spite of her difference, shows Theresa how willingly they have expanded their definition of community membership, which may be read as one result of the North's increased interaction with the outside world during the war years. Yet in the story's final scene, Beckett hints at a difficult future for Deirdre once she grows into adulthood. As Theresa packs away the Communion dress, she reflects on Deirdre's life to come: '"Harry what's going to happen to her when she grows up? How's she going to get married? How's she going to get work? What in the name of God is she going to do?"'.[41] Though Beckett ends the story with Harry's reassurances, Theresa's questions about her daughter's future are left unresolved.

After the war, writers for *The Bell* continued to be concerned about outsiders' perceptions of Irish living conditions under neutrality. As 'The Bellman' wrote in 1947, 'I think the English and American journalists who've been to Ireland and written about us during the past ten years have a whole heap to be ashamed of'.[42] He noted that most visiting journalists had embellished their reports of Irish freedom from the extremes of the food and supply shortages that faced belligerent countries during the war years and afterward. Patrick Campbell, who also wrote as 'Quidnunc' for the *Irish Times*, noted the change in relations between Irish natives and post-war English tourists, who were beginning to arrive in large numbers 'for the food, and for the scenery, and for the sense of ease and independence which they say that only Ireland can now provide'.[43] Yet despite English criticism of Irish neutrality during wartime, Campbell reports that it was now the English themselves who studiously avoided the topic: 'They are here to have nothing but a good time, and seem at once bored and unhappy if the subject of politics arises'.[44] Moreover, he writes, 'Very few of them appear to have any idea of what our neutrality was about'.[45] The influx of English tourists also provoked a tendency, Campbell claims, to play the stage Irishman for English visitors; he reports with embarrassment that he and his friends had been known to punctuate their speech with 'begobs' and 'mushas' when telling stories to holiday makers.[46]

But there were other charges against Irish neutrality which *The Bell*'s editors found more objectionable. In two post-war editorials on 'This Myth of Irish Fascism', Peadar O'Donnell confronted the propensity of foreign journalists to view neutrality as 'hostility to Britain', and the Irish government, therefore, as 'a thoroughly Fascist administration'.[47] O'Donnell makes several references to

40 Beckett, 'Theresa', p. 37. 41 Ibid., p. 38. 42 The Bellman, 'Dublin Revisited', *The Bell* 15:2 (November 1947), p. 29. 43 Patrick Campbell, 'The English in Ireland', *The Bell* 13:3 (December 1946), p. 33. 44 Ibid. 45 Ibid., p. 31. 46 Ibid., p. 36. 47 O'Donnell, 'This Myth of Irish Fascism', *The Bell* 12:3 (June 1946), p. 185.

the number of Irish men and women who volunteered for the British armed forces, and notes that they were treated in a friendly manner by the public at large. In a later editorial he states that 'We do not need to defend our neutrality but merely to prove it'.[48] It seems clear that, two years after the war's end, allegations of sympathy for the Axis powers still rankled.

The Bell's publication of Denis Johnston's war diaries may have been an attempt to dispel accusations of Irish ignorance about the war. Four excerpts, which appeared in the magazine in late 1950 and early 1951, chronicle Johnston's experiences as a BBC radio correspondent in North Africa and Europe, including his visit to the Buchenwald death camp only two days after its liberation. In his diaries, Johnston records his frustration with military censorship and his inability to convey to his listeners 'how hopeless the situation is and how exhilaratingly human are the performers'.[49] He expresses his admiration for the ordinary soldiers that he meets, and states that much of Allied propaganda 'about the fighting man grimly concentrating on his cause, is just so much crap'.[50] Indeed, propaganda seems to have been a central concern for Johnston. Wills quotes Johnston's private diary as stating that while he was bound to present the Allied perspective in his broadcasts for the BBC, in his published journals he aimed to be 'truly neutral'.[51]

Wills writes of Johnston's *Nine rivers from Jordan* that it 'not only questions the possibility of an objective stance on the war. It also warns that a belief in the superior virtue of impartiality can blind people to the real issues at stake'.[52] But this is not the note struck by the diary excerpts published in *The Bell* in 1950–1. In the excerpt 'Buchenwald', written when Johnston arrived at the death camp, the grim reality of Nazi cruelty does indeed shatter his cherished neutrality:

> Worse for me is the fact that I have been made a fool of, in my thirst for fairness and international justice. All the reasonable and sensible things that Hitler has ever said – the virtue of Courage and Order, the justice of self-determination and unity, the fact that we went to war to preserve Danzig for the Poles, the evil of money power, the right of a great people to a place in the sun – all these things were just a cover-up for this![53]

Here the perceived positive aspects of Hitler's pre-war agenda are explicitly considered. But this paragraph was substantially revised for publication in *Nine rivers*

---

48 O'Donnell, 'Our Mythical Fascism Again', *The Bell* 15:1 (October 1947), p. 1.   49 Denis Johnston, 'Meet a Certain Dan Pienaar', *The Bell* 16:2 (November 1950), p. 17.   50 Ibid., pp 16–17.   51 Quoted in Wills, *That neutral island*, p. 405.   52 Ibid., p. 408. See also Terry Boyle, 'Denis Johnston: Neutrality and Buchenwald' in *Modern Irish writers and the wars* (Gerrards Cross, 1999).   53 Denis Johnston, 'Buchenwald', *The Bell* 16:6 (March 1951), p. 40.

from Jordan, where it appeared as a forceful closing statement on the immorality of neutrality:

> Worse for me is the fact that we have been made fools of. Appeals to reason were just a cover-up for this! Our good will has been used as a means to betray us; and that is as great a crime as the degradation of humanity, for it means that good will is a mistake – that destruction is our only means of preservation.
>
>   How did I ever doubt that there is not an Absolute in Good and Evil?[54]

In the *Bell* version of his diaries, Johnston gives considerable space to his description of the horrors of the camp, but he closes with a reflection on Buchenwald's potential use as an instrument of anti-Nazi propaganda, 'a justification for every crime that will be committed in return'[55] – a reflection that does not appear in *Nine rivers from Jordan. The Bell's* diary series ends not with a moral indictment of Irish neutrality, but with a lament for the impossibility of objectivity in the face of revelations about Nazi death camps. In *Nine rivers from Jordan,* on the other hand, Johnston implies that the brutality of the death camps justifies any brutality against those who built them: 'I have done my best to keep sane, but there is no answer to this, except bloody murder'.[56] This sentence does not appear in the excerpt 'Buchenwald' as it was printed in *The Bell.* Instead, Johnston's final lines for *The Bell* contain a foreboding prediction of the moral superiority to be claimed by Allied belligerents after the war, and the admission that 'they will have Buchenwald to prove them right'.[57]

EXTERNAL RELATIONS AND FOREIGN AFFAIRS

In its early years, *The Bell's* editors had stated their intention to keep their focus squarely on Irish life. However, as the war dragged on and the sense of isolation from the rest of the world grew deeper, the magazine's editors declared a break from their original policy and began to venture into the area of international affairs. Initially, the outward-looking impulse took the form of International Numbers, the first of which appeared in March 1943; O'Faoláin's concurrent series of 'One World' editorials first appeared in January 1944. Then, in April 1944, came an announcement: 'This month the feature ONE WORLD does

54 Denis Johnston, *Nine rivers from Jordan* (London, 1953), pp 396–7.   55 Johnston, 'Buchenwald', pp 40–1.   56 Johnston, *Nine rivers*, p. 397.   57 Johnston, 'Buchenwald', p. 41.

not appear, and will not whenever it seems necessary to comment at length on Home Affairs. Otherwise the Feature appears regularly'.[58] The statement that world affairs would henceforth take precedence in the editorial pages of the magazine, unless domestic affairs happened to merit comment, marked a significant shift in focus for *The Bell*. The prioritization of international developments also signals the beginnings of transformation in *The Bell*'s portrayal of Irish identity. In promoting the discussion of international affairs, an area of debate which the editors might initially have categorized as 'blatherskite',[59] the magazine suggested that the new Irish identity would be outward-looking, not isolationist, and that sovereign, independent Ireland would now define herself, in keeping with the vision of Robert Emmet, as an equal player among the nations of the world.

The first international controversy to arise in the pages of *The Bell* was the question of Ireland's membership in the British Commonwealth. O'Faoláin first raised the issue in his post-war editorial 'The Price of Peace', arguing that 'our relationship with Britain is now a dishonourable and a demoralising relationship. In 1920 we knew where we stood. In 1945 we don't know where we stand'.[60] In his characteristically expansive editorial style, O'Faoláin blamed Irish uncertainty on the government's 'shillyshallying, double-shuffling, leg-in-both-camps, can't-make-up-my-mind attitude of evasion' as to whether Ireland would continue as a member of the Commonwealth of Nations.[61] As the war drew to a close, the question of Ireland's political status took on ever greater significance. Alliances were rapidly being formed among world powers, and Ireland would soon be pressed to declare its position. In May 1944, *The Bell* published a long letter to the editor on the subject of 'Eire and the Commonwealth', in which the writer, whose name was signed as 'N.N.', argued that 'No small nation can ever again hope to exist as before the war, isolated and sovereign in its own territory'.[62] 'N.N.' implied that Irish membership in the Commonwealth was necessary for full participation in international affairs, and rejected the idea that Ireland should 'prefer isolation on the edge of a Europe from which we have deliberately cut ourselves off '.[63]

The letter provoked a flurry of responses from fellow readers over the next several months. The first, from Denis Ireland, disagreed with 'N.N.', arguing that Ireland could not remain a member of the Commonwealth as long as the British government persisted in its claims to Northern Ireland.[64] The entire discussion swiftly devolved into a debate over Partition and whether its abolition would be best achieved from within or without the Commonwealth of Nations.

58 Editorial note, *The Bell* 8:1 (April 1944), p. 64. 59 O'Faoláin, 'Answer to a Criticism', p. 6. 60 O'Faoláin, 'The Price of Peace', p. 289. 61 Ibid. 62 N.N., letter in 'Public Opinon', *The Bell* 8:2 (May 1944), pp 171–2. 63 Ibid., p. 173. 64 Denis Ireland, letter in 'Public Opinion', *The Bell* 8:3 (June 1944).

George Gilmore expressed hope that the world's post-war focus on 'Unity and co-operative effort in international politics' would benefit Irish aspirations for a 32-county independent state, stating that it was important not to retreat into isolationism 'when the world is moving our way'.[65] In a later letter, John Ireland compared the Irish case to Switzerland and Yugoslavia, and suggested increased post-war economic cooperation between the two parts of the island.[66] The emphasis on Partition as a central element in the debate over Ireland's status in global politics demonstrates the fact that even into the late 1940s, Irish foreign policy was still centred on relations with Britain, and that these relations were overshadowed by continuing debate over the permanent status of Northern Ireland.

It was exactly this relationship that O'Faoláin set out to question in his own contribution to the discussion of 'Eire and the Commonwealth'. In O'Faoláin's view, the 'Irish fixation' on Britain was harmful not just to the nation's political status, but to the entire definition of Irish identity: 'it is essential for the mental health of Ireland that we should as quickly as possible get to the stage where we do not give a damn about Britain'.[67] He repeated his call for the Irish government to clarify its position on membership in the Commonwealth, and stated that such a move was necessary for the development of Irish intellectual independence:

> If we do not bravely clarify our concept of our relations to the world – and we may as well make a beginning with the British Commonwealth, that being the most pressing part of it – we shall never expand the contours of life, expand our horizons, get room to breathe mentally.[68]

O'Faoláin did not advocate either for or against Irish membership in the Commonwealth; when one letter writer interpreted his position as promoting the continuation of membership, O'Faoláin replied that he wanted only for Ireland to 'make up our minds about it one way or the other'.[69] In his view, it would only be when Ireland stopped defining its identity with reference to Britain that the nation would be free to create a new sense of political independence, one that would redefine its relations with the rest of the world. Indeed, the debate over Ireland's political status would culminate in the passage of the Republic of Ireland Act in 1948, during *The Bell*'s suspension of publication, when Ireland definitively ceased to be a Dominion of the Crown.

Articles on international affairs took up an increasing amount of space in *The Bell* after the end of the war and the lifting of the Emergency-era censor-

65 George Gilmore, letter in 'Public Opinion', *The Bell* 8:3 (June 1944).   66 John Ireland, letter on 'Eire and the Commonwealth' in 'Public Opinion', *The Bell* 8:5 (August 1944).   67 O'Faoláin, 'One World', *The Bell* 8:6 (September 1944), p. 468.   68 O'Faoláin, 'One World', *The Bell* 8:6, pp 469–70.   69 O'Faoláin, editorial note, 'Public Opinion', *The Bell* 9:2 (November 1944), p. 167.

ship. In July 1946, there appeared the first of five 'Foreign Commentary' columns written by Owen Sheehy Skeffington, then a Trinity lecturer, who had written a similar column for *Ireland To-Day* beginning in 1936, and who had been suggested as a political analyst by Vivian Mercier in his 'Verdict on "The Bell"' in 1945.[70] For his first contribution Sheehy Skeffington assembled a series of short comments on international issues: the still unsigned peace treaty, the proposed United Nations Organization, the French Socialist government, German disarmament, western capitalism and workers' unrest in the United States.[71] The freedom with which Sheehy Skeffington attacked American and British capitalists who sold weapons and raw materials to Germany and Japan in the build-up to war is notable for its contrast with wartime commentaries which contained no such criticism of foreign powers: Sheehy Skeffington noted that the use of the atomic bomb was defended on the grounds that it shortened the war, and asked 'What should be done, then, with those who lengthened the war?'[72] Subsequent columns dealt with the history and failure of the League of Nations and with the contemporary French political and economic situation. And it was Sheehy Skeffington's 'Foreign Commentary' on the Jewish-Arab conflict in Palestine that sparked a confrontation in the pages of *The Bell* that eventually led to O'Faoláin's final resignation from the magazine's Editorial Board.

Sheehy Skeffington framed his discussion of Palestine in terms of the British mandate, granted by the League of Nations after the First World War, to oversee the region for a short period until self-government could be established. He compared the continued presence of the British government in Palestine to Irish disappointment over the 1920 Anglo-Irish Treaty, which many had once interpreted as promising a plebiscite on the future of Northern Ireland, and he equated Jewish resistance movements with pre-revolutionary Sinn Féin and the IRB.[73] O'Faoláin immediately took issue with Sheehy Skeffington's view of the situation. In a letter to the editor which marked how far O'Faoláin considered himself outside *The Bell*'s day-to-day operations, the former editor wrote: 'I beg leave to be extremely annoyed with your political expert, Mr Owen Sheehy Skeffington'.[74] Sheehy Skeffington's column on Palestine, O'Faoláin wrote, was 'marred by exaggeration, overstatement and downright inaccuracy', and his focus on Jewish resistance to British rule unfairly skewed his report against Palestinian Arabs.[75] Sheehy Skeffington responded with a vigorous defence of his original analysis, and accused O'Faoláin of distorting the argument.[76]

70 Ballin, *Irish periodical culture*, p. 68; Mercier, 'Verdict on "The Bell"', p. 163.   71 Owen Sheehy Skeffington, 'Foreign Commentary', *The Bell* 12:4 (July 1946).   72 Sheehy Skeffington, 'Foreign Commentary', *The Bell* 12:4, p. 344.   73 Sheehy Skeffington, 'Foreign Commentary', *The Bell* 13:1 (October 1946).   74 O'Faoláin, letter to the editor, *The Bell* 13:3 (December 1946), p. 62.   75 O'Faoláin, letter to the editor, *The Bell* 13:3, p. 62.   76 Owen Sheehy Skeffington, 'Foreign Commentary' *The Bell* 13:3 (December 1946).

In the following month's 'People and Books' section, O'Faoláin, then serving as Book Editor, published Elizabeth Monroe's bluntly anti-Semitic review of Arthur Koestler's *Thieves in the night*, a novel based on the founding of a Zionist kibbutz in Palestine. Monroe's review barely touches on the text of Koestler's novel, but instead criticizes the Jews as an 'elbowing, thrusting people', attributes their conflict with Palestinian Arabs to 'Jewish exclusiveness', and questions whether Irish society would be any more willing to accommodate these 'unwelcome neighbours' than were the Arabs themselves.[77] Not surprisingly, the review elicited several letters to the editor. *The Bell* published two: one from Sheehy Skeffington, and one from Gerald Y. Goldberg, a prominent member of the Jewish community in Cork, who noted that 'there have been Jews in Ireland for hundreds of years', and who accused Monroe of forgetting that 'the greatest "elbowing, thrusting people" in modern history have been and are the British'.[78] Sheehy Skeffington also took issue with Monroe's description of the Jewish race:

> It would be interesting to know whether she would similarly label, say, the English in New Zealand (or in Palestine for that matter), the Irish in America (or in Liverpool), the Scots in Ulster, the Dutch in South Africa, the white races in Asia, or the British who strove to 'elbow' the Irish to Hell or Connaught.[79]

In his published response, O'Faoláin defended Monroe, and accused both letter writers of stooping to personal attack on his reviewer. He rejected accusations of anti-Semitism on Monroe's part, and wrote that 'it is not a question of letting Jews into Eire or Palestine – in both of which countries they are heartily welcome. It is a question of their taking over the whole blessed place as a Jewish National State'.[80]

O'Faoláin continued to insist on questions of scale when Editor Peadar O'Donnell suggested, in an editorial prompted by Monroe's book review and the ensuing letters from Goldberg and Sheehy Skeffington, that the Jewish-Arab conflict in Palestine had direct parallels with Irish experiences in Belfast, the Gaeltacht and the Midlands. Most problematic for O'Faoláin was O'Donnell's hypothetical statement that Jews would be welcome to settle in rural Donegal: 'In my home townland a Jew could buy a small farm and come to live among

77 Elizabeth Monroe, review of *Thieves in the Night*, *The Bell* 13:4 (January 1947). 78 Gerald Y. Goldberg, letter in 'Public Opinion', *The Bell* 13:6 (March 1947), pp 63, 64. Goldberg, who became Lord Mayor of Cork in 1977, told the *Irish Times* in 1998 that he believed the Irish government's policy of refusing entry to Jewish refugees during the war, in the interest of maintaining neutrality, was partly responsible for the decline of Jewish communities in Ireland (Dick Hogan, 'Cork's Oldest Jew Reflects in Sadness on the Slow Death of a Local Community', *Irish Times* 17 February 1998, p. 2). 79 Owen Sheehy Skeffington, letter in 'Public Opinion', *The Bell* 13:6 (March 1947). 80 O'Faoláin, 'Books' Editor's Response', *The Bell* 13:6 (March 1947), p. 66.

us, and we should be neighbours to him'.[81] In a private letter to Hubert Butler, O'Faoláin wrote that 'The shocking and brutal dishonesty of such a statement revolts me'.[82] The following month, an editorial note announced his resignation as Book Editor.[83] In a final letter to the editor on the subject, O'Faoláin asked O'Donnell to consider whether his townland in Donegal would willingly accommodate a thousand Jews, or 100,000, with the prospect of millions more to come.[84] O'Donnell conceded that the Irish would riot, but pointed out that the question served to demonstrate the necessity of 'a new way of life' (a socialist way of life, he implied) for both Arabs and Jews in Palestine, so that racial conflict did not become a camouflage for economic injustice.[85]

Nearly every discussion of foreign affairs in *The Bell* eventually led to comparisons with the Irish relationship to Britain and the continuing debate over Partition. In 1952, five years after O'Faoláin and O'Donnell's debate over Palestine, there appeared in *The Bell* a short story by David Marcus entitled 'Ransom', set in 1920, in which Shamus, an IRA gunman, is ordered to kidnap Mordecai Cohen, a Jewish businessman, and to demand £500 for IRA coffers. Cohen gradually draws Shamus into conversation, however, by stating that he has no intention of handing over the money, and that he believes the battle for Irish independence is a futile, though noble cause. In disbelief, Shamus asks whether Cohen does not feel willing to fight for the Holy Land. Cohen warns him against adopting an inflexible idealism: 'Look how long your country has fought and where are you? No. You'll remain like us – a race with a home they once owned, but now it's a home they can only think about or write about – and pray for'.[86]

Despite his resignation as Book Editor and his privately expressed disgust at O'Donnell's 'concealed communism' in supporting Jewish settlement in Palestine,[87] O'Faoláin continued to use *The Bell* as a platform for expressing his views on political affairs, both foreign and domestic. With the announcement of the Marshall Plan and the American offer of eighteen million dollars in aid to Ireland, activists such as the trade unionist Louie Bennett were arguing that the Irish government should consider whether America wished, by offering aid, to secure Ireland's support for its future military campaigns. O'Faoláin coined the unwieldy term 'Autoantiamericanism' for what he saw as a reflexive Irish reaction against American aid, and launched a campaign in the pages of *The Bell* to expose the weaknesses in Bennett's line of reasoning. O'Faoláin, who as a young man had spent three years in America as the beneficiary of a Commonwealth Fellowship at Harvard, argued vehemently against anti-American prejudices, which he said were based on British influences as well as on cynicism, suspicion

81 O'Donnell, 'Palestine', *The Bell* 13:6 (March 1947), p. 2.   82 Harmon, *Sean O'Faoláin: a life*, p. 149.   83 Editorial note, *The Bell* 14:1 (April 1947), p. 75.   84 O'Faoláin, 'Palestine', *The Bell* 14:2 (May 1947), p. 2.   85 Ibid., p. 4.   86 David Marcus, 'Ransom', *The Bell* 18:6 (November 1952), p. 360.   87 Harmon, *Sean O'Faoláin: a life*, p. 148.

and misapplied patriotism.[88] He felt that the desire to maintain self-sufficiency must come to an end, and suggested that Irish neutrality in wartime must give way to engagement with world affairs in the post-war era: 'We are slipping into the attitude that our hands are too lily-white, our souls too pure, to touch the muck of the world'.[89] O'Faoláin himself embraced the American offer of financial aid, going so far as to script a propagandist film commissioned by the American government, *The promise of Barty O'Brien*, in 1951.[90] In language that recalled *The Bell's* original editorial mission, O'Faoláin accused his fellow Irishmen of 'snoring gently behind the Green Curtain that we have been rigging up for the last thirty years – Thought-proof, World-proof, Life-proof'.[91] In a marked departure from O'Faoláin's first *Bell* editorial, here 'Life' with a capital 'L' does not spring from within Irish society; instead, it has been relocated to an existence outside Ireland, and O'Faoláin now accuses his compatriots of shutting themselves off from both its stimulation and its challenges.

Louie Bennett did not take this accusation lying down. She responded, in the pages of *The Bell*, that she fully appreciated American contributions to human knowledge and human welfare, and did not reject Irish involvement with the outside world. She questioned American motives, however, as did other letter writers to *The Bell*, and speculated as to the return Washington would expect on its investment. Bennett insisted that the preservation of Irish identity depended on maintaining a healthy distance from American influence:

> Ireland, a small, agricultural country with age-old traditions and customs has a different contribution to make to life and must, therefore, receive with caution, and even suspicion, efforts from outside sources to lead her people on the road to civilisation.[92]

Thus she based her objection on the assertion of Irish cultural, political and economic independence.

Other letter writers based their support for Bennett's opposition to American aid on questions of American militarism and the potential Irish obligation to follow future Washington directives. D. Sevitt, described in *The Bell* as 'An Exile', argued that 'Marshall Aid is martial' and asserted that 'America wants to involve Ireland in her plans for conquering the world. She needs Ireland's ports and fields for naval and air bases'.[93] Sevitt closed by stating that 'It is therefore fitting that Louie Bennett, an Irish Trade Union leader, should warn the Irish

---

88 O'Faoláin, 'Autoantiamericanism', *The Bell* 16:6 (March 1951), p. 8.   89 Ibid., p. 18.   90 Bernadette Whelan, *Ireland and the Marshall Plan, 1947–57* (Dublin, 2000), p. 379.   91 O'Faoláin, 'Autoantiamericanism', p. 8.   92 Louie Bennett, letter in 'Autoantiamericanism: Four Comments', *The Bell* 17:2 (May 1951), pp 8–9.   93 D. Sevitt, letter in 'Autoantiamericanism: Four Comments', *The Bell* 17:2 (May 1951), p. 26.

people against America's real motives, against joining Wall Street's preparations for war and conquest'.[94] Brigid Lalor, identified only as 'A Housewife', concurred: 'I want peace, not war'.[95] And Hubert Butler, who by then had taken over O'Faoláin's former position as Book Section Editor, pointed out the difference between O'Faoláin's wartime editorials, which did not argue against neutrality, and his post-war, anti-isolationist stance.[96] O'Faoláin, in his response, summarily dismissed Sevitt's letter as 'a Communist viewpoint' and Lalor's as that of an 'isolationist Nationalist'.[97] He labelled Butler an individualist Liberal, and Bennett a humanitarian idealist. The entire debate, wrote O'Faoláin, could be boiled down to his personal viewpoint on the new world order as it emerged in the post-war era: 'In my heart I hate Communism. That is the beginning and end of it. Mr. Butler and Miss Bennett hate nobody, good souls, and the Editor [i.e., O'Donnell] has his own views too'.[98] In framing the debate over American aid in terms of the struggle between Communism and capitalism, however, O'Faoláin neglected to explore a struggle that was taking place closer to home: the growing tension between tradition and modernization.

MODERNIZATION AND NEW MEDIA INFLUENCES

After the end of wartime censorship, *The Bell*'s writers and editors wrestled with the increasing modernization of Irish culture under the influence of technological advances, especially in the field of communications. As the Irish government struggled to catch up with England and America in the production of native radio and cinema, *The Bell*'s pages chronicled developments in the new media and questioned their potential influence on Irish society. As early as in *The Bell*'s second issue, in November 1940, Flann O'Brien noted that 'The Irish brand of humanity, expansive and voluble, is hardening and contracting under the hammer-blows of international mammon, dealt through the radio, press and cinema.'[99] O'Brien observed that the younger generation of Dublin pub-goers wanted to imitate the drinking habits of actors such as William Powell, who played the detective Nick Charles in the *Thin Man* movies of the 1930s:

> Their cinema-going has taught them the great truth that William Powell does not walk up to a counter, bellow for a schooner or a scoop and ask Mick whether the brother is expected up for the match on Sunday.

94 Ibid., p. 28.   95 Brigid Lalor, letter in 'Autoantiamericanism: Four Comments', *The Bell* 17:2 (May 1951), p. 23.   96 Hubert Butler, letter in 'Autoantiamericanism: Four Comments', *The Bell* 17:2 (May 1951), p. 20.   97 O'Faoláin, 'Autoantiamericanism', *The Bell* 17:3 (June 1951), pp 57–8.   98 Ibid., p. 59.   99 Flann O'Brien, 'The Trade in Dublin', *The Bell* 1:2 (November 1940), p. 7.

> William is modern and drinks out of glasses with long stems in a cush-
> ioned corner with his doxy. His many imitators (what could be more
> flimsy than an imitation of a flat two-dimensional picture-house
> ghost?) have insisted on something similar, since they, too, have to go
> out with Myrna Loy.[1]

O'Brien's account treats the influx of foreign films with derision, but concedes
that their influence has changed the appearance of Dublin pubs, with some pub-
licans being less skilled than others in approximating the meaning of modernization:

> They think that it means just tubes – tubular chairs, repellent alike to
> eye and seat, tubular lighting, tubular effects in decoration. Those who
> have been to prison immediately recognise the lamentable simplicity of
> the decor and the severity of the furnishings.[2]

In his characteristically satiric style, O'Brien questions the trend towards modernization and its manifestation in the aesthetics of the Dublin pub trade. Yet
at the heart of the joke lies the question of Hollywood's influence over Irish
society, and the concern that traditional Irish identity not be lost in favour of
imitation.

Ernest Blythe, the former Minister of Finance, who was Director of the
Abbey Theatre in the 1940s, voiced this concern more seriously in his interview
with 'The Bellman' in October 1941. When asked what his priority would be if
he were Minister of Fine Arts, Blythe replied emphatically that if wartime considerations did not exist, he would invest in the development of an Irish film
industry in order to 'prevent the national individuality of the country being
destroyed' by the influence of Hollywood movies.[3] Blythe suggested that the cost
of establishing Irish film production would be £200,000, and, perhaps most significantly, stated that 'If there were no other way of getting the money I should
scrap the Diplomatic Service and reduce the Army'.[4] For the former Minister of
Finance to state that preserving national individuality through film production
was more important than diplomacy or defence spending indicates the enormous
influence of the new media on popular conceptions of Irish identity.

Later *Bell* contributors took up the idea of an Irish film industry, advocating for the marketing of Irish films in foreign countries as a way of offsetting
the high cost of production. In 1946, Rex Mac Gall, who was also the Film Critic
and Associate Editor of *Commentary* magazine, put forward a detailed proposal

1 O'Brien, 'The Trade in Dublin', pp 7–8.   2 Ibid., p. 8.   3 The Bellman, 'Meet Mr Blythe', *The Bell* 3:1 (October
1941), p. 56.   4 Ibid., p. 56.

for setting up an Irish film industry to employ Irish actors and technicians.[5]
Hilton Edwards, co-founder of the Gate Theatre, was spurred by the 1952 release
of *The quiet man* to write that it was necessary for a native film industry to counteract the image of 'stage Irishry' offered by Hollywood.[6] Edwards echoed *The
Bell's* original statement of policy in proposing that Irish films should represent
an authentic version of Irish identity: 'If it is necessary to perpetuate a kind of
fairy tale Ireland, which is neither accurate, beautiful, or more than uninten-
tionally funny, then let's pack the whole thing up.'[7] His theatre experience had
instilled in him the belief that Irish life could be written about, acted and pho-
tographed, and that there was a market for Irish films. Edwards noted, however,
that laboratory expenses represented one-third to one-half of film production
costs, and that as yet there were no laboratories for cinematic film development
in Ireland.[8] The nascent Irish Film Society ran regular advertisements in *The Bell*,
which included mention of its film school and production unit, as well as list-
ings of European films, such as *Lac aux Dames* and *Chapeyev*, to be shown at the
Classic Cinema in Terenure.[9] Liam O'Laoghaire, co-founder of the Irish Film
Society, chronicled its beginnings in a 1947 article, in which he described the first
Irish Summer School of Visual Education, which taught the basics of film-
making to teachers from all over the country in 1945.[10] But such efforts were, for
the time being, limited by the lack of financial support; the government-spon-
sored Ardmore Studios would not be built in Wicklow until 1958.[11]

Yet even in the absence of a native film industry, *The Bell's* editors were
unable to deny the thrall in which the cinema held Irish society. In April 1945,
the magazine introduced a new feature, film criticism, written by the American-
born Lucy Glazebrook, who was then married to Vivian Mercier. An editorial
note preceding Glazebrook's first column admitted that *The Bell* had resisted the
notion of film reviewing for its first five years of publication. Several reasons
were offered to explain the omission: first, the fact that, given the newness of
the medium, 'there are no standards and few traditions' to guide film criticism;
second, the technical difficulties of printing film reviews in a timely fashion;
and finally, the 'æsthetic difficulties' of incorporating film criticism into a 'periodical with a good opinion of itself' such as *The Bell*.[12] This last reason was a
direct jab at the cinema as being beneath the notice of a literary and cultural
journal. It is also noted, almost begrudgingly, that 'any periodical with a social
conscience has to acknowledge that after the Churchman, the Politician, the

---

5 Rex Mac Gall [pseudonym of Deasún Breathnach], 'Towards an Irish Film Industry', *The Bell* 12:3 (June 1946).   6
Hilton Edwards, 'An Irish Film Industry?', *The Bell* 18:8 (January 1953), p. 461.   7 Ibid., p. 462.   8 Ibid.   9 Irish Film
Society, advertising in *The Bell* 3:1 (October 1941).   10 Liam O'Laoghaire, 'The Film Society Movement', *The Bell*
15:3 (December 1947), p. 61.   11 Harvey O'Brien, 'The Identity of an Irish Cinema', 3rd ed., 2007.   12 Editorial
note preceding Lucy Glazebrook, 'A Tour of Films – I', *The Bell* 10:1 (April 1945), p. 42.

Industrialist, and the Farmer, the next greatest influence in Eire is Mr Sam Goldwyn and all his beautified brethren and sistren'.[13] Thus the inclusion of film criticism is cast as a necessary extension of the magazine's stated mission of representation; to continue to omit the cinema would be to ignore a significant influence on Irish life.

Glazebrook's initial attempts at film criticism attempted to categorize contemporary films by genre. In six monthly columns, she dissected genres such as crime films and musicals, examining their typical components and evaluating their artistic merits. The cerebral quality of these columns may represent Glazebrook's efforts to impose a high standard of criticism on what was essentially a form of mass media. She often interprets popular cinema in terms more fitting to literature or drama, as for example, when she devotes seven pages to the differentiations between mysteries, horror films and thrillers.[14] One particularly interesting column contains Glazebrook's commentary on the glut of war films screened in Ireland just after V-E Day and the lifting of wartime censorship.[15] But it was not until her later columns that she turned to reviewing films that were currently in the cinema, scoring movies on a three-star scale of her own invention:

> *** – Attempts something original and succeeds.
> ** – Does not attempt anything original, but succeeds.
> * – Attempts something original, but fails.[16]

This type of film criticism, however, was short-lived in *The Bell*. Glazebrook's second review of current films was accompanied by an editorial footnote asking 'Is there a place in *The Bell* for a monthly guide to Films?',[17] a question to which readers may have responded in the negative, for the following month, Glazebrook's review of Walt Disney's *Three Caballeros* was followed by a brief editorial statement: 'We are pausing for the present in our experiments in film-criticism. As our readers and circumstances advise we may be able to reconsider the whole of this important problem later.'[18] Indeed, a later attempt at film criticism, in 1948, saw Liam O'Laoghaire, who, besides being co-founder of the Irish Film Society, was a former film critic for *Ireland To-day* and former Gaelic Producer at the Abbey Theatre, bridging two genres of performance with a column entitled 'Theatre and Film', in which much space was devoted to his deprecation of the Dublin theatre scene, and as little as one paragraph given to a mention of current films.[19] O'Laoghaire's column ran for only two issues.

13 Ibid. 14 Glazebrook, 'A Tour of Films: II. – The Crime Film', *The Bell* 10:2 (May 1945). 15 Glazebrook, 'Ireland Sees the War', *The Bell* 10:5 (May 1945). 16 Glazebrook, 'The Films', *The Bell* 11:5 (February 1946), p. 997. 17 Editorial note appended to Glazebrook, 'The Films', *The Bell* 11:4 (January 1946), p. 908. 18 Editorial note following Glazebrook, 'The Films', *The Bell* 11:5 (February 1946), p. 998. 19 Liam O'Laoghaire, 'Theatre and Film',

The cinema was not the only aspect of modernization which *The Bell* approached with some ambivalence. The magazine's editors focused an equal amount of attention on the development of Irish radio and its implications for literary culture. In one early *Bell* article, Frank O'Connor reflected on the challenges of reading short stories for radio transmission and remarked that the new technology was 'the most important thing that had happened the art of literature since the invention of printing'.[20] The transformation from writer to oral story teller, O'Connor wrote, was 'in a sense a coarsening of the writer's trade' in that 'It turns him again into the rogue and vagabond he was in mediæval days, before printing helped him to break the yoke of the patron'.[21] O'Connor acknowledged that the demands of oral delivery changed the shape of stories he wrote for radio broadcast, but argued that the radio would restore the 'resources of the spoken word', and that through the new technology, writers and listeners would 'recapture the vivid speech and fantastic incident which are the joy of the mediæval romances'.[22] Others were less enthusiastic. O'Faoláin wrote despairingly of the influence of the radio on young short story writers:

> The Radio is affecting all modern short-story writers, and as I think very much for the worse. It induces a fake air of intimacy – simulated by the voice and assisted by a number of special tricks – which is destroying the true intimacy and compression of the printed tale, and fast developing the button-holing technique of the Club bore.[23]

O'Faoláin did not exempt himself from criticism, noting that his short story 'The Murderer', though it had been successfully broadcast several times on the BBC and included in the Faber - BBC book of best broadcast stories, 'is *not* a good story, and no story written for the Radio could be'.[24] O'Faoláin clearly believed that the new technology was a dangerous influence on traditional modes of writing. Readers of Michael Farrell's 'Gulliver' columns would likely have agreed. When one reader posed the question, 'Is broadcasting poetry destroying poetry?', Farrell was surprised to report of the responses that 'Every one of them emphatically gives the same answer – "Yes."'[25]

Despite concerns about the effects of new technology on traditional literary culture, *The Bell* made space for those who embraced the new media as a potential tool for the expression of national identity. In October 1944, an article by the English radio critic Frederick Laws titled 'What *Is* the BBC?' was fol-

The Bell 15:5 (February 1948) and 'Theatre and Films', *The Bell* 15:6 (March 1948). 20 Frank O'Connor, 'At the Microphone', *The Bell* 3:6 (March 1942), p. 415. 21 Ibid., pp 418–19. 22 O'Connor, 'At the Microphone', p. 419. 23 O'Faoláin, 'The Craft of the Short Story', *The Bell* 8:4 (July 1944), p. 312. 24 Ibid., p. 313. 25 Michael Farrell, 'The Open Window: A Monthly Perambulation Conducted by Gulliver', *The Bell* 9:5 (February 1945), p. 453.

lowed by four Irish commentaries, solicited by *The Bell*, as to whether Irish radio should adopt a similar structure of governance to that of its British counterpart. Laws described the original charter of the BBC and explained changes in its financing over its twenty years of existence, from its initial funding by the major wireless manufacturers to its dependence on listener licences and occasional government grants. He discussed the question of who controlled the BBC, and how control worked. Stating that it remained to be seen how the BBC would evolve in the post-war era, Laws nonetheless counselled his readers that 'whatever happens some sort of BBC is likely to survive. We have got to get used to it'.[26] The four Irish commentators on Laws' article acknowledged the differences between British and Irish radio, but all four stated the importance of developing the new technology as 'a means of national expression'.[27] Noel Hartnett, a Radio Eireann producer and broadcaster, argued that Irish radio need not try to imitate the BBC, 'but to work along our own distinctive lines on our own distinctive material'.[28] All four commentators agreed that Radio Eireann needed increased government investment, and greater independence from ministerial control. As James Kitchen, who had been the *Irish Independent* radio critic before the wartime paper shortage, wrote, 'a young and growing state like Eire stands in great need of a virile broadcasting service'.[29]

Yet the potentially detrimental impact of the radio on literary culture continued to attract commentary in the pages of *The Bell*. Harry S. Kennedy, radio critic for the *Irish Times*, wrote one article on how radio drama could be exploited in ways that stage and cinema could not, for example in the mobility of actors and scenes, and in the possibilities for historical and documentary drama; he also set out the handicaps of radio drama, which became confusing to listeners if too many characters, for example, or too many different accents were introduced.[30] Patrick Kavanagh prefaced the publication of one of his own radio scripts with the statement that much of what was fit for broadcast was nonetheless embarrassing in print; he singled out Dylan Thomas' *Under Milk Wood* as an example. Kavanagh, like Frank O'Connor, felt that print publication imposed on the writer a different set of strictures than radio broadcast, and wrote: 'I do not think that any Radio Eireann script, creative or otherwise, has met the challenge of print'.[31] *The Bell* printed several radio scripts in its final years, including work by Valentin Iremonger, H.A.L. Craig, and James Plunkett.[32] The issue of

26 Frederick Laws, 'What *Is* the BBC?', *The Bell* 9:1 (October 1944), p. 60. 27 James Kitchen, 'Comments' on Laws, 'What *Is* the BBC?', p. 63. 28 Noel Hartnett, 'Comments', p. 62. 29 Kitchen, 'Comments', p. 63. 30 Harry S. Kennedy, 'Writing for the Radio', *The Bell* 12:5 (August 1946). 31 Patrick Kavanagh, 'Return in Harvest: A Radio Script', *The Bell* 19:5 (April 1954), p. 29. 32 Valentin Iremonger, 'Wrap up my Green Jacket', *The Bell* 14:4 (July 1947); H.A.L. Craig, 'Blame not the Bard', *The Bell* 18:2 (May 1952); James Plunkett, 'Homecoming', *The Bell* 19:7 (June 1954).

broadcasting poetry via radio, meanwhile, became part of a larger debate over 'verse speaking', which was alternately deplored by Kavanagh, who deemed it 'a torture that no people however sinful deserve to have inflicted upon them',[33] and championed by Austin Clarke, who traced the origins of verse speaking to W.B. Yeats, and who described his own involvement in the Dublin Verse Speaking Society, which he had co-founded with Robert Farren, Talks Officer of Radio Eireann.[34] Clarke himself embraced the new medium of radio. Beginning in 1939, he broadcast weekly poetry readings for Radio Eireann, which continued in one form or another until well into the 1960s.[35]

URBANIZATION: THE SHORT STORIES OF JAMES PLUNKETT

For readers, *The Bell* opened windows on aspects of Irish life that were not always found in mainstream media representations: prison conditions, Dublin slums, and the struggles of small farmers, for example. Moreover, at a time when leading commentators on Irish society, such as Corkery and de Valera, were arguing for a return to an idealized way of life that pre-dated colonial influences, *The Bell* was consistent and explicit in advocating the construction of a complex and inclusive Irish identity: a version of Irishness that could accommodate the multiplicity of Irish historical heritages, as well as the diversity of contemporary experiences in a young nation in the midst of modernization. For an illustration of the differ-ence between *The Bell*'s inclusive approach to identity and an essentialist approach, we might return to the discussion of Corkery's famous use of the metaphorical 'quaking sod' to represent the fractured state of Irish consciousness in the early 1930s: 'It is not English, nor Irish, nor Anglo-Irish'.[36] What Corkery saw as an inherent weakness in the formation of Irish identity – a state of crisis that Erik-son might have labelled 'identity confusion'[37] – the editors and writers of *The Bell* embraced as an inherent richness. One can imagine the magazine's editors re-writ-ing Corkery's statement to say that Irish identity *is* English *and* Irish *and* Anglo-Irish, and Norman, and Roman, and Scottish besides – not to mention Jewish, and Quaker, and Catholic, and Unitarian, and Presbyterian.

Corkery's answer to the Irish identity crisis was to retreat into reverence for the three forces which, he wrote, had shaped 'the Irish national being': religion, nationalism and 'The Land'.[38] His choice of these three elements, however, was

33 Patrick Kavanagh, 'A Goat Tethered Outside the Bailey', *The Bell* 18:11 (Summer, 1953), p. 31.   34 Austin Clarke, 'Verse Speaking', *The Bell* 15:3 (December 1947).   35 RTÉ Archives, 'Irish Public Service Broadcasting – 1930s', www.rte.ie/laweb/brc/brc_1930s.html, accessed 7 October 2008.   36 Corkery, *Synge and Anglo-Irish literature*, p. 14.   37 See Erikson, *Identity: youth and crisis*, pp 142–50, for a discussion of identity confusion using the young George Bernard Shaw as a case study.   38 Corkery, *Synge and Anglo-Irish literature*, p. 19.

based more on their historical significance than on their actuality. Corkery justifies his emphasis on 'the Land' by noting that whereas only 6 per cent of the
English population worked the land, the figure in Ireland was a staggering 53 per
cent.[39] This, of course, ignores the 47 per cent of the Irish population who did
not live the life of the rural peasant. In fact, Irish migration from rural to urban
areas rose steadily throughout mid-twentieth century. In 1926, only 32 per cent
of the population lived in towns of more than 1,500 people; by 1951, that figure
had grown to 41 per cent.[40] Statistics from 1951 also indicate that about one-third
of the residents of County Dublin had been born outside the county, and that
the capital city's population had grown by over 100,000 since 1936, an increase of
more than 20 per cent, at a time when the total population of the twenty-six
counties was declining due to emigration and a low overall birth rate.[41]

Yet much of Irish fiction, including that published in *The Bell*, continued to
focus on rural life. John Hewitt, writing in *The Bell* in 1948, quoted a local pundit
who complained that most contemporary Irish short stories fell into one of two
categories: those told from a child's point of view ('Everything seen from knee-
level, with the microscopic vision of a child'); or those told from an old person's
point of view ('And they're always old people in the country who remember the
toad flax and the stains on the calendar').[42] Moreover, Hewitt's speaker pointed
out, such stories presented a view of reality that was often far removed from the
writer's own experience:

> The wee farm at the hill foot, the cabin by the moss side. Yet, mind you,
> the writers are, most of them, townsmen. Never the feeling of a wet
> day in Royal Avenue; the tram tickets stuck like leaves to the pavement:
> the raindark shoulders sheltering in shop doorways, and the green pyja-
> mas on the dummies in the window.[43]

Hewitt's list reveals his poetic eye for the gritty details of the Belfast city centre.
Most *Bell* short stories, however, fall into one of the two categories he describes,
and most remain fixated on the details of rural life, however authentic and various those details may be.

James Plunkett's short stories represent a break with the rural focus. Plunkett, a trade union official whose full name was James Plunkett Kelly, published
his first story in *The Bell* in November 1942, and contributed two others in 1943
and 1945, but the bulk of his writing for *The Bell* appears after the break in publication, with the short story 'Mercy' as his first post-war contribution, in February 1951. In August 1954, in lieu of its usual compilation of essays, poems, sto-

39 Ibid. 40 Brown, *Ireland*, p. 245. 41 Ibid., p. 200. 42 John Hewitt, 'The Laying on of Hands', *The Bell* 16:1 (April
1948), p. 29. 43 Ibid.

ries and book reviews, *The Bell* published *The eagles and the trumpets*, a collection of five short stories by Plunkett, which included 'Mercy' as well as another story that had been previously published in 1951, 'The Half-Crown'. Associate Editor Anthony Cronin explained in his preface to the collection that Plunkett's work had been chosen for the magazine's new venture into book publishing largely because of the author's focus on city life:

> First of all he is an urban writer, dealing with experience against a city background to which he still belongs – instead of, like so many other Irish writers, looking back to a rural or small-town setting which belongs already to their own past and is coloured by the nostalgia and sentiment which we feel for an abandoned and regretted childhood.[44]

Cronin criticized other short story writers for their attempts to recapture the nostalgia of country life, and speculated as to their motives: 'One feels in general in Irish fiction a sense of isolation from the complexities of urban living and of almost deliberate anaesthesia against the dragging pain of the city wage-earner'.[45] True to its original mission of representation, *The Bell* sought not to escape from the difficult realities of urban life, but rather to document the lives of city dwellers, and, especially through Plunkett's short stories, to explore their meaning. As Cronin wrote: 'The comparatively new Ireland of the age of anxiety is in more need of a mirror than its rural counterpart and is less often offered one'.[46]

Plunkett's stories for *The Bell* depict the encroaching tide of modernization and its discontents. In 'The Trusting and the Maimed', which appeared in December 1953, Joe Casey works as a clerk in a newly constructed Dublin office building: 'No views of distant mountains troubled the air-conditioned comfort of the Municipal Insurance Office, no windows allowed the sunlight to challenge the discretion of its artificial lighting'.[47] The separation between Casey's office and the outside world is mirrored in the clerks' separation from the moral judgment of the larger society and from the consequences of their recreational activities. In one scene Casey reflects on the lifelong monotony of his work as an insurance company clerk: 'A salary scale starting at three quid a week and rising by annual increments over twenty-one years to a max. of ten pounds. Sign the clock in at nine and sign it out at five. Three weeks' paid leave every year. That's being a clerk'.[48] In the absence of an extended family or village social structure, the clerks spend their time outside of work in one another's company, drinking, betting on horses, and flirting with women: 'Life was a succession of

44 Anthony Cronin, 'Preface', *The Bell* 19:9 (August 1954), p. 7.   45 Cronin, 'Preface', p. 7.   46 Ibid., p. 8.   47 James Plunkett, 'The Trusting and the Maimed', *The Bell* 19:1 (December 1953), p. 154.   48 Ibid., p. 162.

small deceits and subterfuges, snatched pleasures and social inconveniences. There was only one commandment which demanded absolute regard, the eleventh commandment – don't be caught'.[49] Casey's girlfriend Rita Kilshaw, however, has become pregnant, and the story's action centres on the consequences for her, for Casey, and for Casey's fellow clerk Bob Ellis, who attempts to help Rita arrange an abortion when Casey inexplicably disappears.

Although both Ellis and Rita believe that Casey has run away, Plunkett reveals that Casey has sought respite in a walk in the country, away from the city and away from the difficulties of Rita's situation, and that he has badly broken his leg and is lying helpless on the moors below the very mountains that loom in the distance outside his windowless office. Early in the story those mountains, which serve as a recurring image – they are visible from the office where Rita works as a typist, and from the windows of the boarding house where Casey lives – provide 'some measure of peace' to Casey's troubled mind, and his walk across the moors brings him 'a calm which had not been his for weeks'.[50] He begins to think about marrying Rita, and to work out the financial arrangements. But when his foot catches in a hole and the bone breaks through the skin, Casey finds that his journey into the countryside has left him even more isolated than before. Plunkett makes no mention of Casey's family, and neither his landlady nor his office colleagues know where to look for him, so he lies overnight on the moor. As a second day draws to a close, he reflects on the possibility that he will die within a few miles of the city's hospitals and their modern medical techniques:

> He was within eight miles of the city, within eight miles of hospitals, X-ray apparatus, ambulances, of blood plasma and surgical instruments and anaesthetics. You turned on a tap and you got water, you turned a knob for music, you touched a switch for light. Eight miles was nothing.[51]

The modern conveniences of city life are no help to Casey, alone and exposed, as he contemplates his fate. As the story ends, Casey lies shivering in the rain for a second night on the moor, Bob Ellis gives up searching the pubs for him, and Rita returns home from confession to tell her parents that she is pregnant. A message that Casey tried to send with a racing pigeon he discovered lying injured under the heather is reduced to pulp by the rain, and the pigeon itself, who, in the story's opening scene, lies 'yearning and quivering for the city', has been slated for euthanasia by its owner.[52] In an ending that Frank Ormsby has compared to Joyce's in 'The Dead',[53] the rain beats down on each of Plunkett's

49 Ibid., p. 159. 50 Ibid., p. 161. 51 Ibid., p. 166. 52 Ibid., p. 151. 53 Frank Ormsby, 'The Short Stories of James Plunkett', *The Honest Ulsterman* 20 (December 1969), p. 15.

characters, underscoring their individual isolation in the unforgiving landscape of urban society.

Isolation and frustration are recurring themes in Plunkett's short stories about urban life. In the title story from *The Bell's* collection *The eagles and the trumpets*, Sweeney, another office clerk, lends a colleague the money he had been saving for a weekend trip to the country, then spends the evening with his fellow clerks, in a succession of city pubs, instead of travelling to visit the small-town librarian he had met on a summer holiday. In Sweeney's opening scene, he, like Casey, reflects on the dull life in office work that stretches ahead of him:

> Put into the firm at nineteen years of age because it was a good, safe, comfortable job, with a pension scheme and adequate indemnity against absences due to ill-health, he realized now at twenty-six that there was no indemnity against boredom, no contributory scheme which would save his manhood from rotting silently inside him among the ledgers and the comptometer machines. From nine to five he decayed among the serried desks with their paper baskets and their telephones, and from five onwards there was the picture house, occasional women, and drink when there was money for it.[54]

As noted by critics such as Thomas MacIntyre, 'The Eagles and the Trumpets' owes much to T.S. Eliot, and not just its title, which is taken from Eliot's poem 'A Cooking Egg', on the disappointment of adult life when compared to childhood dreams of success.[55] The office clerks in Plunkett's story move through their days and nights with a sense of futility that is similar to J. Alfred Prufrock's, and they pursue their pleasures with the same joylessness as the 'young man carbuncular' in Part III of *The Waste Land*. We may also note that Sweeney is Eliot's name for the brutish character 'Apeneck Sweeney' who appears in the poems 'Sweeney Among the Nightingales' and 'Sweeney Erect'. By using the name, Plunkett places modern alienation into an Irish context, as Sweeney is also the name of the seventh-century Irish king immortalized in the narrative poem 'Buile Suibhne', which translates as 'Sweeney's Madness' but has been more recently anglicized by Seamus Heaney as 'Sweeney Astray'.[56] Either title makes a fitting description for the story of Plunkett's office clerk, who wanders the city with his colleagues in a drunken daze, and never reaches his intended destination.

As the evening wears on and Sweeney and his fellow clerks become more and more drunk, Plunkett provides scenes of the small-town librarian, waiting

---

54 Plunkett, 'The Eagles and the Trumpets', *The Bell* 19:9 (August 1954), p. 11.   55 Thomas MacIntyre, 'Some Notes on the Stories of James Plunkett', *Studies* 47 (Autumn, 1958), p. 325.   56 Seamus Heaney, *Sweeney Astray: a version from the Irish* (Derry, 1983).

for Sweeney to arrive and losing hope with each successive bus that pulls in from Dublin. She, too, is a victim of isolation, transplanted to a boring rural town in which she feels like a perpetual outsider, even after six years of residence. While waiting for Sweeney, she meets a commercial traveller, another character isolated by his work and by a lack of family connections, and she eventually agrees to have a drink with him in a hotel lounge that recalls Flann O'Brien's description of 'modern' Dublin pubs: 'There were tubular tables and chairs, a half moon of a bar with tube lighting which provided plenty of colour but not enough light'.[57] In these drab surroundings, the librarian, whom Plunkett never names, accepts the fact that Sweeney is not coming, and she and the commercial traveller end the evening together, hand in hand, under the same full moon that Sweeney sees as he leans over a wall and vomits into the Liffey.

When family life does appear in Plunkett's short stories, it does nothing to combat the sense of isolation, nor the spiritual poverty of his characters. In Plunkett's families, it is the financial needs of the dependents that often lead to outright material poverty. In 'The Half-Crown', for example, Plunkett takes the perspective of Michael Kavanagh, the unemployed adolescent son of a Dublin office clerk, a man whose situation may represent a projection of Sweeney's, or Casey's, two decades on. Money is short in the Kavanagh household; though Michael can remember a happier time, when he was the only child in the family, he now resents his parents for being unable to give him the half-crown he needs to spend the day in Bray with a girl he fancies.[58] In another story, 'Janey Mary', Plunkett depicts a young girl whose father has died, and whose mother keeps her out of school on the feast day of the Blessed Bread in order to send her begging at the priory of St Nicholas' church. Her mother rebukes her for 'gallivantin'' when she returns empty-handed: 'Are you after lookin' at all, yeh little trollop'.[59] When Janey Mary goes back to the bread queue, her bare feet are trampled by another beggar's hobnailed boots, and she is taken into the priory parlour, where the priest sees the print of the nails on her feet – a Christ-like manifestation of Janey Mary's martyrdom. In the lives of Plunkett's characters, religion is not much comfort in the face of isolation. In his story 'The Damned', for example, an altar boy who has witnessed his father's death when, drunk, he was accidentally beheaded on an electric train, asks a priest if his father is in hell, and receives only the answer that he must pray for his father's soul. As the story ends, however, he imagines his father's head rolling under the gates of hell, and wishes that he could follow.[60]

Similarly disturbing images appear in Plunkett's short stories 'Mercy' and 'Dublin Fusilier', both of which focus on First World War veterans as they strug-

57 Plunkett, 'The Eagles and the Trumpets', p. 25.   58 Plunkett, 'The Half-Crown', *The Bell* 17:3 (June 1951).   59 Plunkett, 'Janey Mary', *The Bell* 9:5 (February 1945), pp 415–22 at p. 419.   60 Plunkett, 'The Damned', *The Bell* 17:10 (January 1952).

gle to come to terms with their war memories, and to survive on the streets of Dublin in their old age. In 'Mercy', Frederick Toner, having just reached the age of seventy, learns that a war comrade has died, and recalls the day when, together, they murdered a Scottish Borderer in Belgium because he belonged to the unit responsible for the Bachelor's Walk massacre in Dublin in 1914. As Toner dutifully carries out his work as a night watchman near Christchurch Cathedral, he is visited by an apparition of the rotting corpse of his dead comrade, and has an apocalyptic vision of the Cathedral's collapse, which foreshadows his own collapse, due to a heart attack, at the end of the story.[61] In 'Dublin Fusilier', Marty Callaghan, another aging veteran, stumbles through the streets of Dublin in a state of prolonged shell shock, envisioning machine guns and grenade explosions at every turn. When Marty throws himself down onto the pavement outside Stephen's Green in response to an imagined attack, he strikes his head against stone steps, and the story ends as he is carried home to his married sister's house and put to bed.[62]

In all of Plunkett's stories, the urban landscape is more than a mere backdrop for his characters' lives. As his characters meander through the oldest parts of Dublin – Winetavern Street, Nicholas Street, and John's Lane all being part of the original mediaeval city – they struggle to maintain a sense of individual agency against what Cronin called, in his preface to *The eagles and the trumpets*, 'the complexities of urban living'. The economic realities of their lives dictate many of their actions, as, for example, when seventy-year-old Fred Toner hides his new pension from his cronies for fear they will want to drink his money away, or when young Michael Kavanagh steals a half-crown from a child in Stephen's Green while the old man minding her dozes on a park bench. Yet in seeking to preserve his own self-interest, each character only distances himself further from the few friends and family available to offer emotional support. In Plunkett's view of urban Irish life, self-preservation all too often leads to isolation and despair. Urbanization thus bookends *The Bell*'s record of transformations in Irish life in the mid-twentieth century, with Plunkett's portrayals of alienated city workers providing a distinct contrast to de Valera's idealized dream of athletic youths and happy maidens.

61 Plunkett, 'Mercy', *The Bell* 16:5 (February 1951). 62 Plunkett, 'Dublin Fusilier', *The Bell* 19:9 (August 1954).

Conclusion: the legacy of *The Bell*

Throughout the 1940s and into the 1950s, *The Bell* looked unflinchingly on the realities of contemporary Irish life, whether they corresponded with the official version of 'the ideal Ireland' or revealed its cruelties and inconsistencies.[1] As Irish society was transformed by the experience of World War II, by modernization and by urbanization, *The Bell* offered a forum for both the representation of new realities as well as considerations of how they would impact Irish identity. Beginning almost with the earliest issues of the magazine, O'Faoláin and his fellow editors encouraged readers to look for 'Elegance' in everyday Irish life, whether it be found in the design of súgán chairs, or Galway hats, or Dublin window displays.[2] Contributors were urged to write poetry and prose that focused on Irish subjects, using an Irish idiom. All of these efforts were undertaken in the name of 'cultivating our garden',[3] a parallel, perhaps, to Yeats' incantatory injunction:

> Irish poets learn your trade
> Sing whatever is well made [...].[4]

But while Yeats' 'Under Ben Bulben', in keeping with the goals of the Irish Literary Revival, urged Irish poets to 'Cast [their] mind on other days', and to sing of the peasants, gentlemen, and monks of 'seven heroic centuries', *The Bell*'s editors rejected such a fixation on the past, and repeatedly called for Irish writers to document and describe 'all the vigour of the life we live in the Here and Now'.[5] Fanon recognized the need felt by colonized intellectuals (such as Yeats) to 'defend the existence of their national culture' in order to prove that they, like the colonizers, were possessors of an ancient heritage.[6] But O'Faoláin warned that post-colonial 'liberation' would not be fully achieved 'until we have got rid of that Old Man of the Sea – our Glorious Past; and that equally tyrannical Old Man of the Sea – our Great Future'.[7]

While de Valera attempted to build a tariff wall to cut off foreign trade, and the Censorship intercepted books at the harbour in order to shut out for-

---

1 de Valera, 'Address by Mr de Valera, 17 March 1943'. 2 O'Faoláin, 'Answer to a Criticism', p. 5. 3 O'Faoláin, 'Signing Off', p. 1. 4 W.B. Yeats, 'Under Ben Bulben' in *The collected poems of W.B. Yeats*, ed. by Richard J. Finneran (New York, 1989), p. 327. 5 Ibid.; O'Faoláin, 'This Is Your Magazine', p. 6. 6 Fanon, *The wretched of the earth*, p. 168 7 O'Faoláin, '1916–1941: Tradition and Creation', p. 11.

eign influences, *The Bell* argued for the development of a home-grown literary and artistic culture that could help Ireland take its place among the nations of the world. In the beginning, this effort took the form of instructional articles such as 'The Belfry' for poetry and 'New Writers' for short fiction. In later years, the magazine promoted the idea of an Irish film industry which could honourably and artistically compete with the influx of movies from Hollywood studios. It is worth noting, however, that *The Bell* never suggested that foreign imports, be they films, literature, or ideas, be shunned in favour of native culture. On the contrary, beginning with its first International Number in 1943, and continuing with the series of 'One World' editorials and 'Foreign Commentary' features, the magazine made a point of introducing its readers to literary and artistic influences from outside Irish borders. Val Mulkerns remembers that 'it was through *The Bell* that we all learned about Mauriac, Kafka, any continental writer'.[8] During the war, the magazine published poems by Louis Aragon, a Communist and member of the French Resistance, once without translation, and twice with translation in Irish by Dr Pádraig de Brún, who later became president of University College Galway.[9] While *The Bell*'s editors hoped that Ireland would 'think originally, not [...] be imitative, [...] be self-proud and self-dependent', they nonetheless encouraged readers to be open to ideas and influences from outside Irish borders.[10]

Beginning as it did in the difficult years of the Emergency, the story of *The Bell* is a story of editorial doggedness and perseverance. Faced by paper shortages and a chronic lack of funds, editors Sean O'Faoláin and Peadar O'Donnell repeatedly called on commercial sponsors and readers alike to support their efforts to provide literary and critical commentary on the contemporary state of Irish life. They did so because they believed in the need for an independent literary magazine during a time when they recognized Ireland as standing, in O'Faoláin's words, 'at the beginning of its creative history, and at the end of its revolutionary history'.[11] This interstitial awareness of time, as Bhabha has called it, lends itself to the construction of a post-colonial identity that resists the restrictive categories of colonizer or colonized. Clair Wills has summarized *The Bell*'s achievement during the war years as the promotion of 'an Irish literary culture which spread beyond the confines of a small Dublin elite', looking westward and northward without engaging unduly in the language debate or in the politics of Partition.[12] In light of the magazine's fourteen-year span of activity,

8 Mulkerns, interview.   9 Louis Aragon, 'Zone Libre', *The Bell* 6:5 (August 1943); 'Richard II Quarante', *The Bell* 6:6 (September 1943), with translation, 'Riseárd a Dó Bhlian a Dachad' by Dr Pádraig de Brún; 'Trua Bhoithreoireacht na Fraince, 1940', by Dr Pádraig de Brún, translated from the French of Louis Aragon, *The Bell* 8:6 (September 1944).   10 O'Faoláin, 'Ireland and the Modern World', p. 423.   11 O'Faoláin, 'Standards and Taste', p. 6.   12 Wills, *That neutral island*, p. 298.

however, Wills' description may need to be expanded. When we revisit Luke Gibbons' appraisal of the transformation attempted by various forms of Irish popular media in the twentieth century, it becomes clear that *The Bell*, too, aimed at nothing less than 'transformation from within'.[13] In the early stages of the magazine's history, this meant the inclusion of as many voices as possible from across the spectrum of Irish social classes, language backgrounds, religious denominations, professional occupations, and geographical locations. By providing a forum for the experiences of a wide variety of Irish men and women, the magazine explicitly attempted to expand the narrow definitions of Irishness that were prevalent in popular cultural and political discourse.

As World War II drew to a close, *The Bell* portrayed the modernization of Irish society and the many changes taking place both within the country and in its external relations with neighbouring European countries and America. Although its role as an agent of transformation was diminishing, in its later years *The Bell* responded, in a clear-eyed, unsentimental manner, to the post-war transformation of Irish society and culture. The magazine's editors and contributors welcomed the end of wartime censorship and the renewed opportunity to comment on foreign and domestic affairs, especially the American initiative to rebuild Europe – which included funding for Ireland that not everyone wanted to accept – and the increasing discord between Jews and Arabs in Palestine. The American influence in cinema was also frequently discussed, as was the burgeoning field of Irish literary criticism, often written by American scholars: in the last few volumes of *The Bell*, there are a half-dozen comments such as Geoffrey Taylor's disparagement of 'transatlantic Doctors' who 'have spun their obliterating theses' on James Joyce and other Irish authors.[14] (The present writer hopes not to be counted in their number.) Yet *The Bell*'s role in post-war Ireland was not entirely reactive. Its decision to sponsor the publication of James Plunkett's first volume of short stories, for example, demonstrates its intentions both to support the publication of Irish writers and to continue challenging common perceptions of Irish identity.

Successors to *The Bell* took up its preoccupation with definitions of Irish identity to varying degrees. Both *Envoy* and *Rann*, two journals which appeared at the end of the 1940s, declared an almost exclusive focus on literary rather than political content. The initial editorial for *Envoy*'s second volume described the journal's purpose as twofold: to provide an outlet for Irish writers and intellectuals, and to introduce the best of international writing to Irish readers, serving as 'an ambassador in both directions'.[15] Its editor, John Ryan, declared defin-

13 Gibbons, *Transformations in Irish culture*, p. 3.   14 Geoffrey Taylor, review of *The poems of Arthur Hugh Clough*, ed. H.F. Lowry, A.L.P. Norrington, and F.L. Mulhauser, *The Bell* 18:4 (July 1952), p. 249.   15 John Ryan, 'Foreword', *Envoy* 2:1 (April 1950), p. 10.

itively that 'the magazine is interested in all that is vital and creative in the world of art, and is, in the most complete sense of the word, disinterested in either politics or polemics'.[16] Nonetheless, as Shovlin has documented, *Envoy*, like *The Bell*, inevitably confronted issues of production that were linked to Ireland's post-colonial status and its complicated relationship with Britain, particularly in the areas of publishing and distribution.[17] *Rann*, on the other hand, dedicated itself to publishing poetry by writers from the six counties of Northern Ireland. It was edited by poets Roy McFadden and Barbara Hunter. For the first three years of its five-year run, its quarterly issues averaged only eight pages in length. Each was prefaced by a brief editorial statement, and concluded with an instalment in the series 'Ancestral Voices', edited by John Hewitt, who chose poems by nineteenth-century Ulster poets for each issue, in an effort that was similar to that of Geoffrey Taylor for *The Bell*.[18] *Rann* was often a vehicle for Ulster regionalism, as evidenced by its first brief editorial, which declared: 'we are offering this region an opportunity to find its voice and to express itself in genuine accents in these pages'.[19] While *The Bell* had been concerned with the representation of life north and south of the border, *Rann* drew its focus still tighter, and attempted to articulate a poetic version of life in the six counties of Northern Ireland.

In contrast to *The Bell*, both *Envoy* and *Rann*, like *Ireland To-Day*, were short-lived. A critical assessment of *The Bell*'s comparative longevity might be drawn from the words of Valentin Iremonger, whose commentary, in *The Bell*, on the state of Irish writing in 1951 sheds light on the typically short lifespan of Irish literary magazines:

> Here in Ireland a magazine tends to stay and to get into a rut. It is a much healthier sign when magazines only last a year or two, die out and are replaced. [...] A writer's magazine cannot both pay its way and pay its contributors in Ireland. The history of *Envoy* in our day proves that.[20]

Indeed, *Envoy*, on whose staff Iremonger served as poetry editor, ran for only twenty months, from 1949 to 1951, before succumbing to financial pressures similar to those faced by *The Bell*.[21] *Rann* lasted only five years, from 1948 to 1953, when it folded in spite of Peadar O'Donnell's attempts to offer support. Roy McFadden later recalled that it was fatigue, not lack of funds, that forced *Rann*'s editors into retirement.[22] As founding editors of the journal *Threshold*, first published by the Lyric Players in Belfast in 1957, John Hewitt and Mary O'Malley alluded to the economic difficulty of sustaining publication when they stated,

16 Ibid.   17 Shovlin, *The Irish literary periodical*, pp 132–3.   18 Hewitt was then writing a Master's thesis on 'Ulster Poets 1800–1870' at Queen's University, Belfast. See Shovlin, *The Irish literary periodical*, p. 172.   19 Untitled editorial, *Rann* 1 (Summer, 1948), inside cover.   20 Iremonger, 'The Young Writer', p. 16.   21 See Shovlin, *The Irish literary periodical*, pp 131–55.   22 See Shovlin, *The Irish literary periodical*, pp 156–79, especially pp 178–9.

in their first issue: 'The history of Irish periodicals is not encouraging'.[23] Although it survived considerably longer than most of its predecessors, publishing annual issues over the course of thirty years, *Threshold* often took a noticeably hesitant stance with regard to political issues. One is struck, for example, by the passivity and vagueness of its first, brief, unsigned editorial, which declared that 'An attempt will be made to present constructively aspects of the Irish and world scene. [...] Our first issue is, therefore, launched with some hope and a certain temerity'.[24] Given the precarious publishing history of most Irish literary magazines, it seems remarkable that *The Bell* managed to survive as long as it did. The fact that its editors were still proposing new experiments in format and policy even in its final issues indicates their determination not to get into a rut, in Iremonger's phrase, as well as their loyalty to Irish readers and Irish writers, and their unflagging drive towards the re-examination and re-invention of their editorial mission of representation and transformation.

Perhaps the most prominent heir to the legacy of *The Bell* is the Field Day project, a literary and critical movement encompassing theatre, politics, and social commentary from 1980 to the present day. Field Day emerged from the joint efforts of Brian Friel and Stephen Rea, who were later joined by Seamus Deane, Seamus Heaney, Tom Paulin and David Hammond, to examine Irish political and cultural identities in order to address the Northern Irish political crisis, which had been marked by increasing violence throughout the late 1960s and 70s. In its commitment to re-examining Irish society through a cultural and literary lens, Field Day's efforts built upon the beginnings made by Deane, Derek Mahon, and fellow editors of *Atlantis*, a Dublin-based journal that was published annually between 1970 and 1974. In their inaugural editorial, the *Atlantis* editors stated their mission in terms that strongly resemble O'Faoláin's first attempt to delineate the policy of *The Bell*:

> *Atlantis* will be a literary magazine, but not exclusively so. Literature is about life (it is, in a sense, life); and the obsessive tedium of so much Irish writing is a reflection on the society which engenders it. We must, therefore, examine that society, and the larger human society of which it forms such a minute part, in an attentive and critical spirit.[25]

The editors went on to declare their intention to publish articles that would help readers to view Ireland in an international context. They promoted a stance that would not be parochial, nor strictly cosmopolitan, but would be shaped by the contributions of established and emerging writers from Ireland and overseas. While it survived for only six issues, *Atlantis* nonetheless preserved a literary and political perspective that engaged critically with questions of Irish

23 'Foreword', *Threshold* 1:1 (February 1957), p. 5.   24 Ibid.   25 'Editorial', *Atlantis* 1 (March 1970), p. 5.

identity, especially in light of the escalating unrest in Northern Ireland. In so doing, it laid the groundwork for the multi-disciplinary efforts of the Field Day Theatre Company and publishing project, of which Seamus Deane would later become an outspoken co-director.[26]

Like the editors of *The Bell*, the Field Day directors believed that literary, cultural and critical work was crucial to the task of exploring national identity, and, furthermore, that it was needed most in times of political and cultural instability. They stated in an early anthology of their work that they 'believed that Field Day could and should contribute to the solution of the present crisis by producing analyses of the established opinions, myths and stereotypes which had become both a symptom and a cause of the current situation'.[27] Like *The Bell*, Field Day aimed to recruit a wide range of writers, who could speak to the realities behind the myths and perceptions that made dialogue so difficult in the context of the Northern Irish Troubles. The company's directors announced their ambition to produce a comprehensive anthology of Irish writing which would

> have the aim of revealing and confirming the existence of a continuous tradition, contributed to by all groups, sects and parties, in which the possibility of a more generous and hospitable notion of Ireland's cultural achievements will emerge as the basis for a more ecumenical and eirenic approach to the deep and apparently implacable problems which confront the island today.[28]

Here literature is presented as a solution to a divided society, much as O'Faoláin and other *Bell* editors proposed to broaden the spectrum of Irishness through the representational work of writers from all parts of Irish society. When the *Field Day Anthology* was eventually published in 1991, discontent over its exclusion of women writers overshadowed discussion of its ambitious intent: to heal divisions in Irish society by allowing the voices of writers from all religious and social backgrounds to speak to readers from the pages of its three comprehensive volumes.

One might draw a metaphorical line from the young boy in Brian Friel's *Bell* short story 'The Child', who lies awake in his bedroom, listening to his parents argue downstairs, to the powerlessness that would later be felt by many in Northern Ireland as they watched and listened in horror to recurring news reports of atrocities on the streets of Derry and Belfast. In such a precarious political context, literature offers one channel for reasoned response. Friel's story, which took up just two pages of *The Bell* in July 1952, offers touches of modernity not always present in *Bell* stories: the headlights of a passing car illuminate the bedroom, and the cold linoleum floor chills the boy's bare feet as he crouches

26 See Ciarán Deane, 'Brian Friel's *Translations*: The Origins of a Cultural Experiment', *Field Day Review* 5 (2009).
27 'Preface', *Ireland's Field Day*, ed. by Field Day Theatre Company (London, 1985), p. vii.   28 Ibid., p. viii.

at the top of the stairs, praying for his parents to stop their nightly row.[29] Details such as these remind the reader that *The Bell's* reach extends into the contemporary era. In founding Field Day with Stephen Rea, Friel would take the first steps toward combating violence through creative expression; what began as a theatre company became a vanguard for cultural criticism and, later, a central part of the Irish literary establishment. Its influence continues to grow, with the 2002 publication of Volumes IV and V of the *Field Day Anthology*, which were devoted to women's writing, and the 2005 founding of the *Field Day Review*, an annual journal focused on literary and political culture. While the journal offered no founding statement or policy to mirror O'Faoláin's, a review of its contents suggests parallels to *The Bell's* continuing focus on opening windows onto Irish culture as well as influences from abroad.

Throughout the history of Irish literary periodicals, *The Bell* looms large. Shovlin, for example, echoes Brown's assessment of the magazine as having been 'crucial to maintaining high artistic standards' in mid-twentieth century Ireland.[30] Moreover, as this study has argued, *The Bell's* insistence upon opening windows on various aspects of Irish life kept the debate over Irish identity alive in the face of political and cultural pressures to revert to an essentialist version of what it meant to be Irish. The questions of identity explored by *The Bell* in the mid-twentieth century confront Ireland no less urgently in the twenty-first century, as Irish society encounters increasing globalization, and as an unprecedented wave of immigration in the wake of economic boom and bust invites discussion about the very definition of Irishness. Ruadhán Mac Cormaic's award-winning *Irish Times* series 'Changing Places: Migration and the Reinvention of Ireland', for example, concluded in June, 2007 with an article whose tagline was 'The new Irish: part of us? ...and if so, who are we now?'[31] There are several loaded terms in these two fragmented questions: 'new Irish', 'us', and 'now' stand out as links to the issues of identity explored by the editors and contributors of *The Bell* in the mid-twentieth century. In particular, the focus on 'now' recalls O'Faoláin's cautionary stance towards the 'twin mesmerists' of Ireland's heroic past and its imagined future.[32] For the editors of *The Bell*, identity was not a simple question with a simple answer, and Irishness was not defined at any time in terms that could be easily delineated. Rather, identity was, as Erikson posited, a process of becoming, one that required both writers and readers to live in the uncertainty and possibility of the present moment.

The Bell began publication, in 1940, with a commitment to representing 'Life' in the present tense, whether that meant life in a country house, or at the dog

29 Brian Friel, 'The Child', *The Bell* 18:4 (July 1952).   30 Shovlin, *The Irish literary periodical*, p. 195.   31 Ruadhán Mac Cormaic, 'We need vision of who we are and what we want to make migration work', *Irish Times* 27 June 2007, pp 1, 11.   32 O'Faoláin, '1916–1941: Tradition and Creation', p. 11.

tracks, or in an orphanage. It ended, in 1954, with an international issue that included Jean-Paul Sartre's speech to the World Peace Council in Berlin, against the use of the newly developed hydrogen bomb.[33] The magazine's fourteen-year print run provides a wealth of material that continues to be useful to both historians and literary scholars. It is hoped that this study of *The Bell*'s representation of Irish identity in the mid-twentieth century yields further possibilities for discussion and research. After all, to borrow a phrase from O'Faoláin's inaugural editorial, there are few more rewarding areas of literary and historical study 'than to stir ourselves to a vivid awareness of what we are doing, what we are becoming, what we are'.[34]

33 Jean-Paul Sartre, 'A Weapon against History', *The Bell* 19:11 (December 1954).   34 O'Faoláin, 'This Is Your Magazine', p. 8.

Appendix: chronology of *The Bell*

This Appendix provides a chronological list of *Bell* volumes and editors. *The Bell* was published monthly beginning in October 1940, and was organized into volumes of six issues each, so that Volume I ran from October 1940 through March 1941, Volume II from April 1941 through September 1941, etc., with new volumes beginning each year in October and April until the suspension of publication from April 1948 to November 1950.

The system of six-numbered volumes continued until the end of Vol. 16, in March 1951. Subsequent volumes were organized into twelve monthly issues each, beginning in April 1951, April 1952 and December 1953; Vol. 18 was irregularly numbered due to an experiment with quarterly publication, and, later, a printers' strike. Volume 19, the final volume of *The Bell*, was also irregularly numbered, because the magazine missed two months of publication, apparently with no notice given to readers. The final issue of *The Bell* was Vol. 19, No. 11, published in December 1954.

Volume 1, Nos. 1–6
(October 1940–March 1941)

Business Address: 43 Parkgate Street, Dublin
Editor: Sean O'Faoláin
Poetry Editor: Frank O'Connor
Editorial Board: Maurice Walsh, Roisin Walsh, Eamonn Martin, Peadar O'Donnell
(List first appears in *The Bell* 1:5, February 1941)

Volume 2, Nos. 1–6
(April 1941–September 1941)

Vol. 2, No. 4 (July 1941):
Poetry Editor listed as Geoffrey Taylor;
First Ulster Number

Vol. 2, No. 6 (September 1941):
Editorial Board no longer listed in masthead

Volume 3, Nos. 1–6
(October 1941–March 1942)

Vol. 3, No. 2 (November 1941):
New cover design (argyle pattern) by Raymond McGrath, B. Arch., A.R.I.B.A.
(See Editorial note, *The Bell* 3:2, p. 103)

Vol. 3, No. 4 (January 1942):
Announcement of price increase from one
shilling to one shilling and sixpence
(Editorial note, inside cover)

Volume 4, Nos. 1–6   Vol. 4, Nos. 4 and 5 (July and August 1942):
(April 1942–September 1942)   Second and Third Ulster Numbers

Volume 5, Nos. 1–6   Vol. 5, No. 1 (October 1942):
(October 1942–March 1943)   Special Short Story Number
                                Vol. 5, No. 3 (December 1942):
                                First *Bell* Christmas card, by Cuala Press,
                                announced
                                (See Editorial note, *The Bell* 5:3, p. 246)

                                Vol. 5, No. 6 (March 1943):
                                First International Number

Volume 6, Nos. 1–6   Vol. 6, No. 5 (August 1943):
(April 1943–September 1943)   Second International Number

Volume 7, Nos. 1-6
(October 1943–March 1944)

Volume 8, Nos. 1–6   Vol. 8, No. 5 (August 1944):
(April 1944–September 1944)   Special Summer Number

                                Vol. 8, No. 6 (September 1944):
                                Third International Number

Volume 9, Nos. 1–6
(October 1944–March 1945)

Volume 10, Nos. 1–6   Vol. 10, No. 4 (July 1945):
(April 1945–September 1945)   Fourth (and final) International Number

Volume 11, Nos. 1–6   Vol. 11, No. 2 (November 1945):
(October 1945–March 1946)   Announcement of Geoffrey Taylor's resigna-
                                tion as Poetry Editor and his replacement by
                                Louis MacNeice (Editorial note, p. 660)
                                Vol. 11, No. 5 (February 1946):
                                Business address changed to
                                2 Lower O'Connell Street

Volume 12, Nos. 1–6 (**April 1946–September 1946**)	Vol. 12, No. 1 (April 1946): O'Faoláin resigns as Editor, to be replaced by Peadar O'Donnell (O'Faoláin, 'Signing Off', and O'Donnell, 'Signing On', pp 1–7) Vol. 12, No. 2 (May 1946): O'Faoláin listed as Book Editor
Volume 13, Nos. 1–6 (**October 1946–March 1947**)	Vol. 13, No. 3 (December 1946): Note in masthead refers to *The Bell*'s British distributor, Pilot Press
Volume 14, Nos. 1–6 (**April 1947–September 1947**)	Vol. 14, No. 1 (April 1947): O'Faoláin resigns from Book Editor post, after conflict with O'Donnell over Elizabeth Monroe's review of Arthur Koestler's *Thieves in the night*
	Vol. 14, No. 2 (May 1947): Announcement of Earnán [Ernie] O'Malley's appointment as Book Editor (Editorial note, p. 68) Vol. 14, No. 3 (June 1947): MacNeice no longer listed as Poetry Editor
Volume 15, Nos. 1–6 (**October 1947–March 1948**)	
Volume 16, No. 1 (**April 1948**)	*The Bell* suspends publication as a result of British Board of Trade restrictions
Volume 16, Nos. 2–6 (**November 1950–March 1951**)	Vol. 16, No. 2 (November 1950): *The Bell* resumes publication, with a new cover, new subtitle ('A Magazine of Ireland To-Day'), and new business address (14 Lower O'Connell Street)
Volume 17, Nos. 1–12 (**April 1951–March 1952**)	Vol. 17, No. 2 (May 1951): Associate Editor listed as Anthony Cronin; Book Section Editor, Hubert Butler; Music Editor, John Beckett

Volume 18, Nos. 1–4
(April 1952–July 1952)

Printers' strike, August and September 1952

Volume 18, Nos. 5–10   Vol. 18, No. 5 (October 1952):
(October 1952–March 1953)   Associate Editor Val Mulkerns (though not
                                  listed in masthead); no other editors listed
                                  Vol. 18, No. 10 (March 1953):
                                  The Bell announces it will move to quarterly
                                  publication (O'Donnell, 'And Again,
                                  Publishing in Ireland', p. 583)

Volume 18, Nos. 11–12   Price increased from 1s. 6d.
(Summer, 1953–Autumn, 1953)   to one half-crown for two quarterly issues

Volume 19, Nos. 1–9   Vol. 19, No. 1 (December 1953):
(December 1953–August 1954)   *The Bell* resumes monthly publication
                                  (O'Donnell, 'An Announcement – A
                                  Request', p. 137); price listed as 2s.

                                  Vol. 19, No. 3 (February 1954):
                                  Associate Editor listed as Anthony Cronin;
                                  Books and Theatre Editor listed as Val
                                  Mulkerns

                                  Vol. 19, No. 8 (July 1954):
                                  Mulkerns no longer listed in masthead

                                  Vol. 19, No. 9 (August 1954):
                                  Publication of *The eagles and the trumpets*
                                  by James Plunkett as a special issue of *The
                                  Bell*; price listed as 2s. 6d.
                                  No issues for September or October 1954

Volume 19, Nos. 10–11   Price listed as 2s.
(November–December 1954)

                                  Vol. 19, No. 11 (December 1954):
                                  Final issue of *The Bell*

Bibliography

In researching the primary source material for this book, I have relied on printed copies of *The Bell*, letters from O'Faoláin to O'Connor, and interviews with the two surviving Associate Editors of the magazine, Anthony Cronin and Val Mulkerns. Rudi Holzapfel's *Index of contributors to* The Bell (Blackrock, Co. Dublin, 1970) has also been an invaluable research aid. The Howard Gotlieb Archival Research Center at Boston University holds a draft of O'Faoláin's first editorial as well as a list of projected costs for *The Bell's* first year among its collection of letters from O'Faoláin to Frank O'Connor. The Donegal County Library, Letterkenny, possesses one annotated dummy copy of *The Bell* 13:1 (October 1946) as part of its collection of *Bell* volumes which formerly belonged to Peadar O'Donnell. There are, sadly, few other extant materials relating to *The Bell*, such as galleys, dummy runs, receipts or letters to contributors. Thus I have attempted to chart the life of the magazine by way of the articles, editorial notes and letters to the editor contained within its pages.

PRIMARY SOURCES

Æ, 'The Two Traditions', quoted in *The Bell* 1:1 (October 1940), p. 53.

'Announcements', *The Bell* 5:3 (December 1943), p. 246.

'Announcements', *The Bell* 5:5 (February 1943), p. 342.

Anonymous, 'The Life of a Country Doctor', *The Bell* 3:1 (October 1941), pp 19–27.

Aragon, Louis, 'Richard II Quarante', *The Bell* 6:6 (September 1943), p. 519, with translation, 'Riseárd a Dó Bhlian a Dachad' b Dr. Pádraig de Brún, p. 520.

— 'Zone Libre', *The Bell* 6:5 (August 1943), p. 365.

Bailey, Revd Matthew, 'What It Means to be a Presbyterian: Credo – 1', *The Bell* 8:4 (July 1944), pp 298–305.

Barnardo's Furs, advertising in *The Bell* 5:5 (February 1943), p. inside cover page (unnumbered).

Barton, Campbell, 'An Arch Purple Past', *The Bell* 6:2 (May 1943), pp 128–33.

Bayes, Kenneth, 'A £750 Cottage', *The Bell* 4:3 (June 1942), pp 176–9.

Beckett, Mary, 'Theresa', *The Bell* 17:2 (May 1951), pp 29–39.

— 'The Young Writer', *The Bell* 17:7 (October 1951), pp 18–20.

Behan, Brendan, 'I Become a Borstal Boy', *The Bell* 4:3 (June 1942), pp 165–70.

'Bell' Questionnaire, *The Bell* 10:2 (May 1945), p. 187.

The Bellman, 'Dublin Revisited', *The Bell* 15:2 (November 1947), pp 27–34.

– 'Meet R.M. Smyllie', *The Bell* 3:3 (December 1941), pp 180–8.

– 'Meet Rutherford Mayne', *The Bell* 4:4 (July 1942), pp 241–8.

– 'Meet Dr Barton', *The Bell* 3:5 (February 1942), pp 392–400.

– 'Meet Dr Hayes: or The General Censor', *The Bell* 3:2 (November 1941), pp 106–14.

– 'Meet Maurice Walsh', *The Bell* 4:2 (May 1942), pp 131–8.

– 'Meet Mr Blythe', *The Bell* 3:1 (October 1941), pp 49–56.

– 'Meet Denis Guiney', *The Bell* 3:4 (January 1942), pp 268–76.

– 'Meet Christine Longford', *The Bell* 4:5 (August 1942), pp 357–64.

– 'Meet Mr Patrick Kavanagh', *The Bell* 16:1 (April 1948), pp 5–11.

Bennett, Louie, letter in 'Autoantiamericanism: Four comments', *The Bell* 17:2 (May 1951), pp 8–28.

'The Best Books on Ulster', *The Bell* 4:4 (July 1942), pp 249–53.

'The Best Selling Books', *The Bell* 6:1 (April 1943), p. 80.

'The Best Selling Books', *The Bell* 6:4 (July 1943), p. 298.

'The Best Selling Books', *The Bell* 9:3 (December 1944), p. 259.

Bowen, Elizabeth, 'The Big House', *The Bell* 1:1 (October 1940), pp 71–7.

– 'James Joyce', *The Bell* 1:6 (March 1941), pp 40–9.

– 'Sunday Afternoon', *The Bell* 5:1 (October 1942), pp 19–27.

Burke, Ulick, 'Her Only Son', *The Bell* 5:1 (October 1942), pp 42–8.

Butler, Hubert, letter in 'Autoantiamericanism: Four comments', *The Bell* 17:2 (May 1951), pp 8–28.

Campbell, Patrick, 'The English in Ireland', *The Bell* 13:3 (December 1946), pp 31–7.

Carnduff, Thomas, 'Belfast', *The Bell* 4:4 (July 1942), pp 269–73.

– 'The Orange Society', *The Bell* 17:4 (July 1951), pp 26–32.

Childers, Erskine H. 'The Village Planned', *The Bell* 3:5 (February 1942), pp 366–8.

Clarke, Austin, 'Verse Speaking', *The Bell* 15:3 (December 1947), pp 52–6.

Clarke, Desmond, 'Flight', *The Bell* 1:5 (February 1941), pp 56–60.

Collis, Robert, 'The Delicacy', *The Bell* 1:5 (February 1941), pp 33–9.

– 'A Description of Tuberculosis', *The Bell* 8:3 (June 1944), pp 209–18.

'Conversation Piece: An Ulster Protestant', *The Bell* 4:5 (August 1942), pp 305–14.

Craig, H.A.L., 'Blame Not the Bard', *The Bell* 18:2 (May 1952), pp 69–89.

– 'A Protestant Visits Belfast', *The Bell* 7:3 (December 1943), pp 236–44.

'Crime Reporter', 'Crime in Dublin (2)' *The Bell* 5:4 (January 1943), pp 301–7.

Cronin, Anthony, 'Nationalism and Freedom', *The Bell* 18:11 (Summer, 1953), pp 11–16.

– 'Preface', *The Bell* 19:9 (August 1954), pp 7–8.

– 'This Time, This Place', *The Bell* 19:8 (July 1954), pp 5–7.

Cross, Eric, 'The Tailor on the Cleverness of Animals', *The Bell* 1:6 (March 1941), pp 31–8.

D83222, 'I Did Penal Servitude: Journey to Fear (Part I)', *The Bell* 9:1 (October 1944), pp 41–50.

– 'There but for the Grace of God ...', *The Bell* 12:1 (April 1946), pp 23–32.

D.A. McLean, Bookseller, Belfast, advertising in *The Bell* 7:3 (December 1943), p. 276.

Dalton, Martin, 'Monday is Pawnday', *The Bell* 14:5 (August 1947), pp 46–50.

Day-Lewis, Cecil, 'Married Dialogue', *The Bell* 13:5 (February 1947), pp 4–6.

de Brún, Pádraig, Dr, 'Trua Bhoithreoireacht na Fraince, 1940', translated from the French of Louis Aragon, *The Bell* 8:6 (September 1944), pp 525–8.

de Faoite, Seamus, 'Pictures in a Pawnshop', *The Bell* 19:2 (January 1954), pp 16–28.

de Vere White, Terence, 'Wise Man's Son', *The Bell* 4:6 (September 1942), pp 404–12.

Dean of Belfast [William Shaw Kerr], '"Orange Terror": A Rebuttal', *The Bell* 7:5 (February 1944), pp 382–93.

Dearden, John, 'Love One Another', *The Bell* 18:5 (October 1952), pp 302–8.

Delany, Patrick, 'A Concert Hall for Dublin?', *The Bell* 17:10 (January 1952), pp 5–10.

Department of Agriculture, advertisement in *The Bell* 7:6 (March 1944), p. 552.

Derrick Mac Cord, Belfast, advertising in *The Bell* 7:3 (December 1943), p. 276.

Dillon, T.W.T., 'What It Means to Be a Catholic', *The Bell* 9:1 (October 1944), pp 12–19.

Disney, Violet, 'Why I am "Church of Ireland"', *The Bell* 8:5 (August 1944), pp 379–87.

Douglas, W., 'Impossibility of Irish Union', *The Bell* 14:1 (April 1947), pp 33–40.

Dowling, John, 'In Defence of Belfast', *The Bell* 4:5 (August 1942), pp 329–31.

Doyle, Lynn, 'The Burying of Maryanne Corbally', *The Bell* 2:4 (July 1941), pp 47–53.

Editorial note, *The Bell* 2:2 (May 1941), p. 64.

Editorial note, *The Bell* 2:2 (May 1941), p. 72.

Editorial note, *The Bell* 2:3 (June 1941), p. 60.

Editorial note, *The Bell* 3:4 (January 1942), p. 253.

Editorial note, *The Bell,* 5:5 (February 1943), p. 342.

Editorial note, *The Bell* 6:4 (July 1943), p. 337.

Editorial note, *The Bell* 6:5 (August 1943), pp 437–8.

Editorial note, *The Bell* 7:3 (December 1943), p. 200.

Editorial note, *The Bell* 7:3 (December 1943), p. 259.

Editorial note, *The Bell* 7:5 (February 1944), p. 441.

Editorial note, *The Bell* 7:6 (March 1944), p. 495.

Editorial note, *The Bell* 8:1 (April 1944), p. 64.

Editorial note, *The Bell* 8:1 (April 1944), p. 81.

Editorial note, *The Bell* 8:4 (July 1944), p. 317.

Editorial note, *The Bell* 8:5 (August 1944), p. 421.

Editorial note, *The Bell* 9:2 (November 1944), p. 162.

Editorial note, *The Bell* 10:3 (June 1945), p. 207.

Editorial note, *The Bell* 10:3 (June 1945), p. 220.

Editorial note, *The Bell* 13:5 (February 1947), p. 82.

Editorial note, *The Bell* 14:1 (April 1947), p. 75.

Editorial note, 'Time and Poetry', *The Bell* 6:2 (May 1943), pp 162–3.

Edwards, Hilton, 'An Irish Film Industry?', *The Bell* 18:8 (January 1953), pp 456–63.

Epigraphs to 'One World', *The Bell* 8:2 (May 1944), pp 93–103.

Fahy, Edward, 'The Boy Criminal', *The Bell* 1:3 (December 1940), pp 41–50.

– 'The Prisons', *The Bell* 1:2 (November 1940), pp 18–31.

Farrell, Michael, 'The Country Theatre', *The Bell* 1:1 (October 1940), pp 78–82.

– 'More Country Theatre', *The Bell* 1:4 (January 1941), pp 78–86.

– 'Drama at the Sligo Feis', *The Bell* 2:3 (June 1941), pp 88–95.

– 'Plays for the Country Theatre', *The Bell* 1:3 (December 1940), pp 58–64.

– 'Plays for the Country Theatre', *The Bell* 2:1 (April 1941), pp 78–84.

– 'More Melodrama', *The Bell* 2:2 (May 1941), pp 31–8.

– 'Opera for the Country Theatre', *The Bell* 2:6 (September 1941), pp 76–82.

– 'Drama at the Sligo Feis', *The Bell* 2:3 (June 1941), pp 88–95.
– 'A Course for Country Producers', *The Bell* 3:1 (October 1941), pp 71–6.
– 'The Country Theatre', *The Bell* 3:5 (February 1942), pp 386–91.
– 'The Open Window: A Monthly Perambulation Conducted by Gulliver', *The Bell* 6:1 (April 1943), pp 81–9.
– 'The Open Window, A Monthly Perambulation Conducted by Gulliver', *The Bell* 7:4 (January 1944), pp 363–71.
– 'The Open Window: A Monthly Perambulation Conducted by Gulliver', *The Bell* 9:5 (February 1945), pp 453–9.
– 'The Open Window: A Monthly Perambulation Conducted by Gulliver', *The Bell* 9:6 (March 1945), pp 543–51.
– 'The Open Window, A Monthly Perambulation Conducted by Gulliver', *The Bell* 10:3 (June 1945), pp 272–9.
– 'The Open Window, A Monthly Perambulation Conducted by Gulliver', *The Bell* 10:5 (August 1945), pp 457–63.
– 'The Open Window: A Monthly Perambulation Conducted by Gulliver', *The Bell* 12:1 (April 1946), pp 85–90.
– 'The Open Window: A Monthly Perambulation Conducted by Gulliver', *The Bell* 13:6 (March 1947), pp 80–8.
'The Five Strains: A Symposium', *The Bell* 2:6 (September 1941), pp 13–30.
Friel, Brian, 'The Child', *The Bell* 18:4 (July 1952), pp 232–3.
G.M., reviews of *An Sean-Saighdiuir agus Scéalta Eile* by Séamus Ó Néill and *An Aibidil a Rinne Cadmus* by 'Máire', *The Bell* 10:6 (August 1945), p. 456.
– review of *Fir Mhóra an t-Sean-Phobail* by Eibhlín Bean Uí Churraoin, *The Bell* 5:1 (October 1942), pp 69–70.
George Morrow & Son Ltd, Interior Decorators, advertising in *The Bell* 3:4 (January 1942), p. inside page (unnumbered).
Gilmore, George, letter in 'Public Opinion', *The Bell* 8:3 (June 1944), pp 256–8.
– 'The Republic and the Protestants', *The Bell* 16:5 (February 1951), pp 11–15.
Giltinan, D.J., 'Futures for Johnny and Jenny', *The Bell* 11:1 (October 1945), pp 609–16.
– 'Futures for Johnny and Jenny', *The Bell* 11:2 (November 1945), pp 697–702.
– 'Futures for Johnny and Jenny', *The Bell* 11:3 (December 1945), pp 787–94.
Glazebrook, Lucy, 'The Films', *The Bell* 11:4 (January 1946), pp 908–11.
– 'The Films', *The Bell* 11:5 (February 1946), pp 995–8.
– 'Ireland Sees the War', *The Bell* 10:5 (May 1945), pp 437–42.
– 'A Tour of Films – I', *The Bell* 10:1 (April 1945), pp 42–8.
– 'A Tour of Films: II. – The Crime Film', *The Bell* 10:2 (May 1945), pp 139–46.
Goldberg, Gerald Y., letter in 'Public Opinion', *The Bell* 13:6 (March 1947), pp 63–5.
Greacen, Robert, 'The Bird', *The Bell* 2:2 (May 1941), pp 84–5.
Gregory, Michael, 'Poem Atmospherical', *The Bell* 13:1 (October 1946), pp 6–7.
Harrison, Sam, review of *Irish Poems of Today*, *The Bell* 8:5 (August 1944), pp 451–2.
Hayes, Stephen, 'My Strange Story', *The Bell* 17:4 (July 1951), pp 11–16; *The Bell* 17:5 (August 1951), pp 42–51.
Heaney, W.J., 'I Fought T.B. – and Won', *The Bell* 8:4 (July 1944), pp 318–24.
Heron, Barney, 'Irish Cheese: A West of Ireland Venture', *The Bell* 6:2 (May 1943), pp 122–8.

Heseltine, Nigel, 'Welsh Writing To-Day', *The Bell* 6:5 (August 1943), pp 405–15.

Hewitt, John, 'Leaf', *The Bell* 1:4 (January 1941), p. 90.

– 'The Colony', *The Bell* 18:11 (Summer, 1953), pp 33–7.

– 'Hay', *The Bell* 2:4 (July 1941), p. 14.

– 'The Hired Lad's Farewell', *The Bell* 3:3 (December 1941), pp 177–9.

– 'The Laying on of Hands', *The Bell* 16:1 (April 1948), pp 27–36.

– Review of *New Poems, 1952: A P.E.N. Anthology*, *The Bell* 18:6 (November 1952), pp 383–4.

– 'Some Notes on Writing in Ulster', *The Bell* 18:4 (July 1952), pp 197–202.

Hewitt, John, and Roy McFadden, 'International P.E.N. in Dublin: Impressions', *The Bell* 18:12 (Autumn, 1953), pp 73–81.

Hicks, E. Savell, Rev. 'What It Means to Be a Unitarian', *The Bell* 9:2 (November 1944), pp 155–62.

Hill, Arnold, 'The Fisher of Men', *The Bell* 4:5 (August 1942), pp 332–7.

Hutchins, Patricia, 'Pattern Day', *The Bell* 3:2 (November 1941), pp 132–9.

'I Live in a Slum', *The Bell* 1:2 (November 1940), pp 46–8.

'I Was There', 'The Capture of the Magazine Fort', *The Bell* 17:12 (March 1952), pp 81–5.

Inside cover, *The Bell* 3:4 (January 1942).

Ireland, Denis, 'Books and Writers in North-East Ulster', *The Bell* 4:5 (August 1942), pp 317–22.

– Letter in 'Public Opinion', *The Bell* 8:3 (June 1944), pp 254–6.

Ireland, John, letter on 'Eire and the Commonwealth' in 'Public Opinion', *The Bell* 8:5 (August 1944), pp 443–7.

Iremonger, Valentin, 'Hector', *The Bell* 13:1 (October 1946), p. 6.

– 'Louis MacNeice: A First Study', *The Bell* 14:3 (June 1947), pp 67–79.

– 'Poets and Their Publishers', *The Bell* 14:1 (April 1947), pp 78–81.

– 'Wrap Up My Green Jacket', *The Bell* 14:4 (July 1947), pp 3–29.

Irish Film Society, advertising in *The Bell* 3:1 (October 1941), p. 92.

'Irish Publishers Answer Two Questions', *The Bell* 15:4 (January 1948), pp 3–11.

Johnston, Denis, 'Buchenwald', *The Bell* 16:6 (March 1951), pp 30–41.

– 'Meet a Certain Dan Pienaar', *The Bell* 16:2 (November 1950), pp 8–18.

Johnston, William J., 'Sanatorium Death', *The Bell* 18:4 (September 1952), pp 234–6.

Kavanagh, Patrick, 'A Goat Tethered Outside the Bailey', *The Bell* 18:11 (Summer, 1953), pp 27–33.

– 'Jim Larkin', *The Bell* 13:6 (March 1947), p. 4.

– 'Return in Harvest: A Radio Script', *The Bell* 19:5 (April 1954), pp 29–35.

– 'Tarry Flynn', *The Bell* 14:2 (May 1947), pp 5–29; *The Bell* 14:3 (June 1947), pp 14–38; *The Bell* 14:4 (July 1947), pp 53–76; *The Bell* 14:6 (September 1947), pp 7–34.

– 'Three Glimpses of Life', *The Bell* 8:4 (July 1944), pp 334–9.

Kennedy, Harry S., 'Writing for the Radio', *The Bell* 12:5 (August 1946), pp 409–14.

Lalor, Brigid, letter in 'Autoantiamericanism: Four comments', *The Bell* 17:2 (May 1951), pp 8–28.

Laverty, Maura, 'Maids *versus* Mistresses', *The Bell* 7:1 (October 1943), pp 18–24.

– 'Work in Progress, No. 2., Lift Up Your Gates (Extract)', *The Bell* 11:4 (January 1946), pp 848–6.

Lavin, Mary, 'A Story with a Pattern', *The Bell* 12:5 (August 1946), pp 383–408.

Laws, Frederick, 'What *Is* the BBC?', *The Bell* 9:1 (October 1944), pp 54–65.

Leahy, Frederick S., Rev., 'Fears and Convictions of Ulster Protestants', *The Bell* 16:3 (December 1950), pp 9–14.

Lennon, Michael J., 'The Murder of Doctor Cronin', *The Bell* 18:1 (April 1952), pp 20–9; *The Bell* 18:2 (May 1952), pp 92–102.

– Untitled poem, *The Bell* 17:3 (June 1951), p. 59.

Leventhal, A.J., 'What It Means to Be a Jew', *The Bell* 10:3 (December 1945), pp 207–16.

Lynch, Patrick K., 'William Thompson of Cork', *The Bell* 12:1 (April 1946), pp 34–46.

M.P.R.H., 'Illegitimate', *The Bell* 2:3 (June 1941), pp 78–87.

MacDonagh, John, 'Maguire', *The Bell* 1:3 (December 1940), p. 93.

Mac Gall, Rex [Deasún Breathnach], 'How Your Films Are Censored', *The Bell* 10:6 (September 1945), pp 493–501.

– 'Towards an Irish Film Industry', *The Bell* 12:3 (June 1946), pp 234–41.

MacLaverty, Michael, 'Moonshine', *The Bell* 2:4 (July 1941), pp 34–9.

MacMahon, Bryan, 'House Sinister', *The Bell* 1:2 (November 1940), pp 87–9.

MacNeice, Louis, 'Carol' and 'Hands and Eyes', *The Bell* 13:3 (December 1946), pp 1–3.

– 'Enfant Terrible' and 'Aubade for Infants', *The Bell* 11:5 (February 1946), pp 940–1.

Madge, Charles, 'Regents' Park, I' and 'Regents' Park, II', *The Bell* 12:6 (September 1946), pp 464–5.

'Máire', 'From the Gaelic of "Máire"', *The Bell* 13:5 (February 1947), pp 16–20.

– 'Seamus O Neill and his Book', *The Bell* 11:2 (November 1945), pp 725–6.

Mannin, Ethel, letter in 'Public Opinion', *The Bell* 6:5 (August 1943), pp 444–5.

Marcus, David, 'Ransom', *The Bell* 18:6 (November 1952), pp 348–63.

May, Sheila, 'Two Dublin Slums', *The Bell* 7:4 (January 1944), pp 351–6.

McCarthy, Earl, 'Eire's Surplus Doctors', *The Bell* 9:2 (November 1944), pp 119–28.

McFadden, Roy and Geoffrey Taylor, 'Poetry in Ireland: A Discussion', *The Bell* 6:4 (July 1943), pp 338–45.

McFadden, Roy, 'Plaint of the Working-Men' in *Irish Poems of To-day*, ed. Geoffrey Taylor (London: Secker and Warburg, 1944), p. 29.

– 'Public Opinion: Poetry in Ireland', *The Bell* 6:6 (August 1943), p. 534.

McGuinness, Norah, 'Make Your Windows Gay', *The Bell* 1:3 (December 1940), pp 65–9.

McHugh, Roger, 'Dublin Theatre', *The Bell* 12:2 (May 1946), pp 162–6.

McManus, Martin J., 'Publishing in Ireland', *The Bell* 15:4 (January 1948), pp 69–71.

'Memo for Businessmen', *The Bell* 2:4 (July 1941), p. 54.

Mercier, Vivian, 'The Fourth Estate: VI. – Verdict on "The Bell"', *The Bell* 10:2 (May 1945), pp 156–67.

'Mise Eire', *The Bell* 1:3 (December 1940), p. 27.

'Mise Eire', *The Bell* 2:1 (April 1941), p. 45.

'Mise Eire', *The Bell* 2:3 (June 1941), p. 47.

'Mise Eire', *The Bell* 5:2 (November 1942), p. 109.

'Mise Eire', *The Bell* 5:4 (January 1943), pp 299–300.

Monroe, Elizabeth, review of *Thieves in the Night*, *The Bell* 13:4 (January 1947), pp 71–5.

Morrow, H.L., 'The Battle of Scarva', *The Bell* 2:4 (July 1941), pp 15–21.

Murphy, Michael J., 'The Weakness', *The Bell* 16:6 (March 1951), pp 54–63.

Mytton-Davies, Cynric, 'Leave Trains – Victoria Station', *The Bell* 2:1 (April 1941), p. 87.

F.N., 'I Lost a Leg', *The Bell* 12:2 (May 1946), pp 140–7.

N.N., letter in 'Public Opinon', *The Bell* 8:2 (May 1944), pp 169–74.

'Naneen', 'Yacht Racing in Dublin Bay', *The Bell* 7:5 (February 1944), pp 417–24.

'Naosc a' Ghleanna', 'Twenty Years A-Withering', *The Bell* 3:5 (February 1942), pp 379–85.

'A National Teacher', 'Gaelic – With the Lid Off', *The Bell* 3:3 (December 1941), pp 221–8.

New Ireland Assurance Company, Ltd., advertising in *The Bell* 1:1 (October 1940), p. 1.

Nicholls, Nick, 'The Bone and the Flower', *The Bell* 7:2 (November 1943), pp 163–7.

'Night-Shift', 'A Day in the Life of a Dublin Mechanic', *The Bell* 5:3 (December 1942), pp 233–6.

O'Brien, Flann, 'The Trade in Dublin', *The Bell* 1:2 (November 1940), pp 6–15.

O'Brien, Kate, 'A Fit of Laughing', *The Bell* 18:4 (July 1952), pp 217–20.

O'Callaghan, Patrick, 'Irish in Schools', *The Bell* 14:1 (April 1947), pp 62–8.

O'Connell, D.C. (Rev.), pp letter in 'Public Opinion', *The Bell* 8:1 (April 1944), pp 75–6.

O'Connor, Frank, 'At the Microphone', *The Bell* 3:6 (March 1942), pp 415–19.

– 'The Belfry', *The Bell* 1:1 (October 1940), pp 92–4.

– 'The Belfry: To Any Would-Be Writer', *The Bell* 1:5 (February 1941), pp 86–8.

– 'The Belfry: A Matter of Idiom', *The Bell* 1:4 (January 1941), pp 88–9.

– 'The Belfry: On Not Being Provincial', *The Bell* 2:2 (May 1941), p. 83.

– 'The Belfry: A New Poet', *The Bell* 1:2 (November 1940), pp 86–9.

– 'The Belfry', *The Bell* 1:3 (December 1940), pp 92–3.

– 'The Belfry: From a Darkened World', *The Bell* 2:1 (April 1941), pp 85–6.

– 'James Joyce: A Post-Mortem', *The Bell* 5:5 (February 1943), pp 363–75.

O'Donnell, Donat [Conor Cruise O'Brien], 'An Epic of the Thirties: Graham Greene', *The Bell* 13:5 (February 1947), pp 7–16.

– 'Horizon', *The Bell* 11:6 (March 1946), pp 1030–8.

– 'The Pieties of Evelyn Waugh', *The Bell* 13:3 (December 1946), pp 38–49.

– 'A Rider to the Verdict', *The Bell* 10:2 (May 1945), pp 164–6.

– 'The Universe of François Mauriac: I. The Sun and the Rain', *The Bell* 14:5 (August 1947), pp 9–19.

– 'The Universe of François Mauriac: II. Women and Boys', *The Bell* 14:6 (September 1947), pp 45–55.

– 'The Universe of François Mauriac', *The Bell* 15:2 (November 1947), pp 47–59.

O'Donnell, Frank Hugh, advertising in *The Bell* 1:1 (October 1940), p. 4.

O'Donnell, Peadar, 'And Again, Publishing in Ireland', *The Bell* 18:10 (March 1953), pp 581–3.

– 'At the Sign of the Donkey Cart', *The Bell* 12:2 (May 1946), pp 93–6.

– 'Belfast – Village or Capital?', *The Bell* 4:6 (September 1942), pp 390–4.

– '*The Bell* Suspends Publication', *The Bell* 16:1 (April 1948), pp 1–4.

– 'Call the Exiles Home', *The Bell* 9:5 (February 1945), pp 382–6.

– 'Changing the Content', *The Bell* 19:4 (March 1954), p. 5.

– 'Exiles', *The Bell* 13:5 (February 1947), pp 3–4.

– 'Facts and Fairies', *The Bell* 13:1 (October 1946), pp 1–5.

– 'Grand-Children of the Insurrection', *The Bell* 12:5 (August 1946), pp 369–72.

– 'The *Irish Press* and O'Faoláin', *The Bell* 18:11 (Summer, 1953), pp 5–7.

– 'Liberty Ltd.', *The Bell* 12:4 (July 1946), pp 277–80.

– 'Migration is a Way of Keeping a Grip', *The Bell* 3:2 (November 1941), pp 115–19.

– 'The Orangeman', *The Bell* 19:1 (December 1953), pp 178–83.

– 'Our Mythical Fascism Again', *The Bell* 15:1 (October 1947), pp 1–4.

– 'Palestine', *The Bell* 13:6 (March 1947), pp 1–3.

– 'A Recognisable Gait of Going', *The Bell* 16:2 (November 1950), pp 5–7.

– 'Signing On', *The Bell* 12:1 (April 1946), pp 5–7.

– 'Teachers Vote Strike', *The Bell* 11:2 (November 1945), pp 669–72.

– 'This Myth of Irish Fascism', *The Bell* 12:3 (June 1946), pp 185–90.

– 'To Our Readers', *The Bell* 15:3 (December 1947), p. 1.

– 'Tourists' Guide to Irish Politics', *The Bell* 14:5 (August 1947), pp 1–3.

– 'Under the Writer's Torch', *The Bell* 12:6 (September 1946), pp 461–4.

– 'A Welcome to a Contributor', *The Bell* 16:3 (December 1950), pp 7–8.

– 'When a Minority Sulks', *The Bell* 16:4 (January 1951), pp 5–6.

– 'Whose Bridgehead?', *The Bell* 13:5 (February 1947), pp 1–4.

– 'Why Blame the Sea-Gulls?', *The Bell* 1:3 (December 1940), pp 6–9.

– 'A Word to Young Writers', *The Bell* 13:4 (January 1947), pp 1–4.

O'Donoghue, John, 'Fiddles and Bagpipes', *The Bell* 3:6 (March 1942), pp 410–14.

O'Faoláin, Eileen, 'Galway Hats', *The Bell* 1:4 (January 1941), pp 68–74.

O'Faoláin, Seán, '1916–1941: Tradition and Creation', *The Bell* 2:1 (April 1941), pp 5–12.

– 'All Things Considered – I', *The Bell* 11:2 (November 1945), pp 649–57.

– 'Answer to a Criticism', *The Bell* 1:3 (December 1940), pp 5–6.

– 'Attitudes', *The Bell* 2:6 (September 1941), pp 5–12.

– 'Autoantiamericanism' *The Bell* 16:6 (March 1951), pp 7–18.

– 'Autoantiamericanism', *The Bell* 17:3 (June 1951), pp 57–9.

– 'Beginnings and Blind Alleys', *The Bell* 3:1 (October 1941), pp 1–5.

– 'The Bishop of Galway and The Bell', *The Bell* 17:6 (September 1951), pp 15–17.

– 'Books and a Live People', *The Bell* 6:2 (May 1943), pp 91–8.

– 'Books' editor's response', *The Bell* 13:6 (March 1947), pp 65–6.

– 'Books in the Country', *The Bell* 3:6 (March 1942), pp 407–9.

– 'A Challenge', *The Bell* 1:5 (February 1941), pp 5–6.

– 'Childybawn', *The Bell* 19:10 (November 1954), pp 11–20.

– 'The Craft of the Short Story', *The Bell* 8:4 (July 1944), pp 306–14.

– 'The Dáil and the Bishops', *The Bell* 17:3 (June 1951), pp 5–13.

– 'Dare We Suppress That Irish Voice?', *The Bell* 3:3 (December 1941), pp 169–76.

– 'Eamon De Valera', *The Bell* 10:1 (April 1945), pp 1–18.

– Editorial note, *The Bell* 2:1 (April 1941), p. 86.

– Editorial note, 'Public Opinion', *The Bell* 9:2 (November 1944), p. 167.

– 'Fine Cottage Furniture', *The Bell* 1:3 (December 1940), pp 27–30.

– 'Fifty Years of Irish Literature', *The Bell* 3:5 (February 1942), pp 327–34.

– 'For the Future', *The Bell* 1:2 (November 1940), p. 5.

– 'Foreign Commentary', *The Bell* 13:3 (December 1946), pp 62–3.

– 'The Gaelic and the Good', *The Bell* 3:2 (November 1941), pp 93–103.

– 'The Gaelic Cult', *The Bell* 9:3 (December 1944), pp 186–96.

– 'The Gaelic League', *The Bell* 4:2 (May 1942), pp 77–86.

– 'Gaelic – The Truth', *The Bell* 5:5 (February 1943), pp 335–40.

– 'Ireland and the Modern World', *The Bell* 5:6 (March 1943), pp 423–8.

– Letter to the editor, *The Bell* 13:3 (December 1946), pp 62–3.

– 'The Man Who Invented Sin', *The Bell* 9:3 (December 1944), pp 219–32.

– 'New Wine in Old Bottles', *The Bell* 4:6 (September 1942), pp 381–8.

– 'New Writers', *The Bell* 1:5 (February 1941), p. 61.

– 'New Writers', *The Bell* 1:6 (March 1941), p. 67.

– 'New Writers', *The Bell* 3:5 (February 1942), p. 370.

– 'New Writers', *The Bell* 4:1 (April 1942), pp 14–20.

– 'New Writers', *The Bell* 4:4 (July 1942), pp 253–4.

– 'On Editing a Magazine', *The Bell* 9:2 (November 1944), pp 93–101.

– 'On State Control', *The Bell* 6:1 (April 1943), pp 1–6.

– 'One World', *The Bell* 7:4 (January 1944), pp 281–91.

– 'One World', *The Bell* 7:5 (February 1944), pp 373–81.

– 'One World', *The Bell* 7:6 (March 1944), pp 465–74.

– 'One World', *The Bell* 8:4 (July 1944), pp 277–86.

– 'One World', *The Bell* 8:6 (September 1944), pp 461–72.

– 'Our Nasty Novelists', *The Bell* 2:5 (August 1941), pp 5–12.

– 'Palestine', *The Bell* 14:2 (May 1947), pp 1–2

– 'Past Tense', *The Bell* 7:3 (December 1943), pp 186–91.

– 'The Plain People of Ireland', *The Bell* 7:1 (October 1943), pp 1–7.

– 'People and Books: The Irish Conscience?', *The Bell* 13:3 (December 1946), pp 67–71

– 'The Price of Peace', *The Bell* 10:4 (July 1945), pp 281–90

– 'Public Opinion: Pro-Soviet', *The Bell* 13:5 (February 1947), pp 58–9.

– Response to letter in 'Public Opinion', *The Bell* 5:4 (January 1943), pp 316–17.

– 'The Senate and Censorship', *The Bell* 5:4 (January 1943), pp 247–52.

– 'Shadow and Substance', *The Bell* 6:4 (July 1943), pp 273–9.

– 'Signing Off', *The Bell* 11:6 (April 1946), pp 1–4.

– 'The Silence of the Valley', *The Bell* 12:6 (September 1946), pp 466–89.

– 'Silent Ireland', *The Bell* 6:6 (September 1943), pp 457–66

– 'Speech from the Dock', *The Bell* 10:2 (May 1945), pp 166–7.

– 'Standards and Taste', *The Bell* 2:3 (June 1941), pp 5–11.

– 'The Stuffed-Shirts', *The Bell* 6:3 (June 1943), pp 181–92.

– 'The Sugawn Chair', *The Bell* 15:3 (December 1947), pp 22–5.

– 'That Typical Irishman', *The Bell* 5:2 (November 1942), pp 77–82.

– 'Third Year', *The Bell* 5:1 (October 1942), pp 1–3.

– 'This Is Your Magazine', *The Bell* 1:1 (October 1940), pp 5–8.

– 'Toryism in Trinity', *The Bell* 8:3 (June 1944), pp 185–97.

– 'Ulster', *The Bell* 2:4 (July 1941), pp 4–11.

– 'An Ulster Issue', *The Bell* 4:4 (July 1942), pp 229–31.

– 'The University Question', *The Bell* 8:1 (April 1944), pp 1–12.

O'Faoláin, Seán and Geoffrey Taylor, 'Sense and Nonsense in Poetry', *The Bell* 7:2 (November 1943), pp 156–63.

Ó Faracháin, Roibeárd, review of *An Doras do Plabadh* by Seoirse Mac Liam, *The Bell* 1:6 (March 1941), p. 96.

– 'Seosamh Mac Grianna', *The Bell* 1:2 (November 1940), pp 64–8.

O'Flaherty, 'The Beggars', *The Bell* 13:6 (March 1947), pp 5–23.

– 'Two Lovely Beasts', *The Bell* 13:3 (December 1946), pp 4–30.

O'Hegarty, P.S., 'About Ulster Novelists', *The Bell* 4:4 (July 1942), pp 289–97.

– 'Pádraic O Conaire', *The Bell* 8:3 (June 1944), pp 233–9.

O'Horan, Eily, 'Optimists', *The Bell* 7:5 (February 1944), pp 410–17.

– 'The Rustle of Spring', *The Bell* 13:5 (February 1947), pp 28–39.

O'Laoghaire, Liam, 'The Film Society Movement', *The Bell* 15:3 (December 1947), pp 56–64.

– 'Theatre and Film', *The Bell* 15:5 (February 1948), pp 52–7.

– 'Theatre and Films', *The Bell* 15:6 (March 1948), pp 57–60.

O Muirthe, Tomás, 'Caoine', trans. by Arland Ussher, *The Bell* 1:3 (December 1940), pp 10–11.

O'Neill, Séamus, 'The Gúm', *The Bell* 12:2 (May 1946), pp 136–40.

O'Shea, Fionan, 'Doctors for Export', *The Bell* 2:2 (May 1941), pp 47–57.

O'Sullivan, D. J., 'Island Man', 'New Writers', *The Bell* 4:1 (April 1942), pp 14–20.

– 'Servant Boy', 'Time and Poetry', *The Bell* 6:2 (May 1943).

'Other People's Incomes – 3 / Compiled', *The Bell* 7:1 (October 1943), pp 55–62.

'Other People's Incomes – 4 / Compiled', *The Bell* 7:2 (November 1943), pp 149–55.

Plunkett, James, 'The Damned', *The Bell* 17:10 (January 1952), pp 20–9.

– 'Dublin Fusilier', *The Bell* 19:9 (August 1954), pp 54–64.

– 'The Eagles and the Trumpets', *The Bell* 19:9 (August 1954), pp 9–30.

– 'The Half-Crown', *The Bell* 17:3 (June 1951), pp 13–24.

– 'Homecoming', *The Bell* 19:7 (June 1954), pp 11–32.

– 'Janey Mary', *The Bell* 9:5 (February 1945), pp 415–22.

– 'Mercy', *The Bell* 16:5 (February 1951), pp 27–39.

– 'The Trusting and the Maimed', *The Bell* 19:1 (December 1953), pp 150–71.

Power, Arthur, 'The Exhibition of Living Art', *The Bell* 7:1 (October 1943), pp 77–8.

Power, Richard, review of *Earball Spideóige* by Seán Ó Riordáin, *The Bell* 18:12 (Autumn, 1953), pp 129–30.

Quinn, Hugh, 'Old Belfast Street Characters', *The Bell* 2:4 (July 1941), pp 55–61.

Robertson, Olivia Manning, 'Court Circular', *The Bell* 10:5 (August 1945), pp 395–401.

– 'Deformed', *The Bell* 9:2 (November 1944), pp 129–34.

– 'Out Patients', *The Bell* 7:6 (March 1944), pp 510–14.

Robertson, W.D., 'The Postage Stamps of Ireland', *The Bell* 4:3 (June 1942), pp 180–7.

Rodgers, W.R., 'From *Europa*', *The Bell* 11:6 (March 1946), p. 1029.

– 'Ireland' *The Bell* 2:4 (July 1941), pp 12–13.

– 'Song', *The Bell* 12:5 (August 1946), p. 373.

Sartre, Jean-Paul, 'A Weapon against History', *The Bell* 19:11 (December 1954), pp 6–9.

Scott, Michael, 'The Village Planned', *The Bell* 3:3 (December 1941), pp 232–9.

Scrutator, 'Verdict on "The Bell"', *The Bell* 10:5 (August 1945), pp 431–7.

Sevitt, D., letter in 'Autoantiamericanism: Four comments', *The Bell* 17:2 (May 1951), pp 8–28.

Sheehy, Anna, 'The Lino Cut', *The Bell* 2:1 (April 1941), pp 41–2.

– 'Cecil ffrench Salkeld', *The Bell* 2:3 (June 1941), pp 48–51.

– 'Dorothy Blackham', *The Bell* 2:4 (July 1941), pp 30–3.

– 'Harry Kernoff, R.H.A.', *The Bell* 2:2 (May 1941), pp 27–8.

Sheehy Skeffington, Owen, 'Foreign Commentary', *The Bell* 12:4 (July 1946), pp 340–5.

– 'Foreign Commentary', *The Bell* 13:1 (October 1946), pp 64–8.

– Foreign Commentary' *The Bell* 13:3 (December 1946), pp 63–6.

– Letter in 'Public Opinion', *The Bell* 13:6 (March 1947), p. 65.

'Slum Pennies', *The Bell* 1:4 (January 1941), pp 74–7.

'Speaking as an Orangeman, by One of Them', *The Bell* 6:1 (April 1943), pp 19–27.

Stack, C.M., Rev. 'Unity, the Republic and the Church of Ireland', *The Bell* 16:4 (January 1951), pp 7–11.

Stanford, W. B., 'Protestantism Since the Treaty', *The Bell* 8:3 (June 1944), pp 218–27.

Stuart, Francis, 'Frank Ryan in Germany', *The Bell* 16:2 (November 1950), pp 37–42; *The Bell* 16:3 (December 1950), pp 38–40.

Subscription slip from *The Bell* 1:6 (March 1941).

T.D. Sauce, advertising in *The Bell* 5:6 (March 1943), p. 512.

Taylor, Geoffrey, 'A Neglected Irish Poet', *The Bell* 3:4 (January 1942), pp 308–12.

– 'Aubrey De Vere', *The Bell* 4:3 (June 1942), pp 200–4.

– 'Notes Toward an Anthology', *The Bell* 3:6 (March 1942), pp 449–54.

– 'The Best "Nation" Poet', *The Bell* 6:3 (June 1943), pp 237–41.

– 'Country House, Clontarf', *The Bell* 13:5 (March 1947), pp 31–2

– 'The Poetry of John Hewitt', *The Bell* 3:3 (December 1941), pp 229–31.

– 'William Allingham', *The Bell* 4:2 (May 1942), pp 139–44.

– Editorial note, *The Bell* 7:1 (October 1943).

– Review of *Poems from Ulster*, ed. by Robert Greacen, *The Bell* 3:5 (February 1942), pp 403–5.

– Review of *The Poems of Arthur Hugh Clough*, ed. by H.F. Lowry, A.L.P. Norrington, and F.L. Mulhauser, *The Bell* 18:4 (July 1952), pp 248–9.

The Bell, Peadar O'Donnell's set, with manuscript additions, Donegal County Library, Letterkenny.

'The Loveliest Thing I Have Seen: The Artist and the Layman', *The Bell* 1:2 (November 1940), pp 40–3.

'The Open Window, A Monthly Perambulation Conducted by Gulliver', *The Bell* 10:5 (August 1945), pp 457–63.

Tomelty, Joseph, 'A Note on Belfast Slang', *The Bell* 2:4 (July 1941), pp 70–1.

Truden, Bernardine, letter on 'Insanity in Ireland' in 'Public Opinion', *The Bell* 8:3 (June 1944), pp 254–9.

'Ulster: A Reply', *The Bell* 7:6 (March 1944), pp 474–84.

'Ultach Eile', '"Orange Terror": A Demurrer', *The Bell* 7:2 (November 1943), pp 137–42.

Ussher, Arland, 'Can Irish Live?', *The Bell* 9:5 (February 1945), pp 435–9.

Victor Waddington Galleries, advertising in *The Bell* 2:2 (May 1941), p. 82.

Walsh, Maurice, 'Whiskey', *The Bell* 2:5 (August 1941), pp 17–26.

Ward, Patrick Roe, 'In an Ulster Workhouse', *The Bell* 2:4 (July 1941), pp 22–9.

Webb, Stella M.B., 'What It Means to Be a Quaker', *The Bell* 9:3 (December 1944), pp 199–209.

Webster, Eileen F., 'History in Our Schools', *The Bell* 7:3 (December 1943), pp 192–200.

Williamson, Bruce, 'Afternoon in Anglo-Ireland', *The Bell* 12:2 (May 1946), pp 97–9.

Woodlock, Charles, 'Two Years in a Sanatorium', *The Bell* 1:5 (February 1942), pp 40–2.

'The Young Writer', *The Bell* 17:7 (October 1951), pp 5–30.

SECONDARY SOURCES

Æ, letter to Sean O'Faoláin, 20 May 1927, John J. Burns Library, Boston College.

Adams, Michael, *Censorship: the Irish experience* (Alabama: University of Alabama Press, 1968).

Advertisement included in Quarto 2, *Bannered spears*, ed. Jonathan Hanaghan (Dublin: Runa Press, July 1943).

Nicholas Allen, *Modernism, Ireland and Civil War* (Cambridge: Cambridge UP, 2009).

Anderson, Benedict, *Imagined communities: reflections on the origin and spread of nationalism*, Revised Edition (London: Verso, 1991).

Arendt, Hannah, *Between past and future: eight exercises in political thought*, Enlarged Edition (Middlesex: Penguin, 1968).

Baker, Denys Val, *Little reviews, 1914–43* (London: George Allen & Unwin Ltd, 1943).

Ballin, Malcolm, *Irish periodical culture, 1937–1972: genre in Ireland, Wales and Scotland* (New York: Palgrave Macmillan, 2008).

— 'Transitions in Irish Miscellanies Between 1923 and 1940: *The Irish Statesman* and *The Bell*', *International Journal of English Studies*, 2:2 (2002), pp 23–37.

Beetham, Margaret, *A magazine of her own? Domesticity and desire in the woman's magazine, 1800–1914* (London: Routledge, 1996).

— 'Towards a Theory of the Periodical as a Publishing Genre' in Laurel Brake, Alec Jones and Lionel Madden (eds), *Investigating Victorian journalism* (London: Macmillan, 1990), pp 19–32.

'A Bell for O'Donnell', *Time* magazine, 14 June 1948, www.time.com/time/magazine/article/0,9171,854911,00.html, accessed 2 June 2008.

Bennett, Louie, Letter, *Motley* 1:4 (September 1932), p. 16.

Bhabha, Homi K., *The location of culture* (London: Routledge, 1994).

Boyle, Terry, 'Denis Johnston: Neutrality and Buchenwald' in *Modern Irish writers and the wars* (Gerrards Cross: Colin Smythe, 1999), pp 205–18.

Brooker, Peter and Andrew Thacker, 'General Introduction' in Peter Brooker and Andrew Thacker (eds), *The Oxford critical and cultural history of modernist magazines, volume I, Britain and Ireland, 1880–1955* (Oxford: OUP, 2009), pp 1–26.

Brown, Terence, 'Geoffrey Taylor: A Portrait' in *Ireland's literature: selected essays* (Gigginstown, Mullingar: Lilliput Press, 1988), pp 141–51.

— *Ireland: a social and cultural history, 1922–2002* (London: Harper Perennial, 2004).

— 'Ireland, Modernism and the 1930s' in Patricia Coughlan and Alex Davis (eds), *Modernism and Ireland: the poetry of the 1930s* (Cork: Cork University Press, 1995), pp 24–42.

— *Northern voices: poets from Ulster* (Totowa, New Jersey: Rowman and Littlefield, 1975).

Bunreacht na hEireann (Constitution of Ireland) (Dublin: Stationery Office, 1937).

Butler, Hubert, '*The Bell*: An Anglo-Irish View', *Irish University Review* 6:1 (Spring 1976), pp 66–72.

Clarke, Austin, 'A Vision of Glendalough', *Irish Times*, 19 April 1946, p. 4.

— . 'Wanted – A Tradition' [review of *Irish Poems of To-day*], *Irish Times*, 13 May 1944, p. 2.

Cleary, Joe, 'Distress Signals: Sean O'Faoláin and the Fate of Twentieth-Century Irish Literature', *Field Day Review* 5 (2009), pp 49–73.

Clyde, Tom, *Irish literary magazines: an outline history and descriptive bibliography* (Dublin: Irish Academic Press, 2003).

Connolly, Cyril, 'Comment', *Horizon* 5:29 (May 1942), pp 297–300.

– Editorial note, *Horizon* 5:29 (May 1942), p. 300.

Contemporary Irish poetry, ed. Robert Greacen and Valentin Iremonger (London: Faber and Faber Ltd, 1949).

Corkery, Daniel, *The hidden Ireland* (Dublin: Gill and Macmillan, 1924).

– *Synge and Anglo-Irish literature* (Cork: Cork University Press, 1931).

Coughlan, Patricia and Alex Davis, 'Introduction' in *Modernism and Ireland: the poetry of the 1930s*, ed. Patricia Coughlan and Alex Davis (Cork: Cork University Press, 1995), pp 1–23.

Cronin, Anthony, Interview, 3 November 2008.

'Cúrsaí Reatha', *Comhar* 6:2 (February 1947), pp 5–7.

Dawe, Gerald, 'An Absence of Influence: Three Modernist Poets' in Terence Brown and Nicholas Grene (eds), *Tradition and influence in Anglo-Irish poetry* (London: Macmillan, 1989), pp 119–42.

de Valera, Eamon, 'Address by Mr de Valera, 17 March 1943', RTÉ Archives www.rte.ie/laweb/ll/ll_t09b.html, accessed 28 April 2008 (audio clip 5 of 9).

Deane, Ciarán, 'Brian Friel's *Translations*: The Origins of a Cultural Experiment', *Field Day Review* 5 (2009), pp 7–48.

Deane, Seamus, 'Remembering the Irish Future', *The Crane Bag* 8:1 (1984), pp 81–92.

Delehanty, James, 'The Bell: 1940–1954 [1]', *Kilkenny Magazine* 1 (Summer 1960), pp 32–7.

Devane, James, 'Is an Irish Culture Possible?', *Ireland To-Day* 1:5 (October 1936), pp 21–31.

'Editorial', *Atlantis* 1 (March 1970), pp 5–6.

'Editorial', *Ireland To-Day* 2:1 (January 1937), pp 1–4.

Erikson, Erik, *Identity: youth and crisis* (London: Faber and Faber, 1968).

Fallon, Brian, *An age of innocence: Irish culture, 1930–1960* (Dublin: Gill and Macmillan, 1998).

Fanning, Bryan, *The quest for modern Ireland: the battle of ideas, 1912–1986* (Dublin: Irish Academic Press, 2008).

Fanon, Frantz, *The wretched of the earth*, trans. by Constance Farrington (London: Penguin, 1967; repr. 1990).

Ferriter, Diarmaid, *The transformation of Ireland, 1900–2000* (London: Profile Books, 2004).

Foley, Dermot, 'Monotonously Rings the Little Bell', *Irish University Review* 6:1 (Spring 1976).

'Foreword', *Envoy* 2:1 (April 1950), pp 9–11.

'Foreword', *Threshold* 1:1 (February 1957), p. 5.

'Foreword', *Threshold* 1:4 (Winter, 1957), p. 5.

Foster, R.F., *Modern Ireland, 1600–1972* (London: Penguin, 1988).

Frith, Simon, 'Music and Identity' in Stuart Hall and Paul du Gay (eds), *Questions of cultural identity* (London: Sage, 1996), pp 108–27.

Furze, Richard A., Jr., 'A Desirable Vision of Life: A Study of *The Bell*, 1940–1954' (unpublished PhD thesis, UCD, 1974).

Gibbons, Luke, 'Challenging the Canon: Revisionism and Cultural Criticism' in Seamus Deane (ed.), *The Field Day anthology of Irish writing* (Derry: Field Day Publications, 1991), pp 561–8.

– *Transformations in Irish culture* (Cork: Cork University Press, 1996).

Grossberg, Lawrence, 'Identity and Cultural Studies: Is That All There Is?' in Stuart Hall and Paul du Gay (eds), *Questions of cultural identity* (London: Sage, 1996), pp 87–107.

Hall, Stuart, 'Introduction: Who Needs Identity?' in Stuart Hall and Paul du Gay (eds), *Questions of cultural identity* (London: Sage, 1996), pp 1–17.

Hall, Wayne E., *Dialogues in the margin: a study of the* Dublin University Magazine (Gerrards Cross: Colin Smythe, 2000).

Harding, Jason, *The* Criterion: *cultural politics and periodical networks in inter-war Britain* (Oxford: Oxford University Press, 2002).

Harmon, Maurice, *Sean O'Faolain: a critical introduction* (Notre Dame: University of Notre Dame Press, 1966).

— *Sean O'Faolain: a life* (London: Constable, 1994).

Heaney, Seamus, *Sweeney Astray: a version from the Irish* (Derry: Field Day, 1983).

Hogan, Dick, 'Cork's Oldest Jew Reflects in Sadness on the Slow Death of a Local Community', *Irish Times*, 2 February 1998, p. 2.

Holzapfel, Rudi, *An index of contributors to* The Bell (Blackrock, Co. Dublin: Carraig Books, 1970).

— *Author index 3* (Blackrock, Co. Dublin: Carraig Books, 1985).

Hyde, Douglas, 'The Necessity for De-Anglicizing Ireland', speech delivered to National Literary Society, Dublin, 25 November 1892, in Arthur Mitchell and Padraig Ó Snodaigh (eds), *Irish political documents, 1869–1916* (Dublin: Irish Academic Press, 1989), pp 81–6.

Johnson, Daniel P., 'Censorship and Publishing in Ireland in the 1930s and 40s' (unpublished PhD thesis, University of Ulster, 2001).

Johnston, Denis, *Nine rivers from Jordan* (London: Derek Verschoyle Limited, 1953).

Jones, Greta, *'Captain of all these men of death': the history of tuberculosis in nineteenth- and twentieth-cenutry Ireland* (Wellcome Series in the History of Medicine, Amsterdam: Editions Rodopi, 2001).

Kavanagh, Patrick, 'The Old Peasant', *Horizon* 5:25 (January 1942), pp 12–17.

Kearney, Richard, *Transitions: narratives in modern Irish culture* (Dublin: Wolfhound Press, 1988).

Kennedy, Liam, 'Modern Ireland: Post-Colonial Society or Post-Colonial Pretensions?', *Irish Review* 13 (Winter, 1993), 107–21.

Kent, Brad, 'Shaw, *The Bell,* and Irish Censorship in 1945', *The Annual of Bernard Shaw Studies* 30 (2010), pp 161–74.

Kiberd, Declan, *Inventing Ireland* (London: Jonathan Cape, 1995).

Lee, J.J., *Ireland, 1912–1985: politics and society* (Cambridge: Cambridge University Press, 1989).

Lunn, Eugene, *Marxism and modernism: an historical study of Lukács, Brecht, Benjamin, and Adorno* (Berkeley: University of California Press, 1982).

Lynch, Martin, 'Michael Farrell, Carlowman (1899–1962): Writer or "Die, Publish and be damned!"', *Carloviana* 49 (2000), pp 46–7.

Lyons, F.S.L., *Ireland since the Famine* (London: Collins/Fontana, 1971).

Mac Cormaic, Ruadhán, 'We need vision of who we are and what we want to make migration work', *Irish Times*, 27 June 2007, p. 11.

MacIntyre, Thomas 'Some Notes on the Stories of James Plunkett', *Studies* 47 (Autumn, 1958), pp 323–7.

MacNeice, Louis, *Letters of Louis MacNeice*, ed. by Jonathan Allison (London: Faber and Faber, 2010).

Matthews, Kelly A., '*The Bell* and Irish Identity, 1940–1954: Representation and Transformation' (unpublished PhD, University of Ulster, 2009).

— 'Cultivating Our Own Garden: The Cultural Project of *The Bell*, 1940–1941' (unpublished M.Phil. thesis, University of Dublin, 1993).

McCarthy, Conor, *Modernisation, crisis and culture in Ireland, 1969–1992* (Dublin: Four Courts Press, 2000).

McClintock, Anne, 'The Angel of Progress: Pitfalls of the Term "Post-colonialism"' in *Social Text*, 31/32 (1992), pp 84–98.

McDonald, Peter, *Mistaken identities: poetry and Northern Ireland* (Oxford: Clarendon Press, 1997).

McFadden, Roy, 'Plaint of the Working-Men' in Geoffrey Taylor (ed.), *Irish poems of To-day* (London: Secker and Warburg, 1944), p. 29.

McMahon, Sean (ed.), *The best from* The Bell*: great Irish writing* (Dublin: O'Brien Press, 1978).

Mercier, Vivian, 'The Professionalism of Sean O'Faoláin', *Irish University Review* 6:1 (Spring 1976), pp 45–53.

Merejkovsky, D., 'L'Avenir du Christianisme', *Dublin Magazine* 14:2 (April-June 1939).

Montague, John, 'The Siege of Mullingar, 1963' in *Selected poems* (Toronto: Exile Editions, 1986).

'Montalembert: Journal de Voyage en Irlande, 1830', *Dublin Magazine* 15:2 (April–June 1940), pp 44–62.

Mulkerns, Val, '"Did You Once See Shelley Plain?": Dublin, *The Bell*, the Fifties', *New Hibernia Review* 10:3 (Autumn, 2006), pp 9–23.

– Interview, 13 November 2008.

na Gopaleen, Myles [Flann O'Brien], 'Waama, etc.' in *The best of Myles*, ed. by Kevin O Nolan (New York: Penguin, 1983), pp 15–40.

O'Brien, Harvey, 'The Identity of an Irish Cinema', 3rd ed. (2007) www.reelireland.ie/history.pdf, accessed 23 October 2008.

O'Brien, Kate, *The land of spices* (London: Doubleday, 1941).

O'Brien, Mark, *De Valera, Fianna Fáil and the* Irish Press (Dublin: Irish Academic Press, 2001).

O'Connor, Frank, Foreword to *The Tailor and Ansty* by Eric Cross (London: Chapman & Hall Ltd, 1942), pp 5–9.

Ó Crualaoich, Gearóid, 'The Primacy of Form: A "Folk Ideology" in de Valera's Politics' in John P. O'Carroll and John A. Murphy (eds), *De Valera and his times* (Cork: Cork University Press, 1983), pp 47–61.

Ó Drisceoil, Donal, *Censorship in Ireland, 1939–1945: neutrality, politics and society* (Cork: Cork University Press, 1996).

Ó Drisceoil, Proinsias, 'Tragic Fragments Revealed', *Irish Times* Weekend Review (10 November 2007), p. 11.

O'Faoláin, Seán, 'Commentary on the Foregoing', *Ireland To-Day* 1:5 (October 1936), p. 32.

– 'Letter from a Novelist to an Idealist', *Motley* 2:7 (November 1933), pp 3–5.

– Letters to Frank O'Connor, Howard Gotlieb Archival Research Center, Boston University.

– 'Love Among the Irish', *Life* (16 March 1953), pp 140–57.

– Review of *Synge and Anglo-Irish literature* by Daniel Corkery, *Criterion* 11 (October 1931), pp 140–2.

– *Vive Moi!*, ed. Julia O'Faolain (London: Sinclair-Stevenson, 1993).

Oireachtas Eireann, Censorship of Publications Act, 1929, acts.oireachtas.ie/zza21y1929.1.html, accessed 12 November 2008.

Oireachtas Eireann, Emergency Powers (Paper) (No. 1) Order, 1941, signed Seán F. Lemass, Minister for Supplies.

Oireachtas Eireann, Emergency Powers (Waste Paper) Order, 1942, signed Seán F. Lemass, Minister for Industry and Commerce.

Oireachtas Eireann, Emergency Powers (Waste Paper Prices) Order, 1944, signed Seán F. Lemass, Minister for Supplies.

O'Leary, Philip, *Writing beyond the Revival: facing the future in Gaelic prose, 1940–1951* (Dublin: University College Dublin Press, 2011).

Ormsby, Frank, 'The Short Stories of James Plunkett', *The Honest Ulsterman* 20 (December 1969), pp 10–16.

The Oxford critical and cultural history of modernist magazines, volume I, Britain and Ireland 1880–1955, ed. by Peter Brooker and Andrew Thacker (Oxford: Oxford UP, 2009).

Plunkett, Sir Horace, 'Notes and Comments: *The Irish Statesman* Ends', *The Irish Statesman* 14:6 (12 April 1930), pp 106.

Poems from Ireland, ed. by Donagh MacDonagh (Dublin: *Irish Times*, 1944).

'Preface', *Ireland's Field Day*, ed. by Field Day Theatre Company (London: Hutchinson, 1985), pp vii–viii.

Quinn, Antoinette, *Patrick Kavanagh: a biography* (Dublin: Gill and Macmillan, 2001).

Reynolds, Paige, *Modernism, drama, and the audience for Irish spectacle* (Cambridge: Cambridge University Press, 2007).

RTÉ Archives, 'Irish Public Service Broadcasting – 1930s', www.rte.ie/laweb/brc/brc_1930s.html, accessed 7 October 2008.

Salmon, Arthur Edward, *Poets of the apocalypse* (Boston: Twayne, 1983).

Shaw, George Bernard, postcard to Sean O'Faoláin, dated 3 November 1940, John J. Burns Library, Boston College.

Sheehy Skeffington, Andrée D., 'What the Censor did in 1944' in 'The Emergency, a supplement to the *Irish Times*', 8 May 1985.

Shelden, Michael, *Friends of promise: Cyril Connolly and the world of* Horizon (London: Minerva, 1990).

Shovlin, Frank, 'Between the Sheets: Material Production and Cultural Politics in the Irish Periodical Press, 1922–58' in P.J. Mathews (ed.), *New voices in Irish criticism* (Dublin: Four Courts Press, 2000), pp 197–205.

– 'From Revolution to Republic: Magazines, Modernism, and Modernity in Ireland' in Peter Brooker and Andrew Thacker (eds), *The Oxford critical and cultural history of modernist magazines, volume I, Britain and Ireland, 1880–1955* (Oxford: Oxford UP, 2009), pp 735–58.

– *The Irish literary periodical, 1923–1958* (Oxford: Clarendon Press, 2003).

Smyth, Gerry, *Decolonisation and criticism: the construction of Irish literature* (London: Pluto Press, 1998).

Taaffe, Carol, 'Coloured Balloons: Frank O'Connor on Irish Modernism' in Hilary Lennon (ed.), *Frank O'Connor: critical essays* (Dublin: Four Courts Press, 2007), pp 205–17.

Taylor, Geoffrey, 'Editor's Note', *Irish poems of To-day* (London: Secker and Warburg, 1944).

Tracy, Honor, *Mind you, I've said nothing!: Forays in the Irish republic* (London: Methuen & Co., Ltd, 1953).

Untitled editorial, *Rann* 1 (Summer, 1948), p. inside cover.

'W.A.A.M.A. Critic of Radio Éireann', *Irish Times*, 4 December 1944, p. 1.

'W.A.A.M.A. First General Meeting', *Irish Times*, 15 September 1941, p. 5.

'W.A.A.M.A. Week', *Irish Times*, 19 May 1942, p. 2.

Weaver, Jack W. (ed.), *Robert Greacen: selected and new poems* (Cliffs of Moher: Salmon Poetry, 2006).

Welch, Robert, *The Abbey Theatre, 1899–1999: form and pressure* (Oxford: Oxford University Press, 1999).

— *Changing states: transformations in modern Irish writing* (London: Routledge, 1993).

Whelan, Bernadette, *Ireland and the Marshall Plan, 1947–57* (Dublin: Four Courts Press, 2000).

Whyte, J.H., *Church and state in modern Ireland* (Dublin: Gill and Macmillan, 1971).

Williams, Helen, 'Ringing the Bell: Editor-Reader Dialogue in Alexander Herzen's *Kolokol*', *Book History* 4 (2001), pp 115–32.

Wills, Clair, *That neutral Island: a cultural history of Ireland during the Second World War* (London: Faber and Faber, 2007).

Yeats, W.B., 'Under Ben Bulben' in *The collected poems of W.B. Yeats*, ed. by Richard J. Finneran (New York: Macmillan, 1989), pp 325–8.

Index

A searchable index of all articles, poems, short stories, and reviews published in *The Bell* is accessible through the author's faculty website at Framingham State University (www.framingham.edu).